QUEENSLAND

W9-CUJ-174

ulla

rulgoonia

Toulby Gate

Culgoa River

River

an

Weilmoringle

Goodooga

Gerara

onia

Birrie

River

Angledool

Boneda

Langboyd

Muckerawa

Lightning Ridge

Narran

River

apper
Tank

Mundiwa
Collerina

Milroy

River

Collarenebri

Bokhara

Hospital
Creek

Cumborah

River

Narran
Lake

h Bourke
urke

Brewarrina

Mission

Barwon

Walgett

Yarrawin

Castlereagh

Cuddy

Pilliga

Marra
Creek

Macquarrie River

River

underbooka

Byrock

Marthaguy

Coronga Peak

Bogan

Creek

ALES

River

Nyngan

Warren
Cathundral

Gilgandra

Tribe

50 km

Tottenham

Dubbo

The two worlds of Jimmie Barker

The two worlds of Jimmie Barker

THE LIFE OF AN AUSTRALIAN ABORIGINAL 1900-1972

as told to Janet Mathews

AUSTRALIAN INSTITUTE OF
ABORIGINAL STUDIES
Canberra, 1977

Australian Aboriginal Studies
Ethnohistory Series No 4

The views expressed in this publication are those of the narrator and author
and not necessarily those of the Australian Institute of Aboriginal Studies.

National Library of Australia card number and ISBN 0 85575 056 1

Printed in Australia by Southwood Press Pty Ltd, Marrickville, N.S.W.

For Dougal Kennedy,

my grandson and Jimmie's friend

J.M.

Contents

Acknowledgments

I SHOULD like to thank Mr F. D. McCarthy for suggesting that this story should be written, and the Australian Institute of Aboriginal Studies for making the work possible. I should also like to record my appreciation of the assistance given by Mrs Peter Clark, who patiently read the manuscript.

Grateful acknowledgment is also due to the N.S.W. Government Department of Youth and Community Services for permission to quote the extracts from the records of the N.S.W. Aborigines' Protection Board given in the Appendix, and to J. P. M. Long and the Australian National University Press for allowing me to quote from the book *Aboriginal Settlements: a survey of institutional communities in eastern Australia*.

Preface

EARLY IN 1964 I was asked to undertake field research among the Aborigines of New South Wales for the Australian Institute of Aboriginal Studies. My qualifications for this work were musical and I expected to be tape-recording songs only. However, when I was ready for my first field trip the Institute suggested that I should not confine myself to music, but should record languages or any other information that might come to light. For four years I worked in the area between Sydney and the Victorian border, mostly among the Aborigines of the South Coast, with occasional visits inland as far as Gundagai and Brungle. During those years I recorded many Aboriginal songs, but also became intensely interested in recording various languages and other material relating to the Aboriginal way of life in the tribal days.

My first visit to north-western New South Wales was in 1968. Several Aborigines had been helpful when I was collecting names of possible informants in this area which was new to me. Only one name had been recommended for Brewarrina. This was Jimmie Barker, who was reputed to have some linguistic knowledge and was described as a 'key figure' in the district. He was not expected to be there for more than occasional visits as he spent most of his time at Lightning Ridge.

Hoping to meet Jimmie Barker I drove from Bourke to Brewarrina, and on arrival there saw some Aborigines in the local park. My inquiries led to the usual confused situation encountered by a field worker. A husband and wife were sitting on a seat; she was too shy to speak to me but he was very helpful and full of enthusiasm. He assured me that he could produce informants if I would wait in the park for a while. In due course he introduced me to several of the residents and some recording was done. Shyness is always a problem with a person recording for the first time, and this makes it difficult to assess his or her ability. This applied to one old man who took a lot of persuasion before he was willing to record: I secured little of value on the tape owing to his fear of the machine. He died soon afterwards, and I learnt later that he was one of the few fluent speakers and singers of Ngemba in the north-west. Thus a lot of music and language was lost.

Towards the end of the day I was introduced to Jack Barker, who recorded some elementary Muruwari words. I liked him and was immediately interested when he told me that his father, Jimmie Barker, was in Brewarrina for a short visit. The day was over and it was time to return to Bourke. Only a little recording had been done but it seemed worth another visit if I could meet Jimmie Barker.

The next day I returned to Brewarrina and, after some delay, Jack Barker directed me to the river-bank where his father was staying. Jimmie Barker, who was then aged sixty-eight, was shy but quite willing to co-operate. We recorded for some time, but his linguistic ability seemed disappointing. He spoke some Muruwari but was slow in answering questions, and the recording was not a great success. Certainly allowances had to be made for the strain of recording for the first time. It had started to rain and it was obvious that I should leave for Bourke before the road became impassable. Just as I was about to leave, Jimmie went into his hut and brought out a small, old-fashioned tape-recorder. He told me that he had bought this machine so that he could record an English-Muruwari dictionary. It had cost him fifty dollars, a large sum for him, which showed that he had a real interest in his language. He was worried about the price of tapes and asked if I could help him. I noted all particulars and returned to Bourke over a slippery road. Those two days in Brewarrina had been full of the normal frustrations and difficulties which occur in the field; little had been achieved and my recordings were poor. But on consideration, there seemed something very interesting about Jimmie Barker.

As soon as possible it was arranged that the Institute would provide Jimmie with tapes. He and I started corresponding immediately on my return from Brewarrina; he wrote good letters. When he received his first tapes he was worried about how to start recording and appealed for help. I sent him elementary lists of vocabulary; he recorded these then returned the tapes to me. I found his ability and his knowledge of the Muruwari language to be very much better than I had expected. When he could record in his own way and at a speed adjusted to his thoughts, the result was excellent. He followed written lists or suggestions but also had his own method of recording. His original intention had been to record vocabulary only, but in his childhood he had spoken Muruwari constantly, and his memory of the language became clearer. With some persuasion and more lists from me he started constructing sentences. We also started a kind of correspondence course in English grammar, with the idea of making it easier for him to explain the use of grammar in the Muruwari language.

The sound-reproduction of Jimmie's small recorder was not very satisfactory. After I had received sixteen recorded tapes from him I asked the Institute if he could be supplied with a tape-recorder and equipment similar to mine. This was provided for him and he started recording more seriously. In early tapes it had been interesting to note how he digressed from the language and spoke about Muruwari customs or beliefs. Soon I received several tapes on which he had recorded a brief description of his life. When these fragments arrived it was obvious that all the subjects should be investigated more fully. They were many and varied, and included Muruwari legends, tribal boundaries and religion, hunting and fishing methods, food and medicine found in the bush, fighting, human relationships and material culture. Having studied the tape I would list the questions arising from the contents and send them to Jimmie. Sometimes we corresponded by letter, and on other occasions it was more satisfactory to record questions and answers on tape.

Through the Institute it was possible to have photo-copies made of anything that had been written previously about the Muruwari tribe; these helped to stir his memory. Those of most interest to him were written by my grandfather-in-law,

R. H. Mathews, and included *The Aboriginal Fisheries of Brewarrina, The Murawarri and other Australian Languages,* and *Initiation Ceremonies of the Murawarri and other Aboriginal Tribes of Queensland.* R. H. Mathews was born in 1841 and died in 1918. His childhood was spent in the country and he associated with the Aborigines from the earliest age. Later, as a surveyor, he spent many years in the bush and his profession gave him the opportunity to meet Aborigines of many tribes and in their natural state. His entire life was devoted to research into every aspect of Aboriginal life, and the result was a tremendous amount of published and unpublished material. Jimmie and I studied it together, and Jimmie's comments, comparisons and additions were interesting.

Between 1968 and 1972 we spent many hours together recording. Jimmie came to Sydney occasionally and a lot of our time was spent at my home; as well, I visited him in Brewarrina once a year. When recording together we could augment and clarify information previously given. My last visit to him was in April 1972. For four days we sat in his little house and recorded for approximately eight hours daily. Our work was nearly complete; he patiently answered questions and most of his Muruwari topics were explained fully.

A few months later, on 7 July 1972, Jimmie died suddenly. He had recorded a total of 110 tapes on his own and approximately fifty with me. It is from all these tapes, his letters and our discussions that the following narrative has been compiled. Transcribing these tapes and sorting out the tribal material and various subjects was a difficult task; I have endeavoured to place them in their correct sequence. The resulting book is written in the form of an autobiography, and I shall try to tell the story of Jimmie Barker in the way he told it to me. His method of expression was descriptive; he did not exaggerate, and would only comment if he believed he was correct. He was a remarkable man, intelligent and well educated. He was almost completely self-taught, as his schooling had lasted only eighteen months, and he was still learning from books until the time of his death. His recording represented countless hours of work, as he did careful preparation before speaking into the microphone. Fortunately Jimmie enjoyed this work: he frequently said that it had given him more satisfaction and sense of achievement than anything else he had attempted during his life. He knew that I was going to work on his tapes and write the story of his life and his memories of the Muruwari tribe; this gave him great pleasure, and I hope he would have approved of the result.

Jimmie Barker's character was gentle, sensitive, shy and full of courage. He was always able to enjoy the present moment and forget troubles of the past. Unlike many Aboriginals, he did worry about the future for his family. He had the ability to stand apart from the Aborigines and analyse their past and present problems. My admiration and affection for him grew during the four years we worked together, and when he died I lost a real friend.

JANET MATHEWS

Pronunciation of Muruwari words

a :	= *ah* as in f*a*ther	*b*	= *p* or *b*
e	= *ĕ* as in m*e*n	*d*	= *t* or *d*
i	= *ē* as in b*e*	*d* or *dh*	= *th* as in *th*en
u	= *ōō* as in b*oo*t	*dj*	= *j* as in *j*ump
ai	= *ī* as in b*i*te	*g*	= *k* as in *k*ite
au	= *ōw* as in n*ow*	*j*	= *y* as in *y*es
ei	= *āi* as in m*ai*n	*ng*	= *n̄g* as in si*ng*er
oi	= *ōi* as in t*oi*l		

xiv

1 Mundiwa

'All was laughter . . . now so silent'

I WAS born on 28 July 1900 at Cunnamulla, in south-western Queensland. We left there soon afterwards and I have no recollection of the place. My father was German and his name was Bocher, but this had been changed to Barker before I was born. At that time he was working as a boundary rider; he later managed a small property called Gerara. This property, which is now called Old Gerara, is near the Queensland border and not far from Enngonia. We moved there when I was a baby, and it was there that my brother Billy was born in 1903. I can just remember the ramshackle house, the old-time windmill by the spring, the buggies and horse-yards, and also little Billy as he lay in his basket under the verandah. There was an Englishman called Harry Thompson who worked with Father. He loved mushrooms, and after rain would take me out to gather them. He always had some sweets for me, and he remained one of my greatest friends until his death a few years ago.

Until the time of her death my mother was always important to me. She was a remarkable woman who made many sacrifices in order to care for Billy and me. Her father was Jimmie Ellis, a Scotsman, and her mother was a full-blood of the Muruwari tribe. I am not sure whether they were married: many white men lived with dark girls in these country places at that time. Granny Ellis was born at Enngonia, and was still there when Mother was born. When she was young Granny lived near the Culgoa River for a number of years. To Granny, Mother and myself the Culgoa has always had some special significance. Mother was the eldest of Granny's children, followed by Clara, Jimmie

1

junior and Jack. I was told that Granny was buried at Enngonia and Grandpa in Bourke.

Grandpa had started his working life in Brewarrina, where he worked in the hotel. Mother and Aunt Clara both married white men. I never met my uncle Jimmie Ellis. He lived at Longreach, and died before I was born. My only memories of Aunt Clara were childhood ones. However, I knew Uncle Jack better, as he came to live with us for a while in 1940. Later he moved to Goodooga, and he died in Brewarrina in 1950. Uncle Jack had not learnt to speak Muruwari very well, although he could understand it easily. He knew many of the Aboriginal families in the area, and he would have known a lot about their customs.

Granny Ellis had a strong affection for my mother. They used to go camping together, and frequently went walkabout when they felt the urge. Sometimes they would walk from Enngonia to the Culgoa River just to see their people, camping beside the track along the way. Sarah Anthony, a white girl from a well-known family, was one of Granny's closest friends. They often went camping together, and Sarah learnt to speak Muruwari. Although Granny had this white friend and was married to a white man, she had strong Muruwari beliefs. These were passed on to my mother, who was proud of her heritage. Mother was grown-up when Granny died, and had learnt a lot about the Muruwari from her. After this Mother did various domestic jobs around Enngonia and Yantabulla until she was married in 1888. Soon afterwards she and Father moved to Cunnamulla, where in 1890 there was a great flood. Mother told me that Father had rowed a boat all the way from Cunnamulla to Enngonia, a distance of almost a hundred miles. Marcia, the eldest child, was born at this time; then Frederick, Albert and John arrived. They spent a lot of time with relatives in Queensland, and gradually drifted away from us. Although Albert came to see us a few times before he was killed at Gallipoli, the others just seemed to disappear. I resented their lack of concern for Mother and did not bother about them.

Uncle Jack was very good at explaining things. He also sang well, and I learnt most of my Muruwari songs from him. He joined the police as a tracker, was a good horseman, and did a lot of horse-breaking and droving. During most of his life he moved through Muruwari country, and he told me many stories about the tribe.

To my mother and the other old people these places encircled by the Muruwari boundary formed their complete world; they had no wish to go farther afield. I must describe my mother. She was not very dark, but was possibly the darkest of the family. She was almost my colour, and I have become darker as the years have crept on. She was a bright person, and had a considerable store of knowledge although she could neither read nor write. She was active and liked her living conditions to be orderly, and she appreciated her few good possessions. On the other hand, she was very superstitious in the true Aboriginal way. I am too. I think that this happens when one has spent sufficient time with the old people. Learning their language and listening to them talking to one another makes a lasting impression. Mother was ready to learn the new way of life, but her Aboriginal views were very definite. I learnt a lot from her. She only spoke to us occasionally in Muruwari, but expected us to understand her.

Mother seems to be at the centre of all my early memories, and one of the clearest of these dates from just before Christmas 1905. Harry Thompson had been telling me about Santa Claus, and my excitement was growing daily. In later years Mother always confided in me, and it seems she must have started then, when I was five years old. One day she took me into her bedroom and asked me to keep a secret. She told me that she was not getting on well with Father and that we were moving to another place. I do not remember having any Christmas that year.

It was soon after this that Billy and I went with Mother to Mundiwa, a small place on the Culgoa River. The three of us lived there for the next two years. Father visited us occasionally during the first year, sometimes bringing us some food or a present. Gradually these visits stopped and I never saw him again. We heard of his progress, that he had moved to Goondiwindi where he owned quite a large property. In later years he wrote and invited me to visit him. I did not bother to answer these letters, for I had not forgotten, nor was I likely to forget, how he had left us on our own.

I shall always remember how Mother had to struggle to rear us without any financial help from our father. Bill did not share my feelings, and visited him a few times. Whatever the trouble may have been between my parents, I was always on the side of my mother. In 1912 some papers arrived for her and she needed some legal assistance with them. She gave me no explanation, but they could have been divorce papers, as some time later I heard that Father had married again. His second wife was white, and there were two more sons; I think one was killed in the second world war. Harry Thompson, Jack McCormack and others said my father was a fine man, and spoke well of him. On his behalf they asked me to visit him, but I could not adjust myself to liking a man who had left Mother with two children and no financial help. Also, he had no real interest in any of us. As I grew up I realised that Mother and Father had separate lives and there was no future in bothering about him. I suspected that his second wife may have come into his life and caused the trouble with Mother. I have seen a photograph of him, and his appearance was distinctly German. This is all I know about him.

When we arrived at Mundiwa there were only two families living there, both in old shacks on the riverbank. We lived in a tent for some time and moved into a tin humpy later. Mundiwa was called Diraluda in Muruwari, and was forty-five miles from Brewarrina. It was a camping reserve for Aborigines, though I did not know this at the time. Gradually more people came to live there, most of them very old and speaking in Muruwari. This was the last remnant of a large tribe. As time passed I became very fond of these old people, and it was from them that I learnt more of the Muruwari language. They used it all the time, and if I did not understand they would explain it to me in part-English. In the evenings they would sit under the trees and talk; if it was winter they would be crouched around a fire. I loved visiting them and listening to their stories of the early days: mythical stories of birds, animals and constellations. There were some children at the camp but I seldom played with them, as being with the older people appealed to me more. I must have been enterprising, and was certainly inquisitive. It was here that I tried my first experiment with a treacle tin filled with water. I hammered the lid tightly and then put it in the fire. It exploded with a loud noise and I was severely punished.

Our tent was about twelve feet square and kept some of the rain out. Sometimes it was very hot and I can remember that it worried Mother, who had to cook on an outside fire and work hard to keep us clean and fed. Daily living seemed a struggle for her all the time, especially in the summer. We had no furniture or possessions worth mentioning. Wagons came out at irregular intervals and brought us issues of flour, tea and sugar. There might be a small issue of tobacco, but no baking-powder or meat. Occasionally the others would share a goanna, porcupine or emu with us, and we caught fish in the river. Our beds were made of bush timber supported by forked sticks. It was all very rough. Mother stuffed possum skins with emu feathers for our pillows. There was also a type of reed similar to kapok, and this could be used for stuffing. Mother joined kangaroo skins and stuffed them with these reeds, and these were our mattresses. Eventually a couple of blankets were issued to us, but mostly we slept under kangaroo skins.

Gradually more people came to live at Mundiwa, and as it became a larger community we had frequent visitors from outside. Jimmy Kerrigan had been living there for some time before we arrived. He was a very old man and one of the true Aborigines whose life and beliefs had never been influenced by white people. He was a good man, reputed to be a witch doctor; he was kind to us all, and he became very fond of me. During the next few years he taught me many things that I shall never forget. His son Hector visited him frequently and was a good friend of ours. Two old men called Goodooga Billy and Billy Campbell* also moved to Mundiwa, as did Peter Flood, the self-appointed 'King of the Muruwari'. The authorities treated him as someone important, and built a tin hut for him. I do not know if he had been issued with a plate naming him as 'king'. I own one of these, engraved 'King Clyde of the Barwon Blacks'. If ever the old native was ridiculed by the white man it was because he wore these plates. Mrs Horneville* lived there for a little

---

* Billy Campbell and Mrs Horneville recorded Muruwari for A.I.A.S.

while; she is still alive. Her age must be close to one hundred years, and she lives at Goodooga. Old Mrs Bailey* lived there for a while before moving to Weilmoringle. There were also two members of the Wellington family, Old Jimmy and Little Jimmy. There were some other residents and a number who came for brief visits, but I have forgotten their names. They all had to be called 'uncle' or 'brother'; sometimes this was regulated by their totem or mine.

With this larger population more huts were needed. The people made sheds from the bark of the red box-tree. The rough outer part was removed until the red colour was showing, then the bark was heated to make it more pliable. These sheets would then be greased with goanna fat and several sheets would be piled on the ground with a weight on top of them. When dried and flat they were ready for use. The huts, which were low, had been made this way for centuries. Sticks were placed over the roof and tied down with vines or sinews.

None of us had any money or possessions, but these old people knew how to use what nature had provided in the bush. It is probable that the possums were of the most use to us, and they were easy to catch. A loop of sinews or vines would be attached to the trunk of a tree in what was expected to be the path of the possum. It might be caught by the head or a foot, but the more it struggled the tighter the noose became. Another method was for a man to climb a tree carrying a long, flexible stick. He would cut a small hole in the tree and poke the stick down the hollow. When he felt a possum he would measure the distance, cut another hole and remove the possum easily. This method must have been tedious with a stone axe.

Apart from the meat, we needed possums for other purposes. The fur was used for many things, and it was the job of the old women to make it into lengths of twine. They teased the fur with their fingers, then rubbed it on their bare thighs: the warmth of the skin made it pliable. In some cases they would put beeswax on their legs and rub the fur on that. It was necessary to remove the fur immediately the possum

Mrs Bailey's daughters have all recorded Muruwari for the A.I.A.S.

had been killed, otherwise it would be impossible to separate the fur from the skin. Sometimes they only plucked out the fur and kept it until they were ready to treat it. After the rubbing it was possible to make it into very long lengths, possibly thirty or forty feet long. We used this for fishing lines, and it was strong enough to catch large fish. This twine was also knotted with two bones and made into mesh nets which were used as animal traps or bags in which babies were carried.

We used the possum skins for water bags. The skin was opened near the hind legs and pulled over the body. The two open ends near the head and hind legs were tied with kurrajong bark or kangaroo sinew. Then the roughness would be stripped from the wattle bark and the smooth inner bark placed in the possum-skin bag, which would be filled with water. Tannin comes from this bark when immersed in water, and this gives the skin strength and also preserves it. An untreated possum skin rots and becomes unpleasant when wet for any length of time. When sufficient tannin had been absorbed the old women would rub the skin strenuously to make it pliable. The two hind legs were tied together to form the handle. We took these bags when we went camping or used them to carry water up from the river. There were not many napkins for babies in those days, and the possum skins were also used as cleansers.

The old people realised how much I enjoyed being with them, and I spent many hours of the day and night in their company. They also took me on their camping and hunting expeditions. I spent many hours a day with my arms around Jimmy Kerrigan's neck or sitting on his shoulders as he carried me. During these years he seemed to wear me like a jacket, and where he went it was fairly certain that I would be there too. One day Mother asked Jimmy's son, Hector Kerrigan, who was aged about thirty years, to take us to Enngonia. She wanted to see Uncle Jack Ellis, and Hector had an old buggy. When we arrived in Enngonia I was terrified when I saw Uncle Jack coming to greet us in a policeman's uniform. I had heard so much about police taking people away and locking them up that his uniform was a thing of horror to me. Uncle Jack was so good to me that I was eventually reassured. I met a lot of people in this district and my uncle kept introducing me as 'my boy, Jimmie'. After several weeks we moved back to Mundiwa again. Bill Campbell was aged about twenty, and he took me out fishing or hunting frequently. Playing with the children seemed a waste of time to me and usually ended in fights, arguments and abuse.

Despite being with the older people so much of the time, I still managed to get up to mischief. In those days most of the men and women smoked clay pipes. One day I found one on the ground in fairly good condition. The stem was broken but I managed to extend it. The next problem was to find tobacco, so I went across to an old cripple we all called Puffy because she smoked a lot. I told her that Mother needed some tobacco and matches. When she gave them to me I pretended to go home and then dodged down to the river and lit my pipe. Towards the end of my second pipe things seemed to be moving and the bank was rolling under my feet. I buried the pipe, started vomiting and staggered home to bed. The bed seemed to sway in all directions and I felt horrible. Mother spoke to me, and I may have admitted that I had been smoking, because she did not have much to say about my illness. I felt fine the next morning. It was some time before I tried smoking again, but eventually I got into the habit of having a puff of someone's cigarette or smoking the occasional one. In this way I became an addict and have smoked all my life, but I shall never forget the day I told old Puffy that awful lie.

It is hard to describe Jimmy Kerrigan. During those few years he spent countless hours telling me about Aboriginal laws and customs. He was aged about eighty-five then, and he enjoyed having an interested listener and loved talking about the past. I knew three Kerrigan brothers, Jimmy, Tommy and Billy. They lived on the Culgoa, while others in the family lived at Enngonia. They came from the same Muruwari group as Mother. When she left Gerara she chose Mundiwa because Jimmy Kerrigan was there. Billy Kerrigan changed his name to Billy McCann, and I shall talk about him later. My memories of Tommy Kerrigan are not very precise.

Jimmy was much older than his brothers. He had been a remarkable tracker in his youth and had tracked the bushranger Midnight. Through Jimmy's tracking, Midnight was found asleep one morning in the bush between Enngonia and Ledknapper Tank. He had no chance of escape, and the trackers wounded him and captured his horse. They then took him to a station called Wapweelah, where he died soon afterwards. He was buried there.

During those years at Mundiwa we needed food from the bush and Jimmy Kerrigan showed me how to collect it. His knowledge of the bush was a great help to us all. Everyone spoke of him with respect and admiration, and that continued for years after his death. My feeling for him was different: I looked up to him with a sort of reverence as a person above all others. I called him 'uncle', and I think he was the brother of my Muruwari grandmother. He was a full-blood, and reputed to be one of the last true witch doctors of the Muruwari. I did not see him doing anything spectacular, but everyone spoke of his ability to remove the bad spirits which could have caused the death or serious illness of the victim. He owned a *wilida*, which is a stone axe with magic properties. This was believed to have been given to him by a spirit in the night, being an implement which may only be used by witch doctors or specially initiated men. Others could never use it because it had to be a gift from a spirit. When using it the owner sang a secret chant which made chopping easier. With the *wilida* a man must use only one blow when killing,. and it could not be used twice for the one action or deed. When the owner died it had to be buried with him or hidden where no one could find it, perhaps in the middle of a river where it would be covered with silt. If this were not done an illegal owner would find himself cursed with some sickness or evil.

Of course I did not know very much about witch doctors in those days, but the old people spoke to children as equals and it was surprising how much I learnt. The witch doctors had dilly bags in which all kinds of secret possessions were kept. Jimmy Kerrigan had some magic stones which appeared to be a type of quartz crystal. They were out of his bag one day, and he was furious when he saw me staring at them. In later years some old Ngemba men told me about them. As with the *wilida*, they were supposed to have some magical properties.

Old Jimmy told me the mixture for a secret poison. He should not have done so, as the secret was only to be revealed to the initiates at the *bora* ceremonies. So many years have passed that I cannot remember the details. Dried *bundhabundha*, or caterpillar, was mixed with various herbs. Another insect and a variety of grubs were dried out and the whole mixture was ground into a powder. The witch doctor would supply it when requested and it would be hidden in the food of the intended victim, who would become ill within hours of eating it. This recipe of Jimmy's was known to very few, but most people were aware of its use. At all times an Aborigine had to consider the possibility of poison when a stranger or witch doctor was present.

In his day Jimmy Kerrigan was the most respected and feared man of the Muruwari tribe. He led them in fights and battles, and his word was law. A number of times he visited people who were presumably very ill and the next day the patient would be seen walking about. Mother had a strong belief in him as a 'clever man'. For myself, I often had doubts about the real power of witch doctors, but there are some memories of old Jimmy which are hard to explain. My other memories are of a man who was very kind and patient with a small boy. He used to draw pictures on the ground for me, talking a lot at the same time. He would tell me that a dot was an emu and continue to explain that a man was behind the tree which he had drawn. As the man was hidden he was not drawn. A line might represent the river and several others were a waterfall. Fish might come into the story, but as they were under the water they were not drawn. The trouble with Aboriginal art is that we cannot get the true story when it is only represented by a primitive picture.

We used to camp out a lot. I loved it in the bush, and still have a special feeling for it. Sitting under the brigalow trees at night was wonderful, especially after rain. The smell of gidgee or brigalow seemed to put life into me; it did then, and has done so throughout my life. Frogs croaked in the water holes, and the clear water we drank tasted very good. It made good tea, which we sometimes drank after a large meal of kangaroo or emu we had caught and killed ourselves. The men caught emus in the same way as their ancestors had. The fact that emus are such inquisitive birds helps considerably when catching them. Old Jimmy used to make me lie on the ground and pedal with my legs in the air. The emus would come to investigate this odd sight; the men would jump out from hiding and hit them with a bundi. The result was a good meal for us all.

There was another method of catching emus which needed more skill. A *murrkarr* or net was made of kurrajong bark. This had to be very strong, and was made in a long strip approximately eighteen inches wide. At intervals there were special nooses made of kangaroo sinew. The men dug a circular pit ten feet in diameter and three feet deep. Sandy ground was preferred, as the digging was easier. Pegs, called *bidjili*, were made from green saplings and driven deep into the ground several feet out from the edge of the hole; the *murrkarr* was placed round the outer side of the *bidjili* and fastened at the top and bottom. Then the whole thing was camouflaged with brush or leaves. The currant-bush is the most satisfactory for this purpose, as it has a mass of small branches and twigs; this makes it more permanent — there are no leaves to drop and it does not have to be replaced too often. Special holes were left in the brush, and the nooses and slipknots were cunningly set. Special branches were also placed so that the men in the pit were concealed. One man would have an instrument slightly resembling a didgeridoo and called a *burrba*, which was made from a 'shelly' or hollow log approximately three feet long and six inches in diameter. (A shelly log is one which has been eaten by white ants and only the shell remains.) Pine resin was warmed and a funnel-shaped mouthpiece was attached to the log. The man made a call through this which was similar to 'brrr-brrr'; this sound was amplified and could be mistaken for the drumming of an emu. While the three men crouched low in the pit an emu would come to investigate. It would find a hole and push its head through, which would tighten the noose around its neck. When it was restrained the men would jump out and kill it with a bundi.

The usual procedure was to kill one bird at a time, even though there may be more curious emus in the vicinity. These would never run away, but would retreat a short distance and come back again and again to observe what was happening. The men sometimes threw a *gudjuru* (a type of nulla nulla) at their legs. If these efforts were unsuccessful it did not bother them as they knew they had one safely trapped in the *murrkarr*. There are still a number of these excavations to be seen around Brewarrina. In more recent years the shelly log has been blown to bring emus within the range of a gun.

At Mundiwa everyone helped with the preparation and cooking of an emu. It was at this early age that I was taught the strict rules of killing, cooking and eating meat. Each tribe had its own method, and strangers or visitors would have to conform: if not, there would be a fight. The belief behind this was that a totem would be abused if not handled in the correct way, and the owner of that totem would be insulted.

The Muruwari cooked an emu on its back; the legs could not be broken off, and the sinews had to be carefully cut at the joints. The cooking involved a routine procedure, and everyone was kept busy. The children gathered firewood and leaves; other people were responsible for digging a hole and lighting a fire in the bottom of it and a smaller one beside it. In the meantime others would be plucking and cleaning the bird, and blood would be rubbed over the skin. If stones could be found they were heated in the outside fire, wrapped in green leaves and placed inside the bird. The emu would never be placed on hot coals; the procedure was to wait until ash had formed on top of the fire in the hole. Then the emu was wrapped in leaves from a box-tree and lowered on top of the fire. Gradually coals and hot ashes were removed from the outside fire and placed on top of the bird, then everything was covered with tightly packed earth. The outside fire would continue to burn, and it was sometimes necessary to add more coals or ashes during the cooking time. Eventually the cooked emu would be lifted out and cleaned with leaves. The outer skin had become crisp, due to the earlier coating of blood. Then the food was distributed in the usual way; this meant that the youngest present had the toughest and least attractive part and the old people had the best. The tail part, which is considered a great delicacy, was never given to the young people. They were told that their hair would go grey if they ate it.

When we had eaten we would still sit around the fire, and the old people would talk to one another and tell us stories of long ago. The other children might fall asleep, but I always listened to the stories even if I pretended to be asleep. They usually spoke in Muruwari, and it was easy for me to understand as I was speaking it most of the time. Even Billy could understand it now. They talked about the seasons of the year; these were recognised by the ripening or withering of various types of fruit or growth. Spring was welcomed as the fruit ripened and the animals moved more freely. Autumn was the time of withering, and scarcity of food would follow. These old people were not governed by the passage of time as we are today. On the other hand, they studied the movement of the sun during the day and would refer to the four phases of the moon if some specific time had to be nominated. They were always aware of the movement of stars at night, and noted their height and position in the sky. The movements of Jupiter and Venus were important; one position at night and another in the early morning were definite events. By watching the stars they could always guide themselves through the bush. In those days time did not need to be very accurate, but it was possible to have a reasonable knowledge of the passage of time.

These stories of the skies were wonderful to hear, especially when told in Muruwari as we sat around the fire. The fire would die down and we could see the sky more clearly. Many of the stars represented animals. Jimmy Kerrigan would say, 'Here comes Gambi the spider,' or perhaps he would point to a kangaroo, possum or porcupine. Binambinam the butterfly was beautiful. The brightest stars all had names. The old people knew nothing about planets: everything in the sky was a star, with the moon the only exception. There were a number of stories about the southern groups and those overhead, but there was very little interest in the northern skies. This was the beginning for me, at the age of seven years, of a great love for the bush and the skies at night. During the next few years the old people told me many of these stories, and they were better than any adventure story. I shall try to remember some of them.

There was the story of the Gambugambu, which I learnt later were the Pleiades. Gambugambu are very shy virgins, some so shy that they can be seen only by people with very good sight, as they are trying to hide. The others can be seen by average eyes, and during mid-winter they rise about three hours before the sun. When they were in this position the Muruwari believed that they were urinating and the *giwa:* (urine) wet the ground. The Gambugambu were so pure that all their *giwa:* would have turned into ice or frost by sunrise. I used to put out a dish of water at night and eat the ice which had formed in the morning. Mother would say: 'Jimmie, you are eating Gambugambu *giwa:*!

Gemini was known as Gidara Galga:, and represented twins who were bound together. I loved the story of Orion's shield. Although the Muruwari recognised that Orion wore a belt with a sheath that carried his knife, the shield was of more importance. This shield, or *burrgu,* is in one hand and his tomahawk is in the other. He was called Jardijardi, which means a strong man. The word also means cyclone, but this did not indicate that Orion had the power to create cyclones. In the sky Orion faces Taurus; the Muruwari interpreted this as the strong man facing a spirit dog. This spirit dog was called Jugi or Guwinj Jugi (ghost dog). The Ngemba tribe called him Mirijula, which also means a fearsome, dingo-type spirit dog. Before Jugi rose into the sky, he lived on earth in places that were frightening to humans, such as dark caves and eerie holes in the ground. The fight between Jardijardi and the Jugi has continued for centuries; a bright red star is the eye of the Jugi. Several other Jugi can be seen in the sky: one perfect head is near the 'false cross'. Another Jugi can be seen chasing a kangaroo. When living on earth the Jugi had an awesome reputation and were controlled by Juriga, the spirit man. Other tribes had similar beliefs about these fabled dogs.

Although the Jugi were reputed to live in caves when on earth, it is hard to be specific about this. At Gerara there are holes in the ground, and this is believed to be the place where some of them lived. Mother told me this, and when we walked on the ground there was a hollow sound. At other times it was said that they lived in dense scrub. As Aboriginal children we were frequently warned about visiting such places because of the presence of Jugi, so the belief could have been fostered by the warnings. I remember a very old man who warned everyone to avoid a certain area as he had seen a Jugi there. He stressed that it was unsafe for anyone to visit the locality. Later it was discovered that it was opal-bearing ground, and he wanted the opals for himself. The natives knew about opals, and called them *wiyi bagul*, or fiery stones. There was some feeling of superstition about them, and children were never allowed to handle them. The reason given was that they came from the home of the Jugi.

These stories and legends seemed easy to believe when surrounded by the bush, sleeping in the open, talking at night with the stars and moon overhead. I used to ask the old people where the moon had gone when it left the sky. They said that the moon was a man who had died and was underground. He liked to come out and look at the people and the world, then as death came upon him again he returned under the earth. For many years I believed this story of the movements of the moon. The phase when the sky was moonless was called *deringa*.

It was in 1907, when I was aged seven years, that I first heard the story of Giyan, the Moon. Since then I have heard it many times, and I understand it very much better now than in those days. This is a Muruwari story and is believed to go far back into the Dreamtime. It happened soon after Bida-Ngulu, the Muruwari creator of all things, had given the Aborigines the *duwadi* or spirit of man. He had also given the *widji bidjuru* or spirit of life to animals, birds, fish, reptiles and insects.

Long, long ago, Giyan* lived on earth. He was a smart and handsome man. He was also very clever and could change his form as he wished or make himself invisible. One day, when travelling, he came to a place where there were many people. He made friends with them and lived there for a while. He gave them new ideas, as he was so clever in every way. He was the best boomerang thrower and the strongest man with a spear. His athletic abilities were wonderful; none of the young men could defeat him at anything. Because of this superiority he had influence over all the men, and the women were attracted to him and applauded all his achievements. His main admirers were two young women

* This story was recorded in Muruwari.

with very large bosoms; they always cheered or laughed when others had lost or fallen to the skill of this visitor to the tribe. Giyan was very clever and boasted of his triumphs, but he carefully guarded one secret. He could not swim, and as there was no river near the camp this fact could not be tested. Although he moved amongst these people he could not select a wife as he came from an unknown tribe. This was another secret and he never revealed his origin or past; this mystery seemed to make him even more attractive to the women.

After a successful day of winning every contest, the two young women with large bosoms came to Giyan and laughed and talked with him; the three of them had many jokes together. For some time he had planned that he would ask these two girls to elope with him, and on this day he had his opportunity. He asked them to come away with him, they agreed to his request, and they decided on a secret meeting place.

That night when all was dark and quiet, they moved away from the tribe. They walked until they came to a very wide and deep river which had to be crossed before they could escape. It was then that Giyan admitted that he was unable to swim. This was a great surprise to the girls, but they helped Giyan search for a log on which he could float across the river. No log could be found, and the girls made another suggestion. They told Giyan to stand between them and to place his hands on their backs; if he did this they should be able to get him across the river safely. All went well until they reached mid-stream where the water was deepest. Giyan, being a man who liked to play with girls, started to tickle his escorts. They warned him that this was dangerous, but he took no notice and tickled even more. This made the girls swim well apart, and Giyan sank to the bottom of the river. The girls turned and swam quickly to the river-bank and returned to their tribe.

Giyan lay under the water as though he had drowned. He was there for several days, then floated to the surface. He happened to float on to the river-bank from where he had started. He rolled into the silt and lay there for a while. As he was not completely dead he revived gradually and became a new man. Now he was a much superior person, a supernatural being who could do many things he had been unable to do before. He could change the identity of anything or anybody and had many new powers.

He changed his own appearance and selected a new name for himself, then he walked away from the river and returned to the tribe. Giyan told the people that he was from a distant land, and used his new name when he introduced himself. He told them he knew many songs and dances he would like to perform for them. They were all interested and started making the preparations he requested. He asked the people to collect as much wood as possible and to place it in a heap; he told them this was for a tremendous fire which would be lit when his performance began. While they were gathering the wood he made a very heavy and sharp tomahawk, then he cut a large coolamon of bark from a tree and left it at his camp, which was apart from the others.

That night the fire was lit, and he told the people to sit close to one another and to stay on one side of the fire. Although he was not recognised by the people, it was as Giyan that he began his performance. He danced many different dances, and after each one moved around the fire and disappeared from sight. Each time he receded into the darkness he moved the bark coolamon a few yards closer to the fire. Then he told the people to bow their heads. When he was ready to dance again he asked them to lift their heads and watch him. This continued through many dances until the coolamon was close to the fire. The dragging of the coolamon had left a long scar on the ground. When he was ready to perform his last dance he told them to put their heads low on the ground and he would say when to raise them again. When they were allowed to lift their heads he was at the back of the fire with the coolamon. Owing to the light from the fire they could not see beyond it. Once again he raised the coolamon: with his magic the bark became very large and moved towards the sky. During this time he was chanting: 'Loja, loja, badu, badu, loja.' All heads were down when he made the large disk of bark fall on them. Then he jumped on top of it and with his weight and the heat of the fire held everyone beneath it. If a head appeared near the side of the bark he chopped it off with his tomahawk. None of those who were caught under the bark survived, although two young men had run off into the darkness as the bark was falling. These two were the only ones to survive Giyan's murderous plot; they moved among the other groups of the Muruwari tribe and described the dreadful event. They also warned neighbouring tribes, and it was not until they gathered together that they realised it must have been the work of Giyan.

The men made a great effort to pursue him, but he was still too clever for them. He went up into the sky and today he still lives up there: Giyan the moon. He disappears and comes out again every month. He gets smaller, then becomes larger and larger, and when his size is greatest, he looks around for several days. Then he becomes smaller again and disappears. He has been living in the sky ever since the massacre of one group of the Muruwari tribe. The story of Giyan will always be remembered during an eclipse of the moon, when it becomes red: the redness is said to be the blood of Giyan. Another reminder of this story is the large ring sometimes seen around the moon: this is supposed to show the size of the bark and the area of ground it covered. The moon, or Giyan, is standing in the middle holding his tomahawk.

There is a second and slightly different version of this story of Giyan. The first part is similar to the original, but for the last act it is thought he may have been blamed wrongly. In this story Giyan was reputed to be a very clever man in all magic, but he was also a man with a poor reputation morally. Two sisters went to the Culgoa River and were digging for mussels late one afternoon. Giyan came to the river and went into the water. He molested the girls; they did not like it and so they retaliated. They hit him and held him under the water until they thought he had drowned. He was a big man, but they pulled him out and left him on the river-bank supposedly dead. When they returned to the camp they told the people about this occurrence, and some men went back to the river. They could not find Giyan. They dived into the water and looked everywhere; then it became late and they returned to the camp. Next morning they all searched but Giyan could not be found. Some said that he would float to the surface in a few days if he was really drowned. Others said he was too clever to be dead.

Many days passed and still Giyan was not found. Some time later a man visited the camp and said that he had seen Giyan in the bush. The people were still annoyed because he had molested the girls, and they decided to search again in the morning. Before the night was over a large fireball from the sky struck the earth and tore away the river-bank where Giyan had last been seen; then it rolled over the camp-site and killed all the people. When other natives came to investigate and saw what had happened, they blamed Giyan. Gathering all their weapons they searched the bush for him, and when they found him they speared and clubbed him to death. Later he rose to the sky and they believed that the moon was Giyan. The deaths of those Muruwari might have been caused by a meteorite, but Giyan had paid for them with his death.

This second version was told by Ngemba people. Mother and Jimmy Kerrigan told me the first story. I was only a little boy when we were at Mundiwa, and I remember being taken by Jimmy Kerrigan to the place on the Culgoa where Giyan was believed to have drowned. It is called 'Giyan bawuma:l', 'the place of the resurrection of the moon'. Leading from this place is a long barren strip rather like a road, which terminates in a large, arid and circular space. The entire area is shaped like a frying pan with a long handle. This is where the Muruwari were slaughtered. It is not far from Boneda, but might be difficult to find again, although I have heard people talking about it in recent years. Perhaps the scars were made by a meteorite, but that was not the Muruwari belief.

I have mentioned Peter Flood before. He was a rough sort of a man; he swore a lot and spoke about unpleasant things which I should have preferred not to hear. Aboriginal children are not ignorant of the facts of life for long. At the earliest age they are told a certain amount, and by the time they are eight years old they know everything. Peter was younger than Jimmy Kerrigan and was supposed to be a witch doctor, although I doubt if many people had much faith in him. He was a self-appointed 'king' and the whites treated him as an Aborigine of some importance. They built a galvanised-iron house for him at Mundiwa; it was larger than our hut and quite comfortable. For some reason he preferred to live in a bark hut in the bush, and gave us his house. This change was good for us and it pleased Mother a lot.

Nobody really believed in old Peter, but he felt that he had some influence in the Culgoa region. In Muruwari he was known as 'Midjin midjin', which meant 'big liar'. They also called him 'Badanj badanj midjin midjin', which meant 'father of lies'. He knew a lot of songs and probably he composed them himself, although he said that the spirits came by night and taught him.* The people enjoyed the songs but were unimpressed by his magic or skill, despite the fact that he was reputed to have killed several people by magic. It was also said that he had killed someone with poison made from hairs and bone and that two other victims had been killed by his bundi and then burnt. Despite all these stories, I learnt to like old Peter. He was good to me and was always willing to take me camping with him and to carry me when I was tired.

Peter was aged about sixty years when we first knew him. He had only one eye; the other had probably been knocked out in one of his many fights. He thought he was a great success with the girls and often joked with them, especially when their husbands were away. He had been married in the Muruwari way but his wife was a cripple and very old. Some people said he had broken her legs so she could neither leave him nor chase him. He collected his rations at Milroy Station and always wanted more than anyone else. He would threaten to stop the rain, bring a flood or produce some other dire calamity if his wishes were not granted.

Old Peter believed he knew everything. He could not read, but would take a newspaper and hold it upside down while moving his lips slightly. After that he would move amongst the people and tell them the news of the day as he had read it. He was cunning and had probably asked a white man for the news, which he passed on to us hoping that we would be impressed. He was not a very good character, although he would give some warning of his misdeeds. He might ask for food at a station, and when he was refused would warn them that they might find a sheep was missing.

* Two of these songs were recorded by Jimmie Barker for A.I.A.S.

At Mundiwa a large number of Muruwari and Ngemba people came and went as they pleased. In those days most of the Aboriginal population enjoyed moving about. Late in 1907 old Jimmy Kerrigan died and was buried in the sandhills near the Culgoa River. This place was a recognised Aboriginal burial ground. No children were allowed near it: the old people indicated a definite point beyond which we were forbidden to go. I was very sad when old Jimmy died. The mourners followed his body to the burial ground while all the children remained in the camp. When the adults returned they made fires with green branches and leaves, which gave off a tremendous amount of smoke. The natives believed that when a man died his spirit lingered for some time around his camp and home. This spirit would try to take away the spirit of one of those the dead man had loved best, especially a favourite child. After some time the spirit would depart for ever and join the other spirits of the dead. The purpose of the smoke was to confuse the spirit and make the identity of those living appear different. The spirit recognised those he knew by their smell, and the smoke made this difficult. All the adults and children were put through the smoke. It is said that the smoke from burning dogwood is the most effective.

This was done to us all after the death of old Jimmy Kerrigan. After that we all moved away from the camp for some days, to avoid any interference by his spirit and because different surroundings made it easier to forget our sadness. Our return to the camp was only brief, as the death of old Jimmy meant that the small settlement at Mundiwa was finished. We all moved to other places, except Peter Flood, who remained alone there until his death in 1912.

It was early in 1908 that Mother told me we were leaving and going to a place called Milroy. This was a station about seven miles from Mundiwa and forty miles from Brewarrina. I remember telling Mother that I refused to leave. She asked me the reason and I explained that I did not want to leave the old people. She reassured me and told me that I would still see them as some were moving to Milroy or to other places on the Culgoa River. This comforted me a little.

During the days before we left Mundiwa I marked a few trees, then filled some bottles with marbles and old mechanical parts and buried them. There had never been any fights at this camp; the people sang together and had some corroborees, and every day they seemed happy. I had been too young to join in the corroborees but often went to watch the dancing. I had enjoyed the singing. Even now I find myself singing scraps from those old songs, although I have forgotten most of them.

Two old people had died when we were there and all their relatives had left soon afterwards. It was at this time that the dark people were moving around and settling in Weilmoringle, Enngonia, Goodooga and Bourke. I was miserable, though Mother tried to assure me that we would be happy at Milroy. She was to be a housemaid at the station homestead.

For many years after we left I dreamed of returning to Mundiwa, but it was fifty years before I saw it again and then I could not find the bottles, although the marks on the trees remained. I wandered through the old familiar places and thought of the time when all was laughter where now it was so silent. It was hard to restrain tears when those memories returned.

2 Milroy

'The spirits created by Bida-Ngulu were near'

I SHALL never forget the journey to Milroy. We travelled in an old sulky; I think I cried all the way, and I was very tired when we arrived in the darkness. Mundiwa had gone and I felt that nothing could replace it. I do not remember having any food that night, but I was out of bed early next morning curious to see our new surroundings. The house, which was to be our home for the next four years, was very old. It had three rooms and a couple of tanks beside it. The roof was tin and the walls were made of timber which had come from the surrounding bush. It was a ramshackle type of a log cabin, and was probably one of the first houses ever built at Milroy. The rooms were small: kitchen, bedroom, and tiny living-room. It was little more than a hut, but there was a stove in the kitchen, which was a help for Mother.

After breakfast Mother went to see Mrs Armstrong, the lady of the Big House, as it was always called. When Mother returned she told us she was to start work the next day, so we had this first day to settle into our new home. The following day, while Mother was at work, Bill and I just played in the hut. I know I spent a lot of the day crying. My sadness was caused by the absence of my old friends. Billy did not worry, then or in later years. He said when he was much older that one had to face the world with a strong heart and never give way. He was right, but I have always been very emotional.

In a couple of days Billy and I became more daring and decided to look inside a big shed. There we saw a man fixing some harness. He told us to call him Tommy, and that this was a buggy shed and horse stables. I asked Tommy many questions and sometimes he answered, then it was morning-tea time and he asked us to join him. We tried to refuse but he told us there would be lots of cakes; and he took us to the kitchen, where the old cook spoke kindly to us. Billy did all the talking; I just answered questions if they spoke to me, as I was always shy and nervous with strangers. The cook gave us a lot of hard biscuits, and when we were out of sight we threw them away because we thought they were very old and much too hard. We had never seen gingernut biscuits before. I used to think of Tommy's kindness and hoped I could spend more time with him. As the days passed I did see him often, and he read me many stories. I think his age was about thirty, but I doubt if he is alive today as I was only eight years old at that time.

Mother worked at the homestead and Mrs Armstrong was very good to her. Her wages were seven shillings and sixpence a week. The station butcher was close and we could get meat daily if we wanted it, and a lot of food was also given to us from the Big House. Life was really comfortable; we were well fed and free to roam about the station buildings. One day I was wandering and found Tommy. He was raising water by a hand pump which slowly filled the tank. When he had finished he took me into a shed and showed me a large carbide generator which produced the gaslight used at that time. I heard loud bubbling sounds as the gas was generated. As the inner cylinder rose above the water-line of the outer tank, I was frightened and rushed to the door. Tommy laughed and called me back to reassure me. After this, I was in there with him every morning.

As the days passed I wandered more widely. There was an old blacksmith's shop near the horse-yard, and I explored that. I had never seen such tools and gear before, and the big bellows fascinated me. One day Mother took us to the Big House, where we met Mrs Armstrong for the first time, also her daughter Amy. They both spoke to us kindly and took us into the garden. As long as I can remember I have always been extraordinarily fond of flowers, but before this I had seen only wild flowers. Here we saw vast beds of cultivated flowers and shrubs, and I was tremendously excited. Mrs Armstrong asked me if I would water the garden for her each morning. I agreed to help her, then she took us to the kitchen and asked the old Chinese cook to give us tea and cakes.

Somehow I was afraid of him, as I had heard stories of how he could chop off a head or do other unpleasant things. Billy and I just stood near the door and watched him. When the food was ready he put two chairs near the table and asked us to sit down. Our behaviour was not good; we grabbed the tea and cakes and rushed outside on to the verandah. Later when we took the cups back the old man looked at us and said, 'Funny boys, you.'

The next day Mrs Armstrong showed me how to use the hose. This was fun, and the watering took more than an hour. Gradually I learnt the names of the flowers; chrysanthemums and stocks have been my favourites since that time. When the watering was finished Mrs Armstrong came out with a large box of toys and led us to a summer-house. She told us to take care of the toys and to leave them there and said that Billy and I could come and play with them whenever we liked. We spent many happy hours with those toys, and she gave us more to add to the collection. I never regretted the day I promised to water the flowers.

Each afternoon I made an effort to get away on my own, and it was an exciting moment when I found the main rubbish dump, which must have been there for many years. There were lots of things I could use: old sewing machines, bicycles, clocks and hundreds of old food cans, which in those days were soldered. Billy helped me make a firing-place for the cans, and we stacked as many into it as possible. The next day we collected the solder, which we called 'lead', melted it down in old frying-pans, and set it in clay moulds. We had stacks of this 'lead' close to our house, and it is probable that there are some pounds of it still hidden in the dust today. As the weeks passed I had other ideas, and Billy became more useful; he was able to help me carry many loads from the rubbish dump. Sometimes we spent the day carrying things for Miss Amy when she went out painting; she was a fair artist. Frequently we went for long walks on our own and gathered berries or wild oranges.

My collection of rubbish and other materials grew larger and I kept them in a special place which I called my workshop. With old rusty tools the blacksmith had given me I was able to make many things. There were mechanical toys made from old clocks, and I shall never forget the first tin boat I made. It was powered by an old clock and had a three-blade propeller. As I had seen only a rowing boat on the Culgoa River, this was my own invention.

Hector Kerrigan had come to work at Milroy, and we were beginning to make other friends. On Sundays the workers had nothing to do, so we just dressed up in our best clothes and stayed at home. One day when I was dressed in my best sailor suit I took my little boat to a large dam. It ran well for a few minutes and then stopped about ten feet from the shore. I made several attempts to reach the craft with a long stick, and then I fell into the deep water. I could not swim, and had been under water for what seemed a long time when strong arms grabbed me. It was my good friend Hector; he saved my life. He asked me how I felt and when he was sure I was quite well he took off his belt and gave me a couple of hits with it. Then he told me that I must never go near deep water again. He did not return my boat, but would take me to the dam for a couple of hours when he had time and let me see it in action. I think he enjoyed it as much as I did, and I loved him for saving me. The following year he married and moved to Weilmoringle, where I visited him for a couple of weeks in 1910. When we parted we talked of our next meeting, but this never took place because Hector died during the influenza epidemic of 1919.

In December 1908 we had been at Milroy for almost a year. I knew all the places of interest within reasonable distance and had made many friends. I spent many hours in my 'workshop' fabricating various contraptions. I had added to my assortment of tools and most of the rubbish dump had been moved to my workshop. I had attached some wire to a large sheet of galvanised iron, and Billy helped me to load it and drag along the things I wanted to salvage. I used to stay there until late at night, despite warnings from some of the older dark people that a ghost might come and take me away. A new manager had arrived at the station; he had five children who pestered me to play with them but I preferred working on my constructive jobs and tried to escape from them. Billy and I made soap from all the scraps we could find, and I managed to make a bird that could fly. This was made possible by finding an old golf ball, unwinding the rubber and fitting it to a type of propeller.

Many new people arrived at Milroy, most of them station hands or fencers who worked in the bush and only visited the station occasionally. Old Jimmy Wellington arrived; he was a good stockman and we had known him at Mundiwa. His wife was Eileen Buckley, a Muruwari full-blood who seldom spoke in English. Two other arrivals delighted me, Hippai and Maria; they were also Muruwari. Hippai might have had another name, but I did not know it. I had met them occasionally at Mundiwa, so we were not strangers. They were very old dark people and I learnt to love them, especially Maria, who was always kind to Billy and me. She worked for a couple of days weekly at the homestead, and Hippai was a station hand. When they were not working they took me to the Culgoa or Birrie rivers to fish, and frequently we camped out together. When Hippai was away Maria used to ask Mother if I could stay with her for company. She used to drag me away from my workshop late at night as she was always afraid the ghost would take me. Several hours a day were always spent with Maria; we spoke in Muruwari and she told me a lot about our tribe and their customs. She knew many of their songs, and always sang a Muruwari lullaby* for me when I was going to sleep. Jimmie Kerrigan had taught me a lot, but now I was nine years old and could understand better. Hippai and Maria seemed to consolidate those things I had partly learnt earlier. They told me how the tribe was divided into groups, and spent many hours drawing in the dust with a stick and explaining their position.

The word *gari* means 'belonging to', and was a suffix used in most of the group names. The area of the lower Culgoa people extended from forty miles above Brewarrina down the Culgoa River to the junction, then followed the Darling River to North Bourke. This group was called the Nandugari, *nandu* meaning 'at times there is nothing there'. The word *nandu* also appears in the name Dinandu, a very small group who lived near the Barwon River just before it

* This lullaby was recorded for A.I.A.S.

joins the Culgoa. The North Culgoa people's boundary followed the Culgoa River past Weilmoringle and then north to the Queensland border on the western side of Toulby Gate; the eastern boundary was the Birrie River. These people were called the Gandugari. These groups spoke Muruwari, but in a completely different manner. The northern people spoke much faster and used a heavily rolled 'r'. There was sometimes a slight difference in pronunciation, and it was easy to identify the group from which the speaker originated.

Mother's group was found near North Bourke, at Ford's Bridge, Yantabulla, Enngonia and south to a small place called Dry Lake. This group could have lived there for centuries; they were called the Gangugari. Above Yantabulla and continuing to the Paroo River they were called the Baragari or Badaragari. Between Collerina and Weilmoringle is a small place called Boneda. This was the boundary of a small but important group, the centre of the area being at Ledknapper Tank. They were called the Dinigada.

The groups found on the actual Muruwari boundaries used words which were unknown to the central people. They had adopted words from the Galali, Gu:rnu, Baranbinja, Guwamu and Ngemba languages. Mother spoke Gu:rnu, Badjari, Baranbinja, Galali, Muruwari and a little Guwamu. Guwamu was spoken north of Weilmoringle, and became mixed with the Muruwari language.

Brinundu was the name of a small group near the northern boundary. The word *bri* means acacia, and this name would mean 'at times there are no acacias'. This word for acacia has also been used in the name Brewarrina, which in Muruwari means 'the place where acacias grow'. The Birrie River derives its name from the same word. In Juwalarai the word for acacia is also *bri*. Bama was the name given to the Barwon River before it is joined by the Culgoa. From this junction to the Queensland border the Culgoa River was called Ngarndu by the natives.

I shall try to describe the boundary of the Muruwari tribe, and it will be seen that these groups were small sections of the entire area. Starting at North Bourke, the line moves along the Darling River to the east, then it continues along the western bank of the Culgoa River to Collerina. Here it moves to the western bank of the Birrie River until it is level with Langboyd. At this point it moves north-west and crosses the Culgoa again, approximately twelve miles north of Weilmoringle. It is here that the border adjoins the Juwalarai tribe. The boundary crosses the Queensland border a few miles west of Toulby Gate, and Guwamu is the neighbour here. The line then moves north-west and crosses the Warrego River south of Cunnamulla, continuing to the eastern bank of the Paroo River, where it turns south through Caiwarro. Soon after this point the direction becomes south-easterly. The line passes through Warroo and slightly west of Yantabulla, then just south of Goombalie it moves due east to join the starting point at North Bourke. The Gungari tribe adjoined the Muruwari in Queensland, and on the western side was the Badjiri. The Baranbinja tribe was adjacent at Bourke. Many people from the Ngemba tribe appeared to have moved into Muruwari territory at the end of the last century, as did a number of other adjacent tribes. There was always a close association between the Juwalarai and the Muruwari, and in some cases they appear to share the same legends. This also applies to the Ngemba and the Muruwari. These three tribes could speak or understand their respective languages and frequently joined each other for corroborees.

In this Muruwari tribal area a number of places had special significance. Tinnenburra and Yantabulla were two of the main centres. Enngonia, Maranoa and Barringun were others of importance. It might be more accurate if the boundary were extended to come a little closer to Talyealye. Hungerford was a place of Aboriginal importance but did not belong to the Muruwari. I have heard that many years ago the correct pronunciation was 'Muruwurari'; this was believed to mean 'fall with fighting club'. In this tribal area many Muruwari place-names are no longer used, having been changed by property owners and other residents. I shall list those that remain and are known to me.

Tinnenburra was Dininburu in the old days. The name came from some edible berries which grew in profusion in the district.

Goombalie means 'a place to bathe'. It was the scene of the last of the tribal fights, against the Badjiri and Galali. Many people were buried here as the result of this battle.

Wirrawarra means 'fallen fire'.

Thurrulgoonia means 'pig-weed excreta'.

Maranoa means 'put out hand'. It was originally pronounced Maranguwa.

Talyealye is not within the boundary, but is a Muruwari word meaning 'eating place'.

Kerribree Creek. The original word was Giribiri, and means 'dancing place'. On the banks of this creek large corroborees were held.

Cuttaburra. The whole meaning of this name is not known, but 'burra' means 'very big'.

Weilmoringle means 'old man saltbush'.

Enngonia. This name came from an Irishman who settled there. He learnt that 'gunya' meant 'camp' and, thinking of home, he called it Eringunya. There was confusion over this name and in the past the natives called it Yangunia, which was later changed to Enngonia. It was a popular gathering place owing to a large sandhill in the vicinity. Sand usually indicated that water was close; berries grew in this type of ground, and goannas, porcupines and other animals were likely to be found. North Bourke also had the attraction of sandy soil beside the Darling River. The original name was Widumardi, but I do not know its meaning.

The Muruwari tribe had strong religious beliefs, and their religion was mine during all those years. It was not until I reached the age of twelve that I heard much about Christianity. The Muruwari believed that Bida-Ngulu, sometimes walled Wi-Bida-Ngulu, was the creator of all things and the supreme being who could never be looked upon. The old people used to talk about him, and drew a symbol in the mud or dust which represented him. This symbol was a circle surrounded by rays, resembling the sun. The sun had no part in their worship however; the rays represented Bida-Ngulu's countenance, which was like fire:

it was said that his name meant forehead of fire'. When the Aborigines were in trouble they believed that Bida-Ngulu would protect them from evil.

Although Bida-Ngulu was never seen, he was believed to have human form. He lived in the sky, and spoke with a booming voice when thunder was heard. *Ja:ndibu,* the Muruwari word for thunder, also means 'he speaks'. Lightning was recognised as being dangerous but had no association with thunder or Bida-Ngulu in the minds of the natives. The son of the creator was Ngulu-Bida, and it was believed that he came down and lived with the Muruwari people for some time. I cannot remember in what way he was supposed to have returned to his father. Neither of these gods had wives; in this our religion differs from the Euahlayi (Juwalarai) beliefs described by Mrs Langloh Parker. There Byamee and his favourite wife, Birrangbooloo, are frequently mentioned. The tribes of Juwalarai, Kamilaroi, Ngemba and Wiradjuri believed in Byamee.

It was not often that the Aboriginal looked ahead to his life after death, as he lived only from day to day. However, it was believed that the man who had been created by Bida-Ngulu would return to him soon after his death. As I have mentioned earlier, this spirit would remain near the dead man's home for a while and it might claim the spirit of one of those who were living. My interpretation of the thoughts of the dead man is: 'I loved my child so dearly that I want to take him with me.' *Jerebin* was the name for this air- or wind-like spirit which can penetrate anything and move anywhere, can appear in a visible form then quickly disappear. Once Bida-Ngulu had regained control of this spirit it would never appear again.

When Bida-Ngulu created men and women he gave them a <u>d</u>uwidi or living spirit which had a connection with dreams — this word also means 'dream'. A native might describe a dream in which he saw someone who was far away, and he would say that this person had visited him in spirit. It was believed that all dreams were of a spiritual nature. Bida-Ngulu also gave the people their totems, which were the spirits of animals, reptiles or birds and were called *bidjuru.* In other cases they would just be called *widji,* which means 'meat'. My totem is kangaroo; I inherited it from my mother. The superior totemic groups were the emu, kangaroo and goanna, which represented the birds, animals and reptiles respectively.

Frequently I have been with the old people when they prayed to the surrounding good spirits created by Bida-Ngulu. They stood silently for a few moments before asking to speak to the spirit, then they made their request. The prayer was offered when a change of weather was needed, or good hunting, or they might quietly call 'guya nguwa', which means 'give us fish'. Sometimes the prayers would be in the form of a song, possibly asking for rain; the rain-makers were reputed to be particularly clever people. Old Maria and Jimmy Kerrigan used to sing rain songs, and the words they sang most often were:

> Have you forgotten us?
> We have not done any wrong.
> There is nothing growing here,
>   it is all dust.
> Everything is drying out;
>   when are you going to send rain?
> Have you forgotten us?
> If someone has done wrong to you,
>   it is not us. *

The custom of the Muruwari required that the oldest people sing this song; the younger ones may have learnt it but were not allowed to sing it. When singing songs the Muruwari held their breath for as long as possible; this resulted in great breathlessness for the older singers.

Songs were also sung when a wind was wanted — often after a death, when the swirling dust would confuse the spirit of the dead man; or it might be wanted to blow away all the old tracks and make the fresh ones more easily visible when hunting.

After prayers for good hunting or fishing, the spirits were never blamed if the results were unsuccessful. The men grumbled that someone else must have been wishing them bad luck or been disobeying the rules. Sometimes I have been

* This song was recorded for A.I.A.S.

fishing with the old people when a group of boys has walked past; they have been quiet and made no noise. Although they were so silent, they could be blamed for interfering with the wishes of the spirits. There was always some reason for lack of success, and the spirits were never the cause. The old people of today still feel that the spirits created by Bida-Ngulu are near them. The Shillingsworths, the Baileys and Robin Campbell of Weilmoringle would still believe in this.

There were also bad spirits who had revolted against Bida-Ngulu; they were called Brena:di. They had broken the laws of the Aborigines and this was their punishment. These rebellious spirits had caused all deformities, whether of humans, animals or plant-life. Cannibalism was not known to have been practised by the Muruwari; I think their fear of the spirit of the dead was too great. I was always told that burial grounds were guarded by the Jugi or the Mirijula, the spirit dogs of the Muruwari and the Ngemba, and this belief made people reluctant to go near them.

It was believed that the Sacred Fires of the sky had been given to the Muruwari by Bida-Ngulu. Previously they had been on earth and in the care of special witch doctors or *gubi,* and only those who were fully initiated could view them. We believe that another tribe tried to steal our Sacred Fires, and as they were being removed from Muruwari country both the fires and the thieves were lifted up into the sky by Bida-Ngulu.

These fires can be seen when the Southern Cross is just rising and low in the sky; they have to be viewed from an open space as their position is just above the horizon. On a very dark night it appears as if a number of men carrying spears almost upright are standing in the sky. The two pointers to the Southern Cross are believed to be two particularly clever witch doctors who are guarding the fires. Their names are Da:daga:mba and Gidjuga:mba, and one star is brighter than the other. The men with spears cannot pass these guards, although they are reputed to be the protectors of the Sacred Fires. At certain times these fires look like distant flames. A little apart from this fire-like glow other stars can be seen; these represent the spirits of the men who stole them. The old men would look into the sky when the night was dark and say: 'The Fires are low tonight, but they are still there. Those men lived here long, long ago, and now they are up there, still on guard and chasing the people who tried to steal the power of the Sacred Fires.'

At another time during the night, a different story is told about the stars in this part of the sky where the Sacred Fires are seen. At this time the Muruwari call it Nurrunjgu Bambu (head of an emu), and it is thought to be the neck of an emu which stretches away from the two pointers, close to which the body can be seen. The natives said the emu was sitting on eggs with its neck stretched parallel to the ground, from which it is picking food. Much later in the night, when the emu is in the west and the Southern Cross is sinking, another story is told. The body of the emu and a large part of the Milky Way, including the Coal Sack, belongs to Gambalaga:n, the great water snake. This water snake represents all the evils of darkness. What had previously been called the body of the emu is now believed to be men standing and fighting to prevent this evil approaching: they are throwing spears and boomerangs at the water snake. Behind them are the two pointers, who give the fighters more power to combat the monster. As in the story of the Sacred Fires, these two pointers are believed to be very clever witch doctors.

All these stories were told to me in Muruwari, and it is hard to remember the exact words that were used. There is another story which has been believed for many years and which a number of the old people have told me; to them it has some religious significance. It happened many centuries ago when some Muruwari people lived on a slight rise in the ground. Near this were some rocks and a very deep hole containing water, which made the existence of the people possible. There was a very long drought and it was a bad time for everybody. This group of people gradually used the water, and the level became steadily lower until the hole was dry. The tribe talked amongst themselves, saying it was too far to walk to any other place where there might be water. Some were too old to make the effort and others were too young. They knew that they might die anyway and that their decision made little difference, so they just sat on the hillside and waited for the rain, but no rain came.

This was during the time that Ngulu-Bida was living with the Muruwari, and when he was told of these troubled people he decided to visit them. When he arrived they swarmed around him and told him of their great thirst and the lack of water. He replied, 'There is water'. They murmured amongst themselves and asked him to look into the dry hole; he must have seen that it was empty but made no comment. He wandered around the area and gathered some smooth, flat pebbles, which he placed near the hole; then he sat down beside them. Once again he said, 'There is water in that hole', and again the people disagreed. Ngulu-Bida said, 'Listen', and dropped one of the stones into the hole. As it hit the bottom it made the sound of striking mud, not rock. He continued dropping more and more stones until the sound indicated a small quantity of water. Then, as he dropped still more stones, the splashing sound increased and was heard by the natives as 'chunk-chunk'. The water rose to the surface and a great volume of it spread around the hole. The people rushed to drink; they were saved and would live. Ngulu-Bida joined them and they all bathed for many hours and were refreshed.

This happened back in the Dreamtime when everything began. The hole was near Goombalie, and has been associated with memories of Ngulu-Bida for all these years. Today the robin redbreast in the bush says 'chunk-chunk' before he begins his song. When the older Muruwari people hear this sound they think of the time when Ngulu-Bida dropped stones in the well, and remember that he chanted the words *gumbal gumba:li*. The meaning of these words is not known, but they have been used as a name for a game which is played by some of the older people. They play on the river-bank, and stones are thrown high into the air. The size of the stone may vary according to the ability of the player, but they are usually between two and four inches in diameter and have sharpened edges. The smaller ones only make a slight sound when hitting the water; the larger stones make a louder sound with a higher pitch. In both cases one seems to hear 'chunk-chunk' as they fall into the river.

My life was very full at Milroy. Many of the children spent most of their time playing games; I joined them occasionally, but their games always seemed to lead to trouble and arguments. I remember we were all making a lot of noise óne day playing on a woodheap near the homestead kitchen, and Bing, the old Chinese cook, came out and asked us to be quiet. The girls, who could be very badly behaved, called him many names, which made him annoyed. He threw his long knife at us and we all left hastily. I avoided the kitchen for many weeks after that, until I was asked to take some meat from the butcher's shop to Bing. I could not refuse, and trotted off hoping he would not be in the kitchen. However, he was there and greeted me pleasantly, saying, 'It long time since I see you; why?' I just stood still, speechless. Then he said he was sorry he had thrown the knife, but the other children had been very cheeky and had annoyed him. He asked me to visit him at any time, as he liked someone to talk to. I did this and we became good friends. I can remember feeling very sad when I heard of Bing's death a few years after we had left Milroy.

In 1910 there was a change of managers and we lost all our playmates. I remember how we all cried, Mother included, because the family had always been so good to us. Although the children's absence gave me more time for my workshop jobs, I missed them a great deal. To our delight the new manager and his wife were very kind to us. They had a four-year-old son, and Billy and I grew to love him. In fact Billy almost lived at the homestead, so he was occupied when I was busy in my workshop or spending time with Hippai and Maria.

I spent many days and nights with Hippai and Maria, either camping or staying with them in their hut. They would light a fire in the bush near the hut; we would cook our meal and then sit near the fire for hours. They would both sing and dance corroboree dances, and I loved listening to their stories. Maria often asked me to corroboree with her, but for some reason I have never liked joining in corroboree dancing, preferring to watch. Quite a number of people joined Hippai and Maria in what were probably the last performances of Muruwari tribal dances.

Whereas the Ngemba had quite impressive dances which were usually a re-enactment of the tracking and kill, in most cases the Muruwari motif was related to their way of life, and there was always plenty of mime. It might be the hopping of a kangaroo, or perhaps hands were held in a certain position which represented the head of an emu. Different names were used which indicated the speed of the dance: *bagada:* was a fast corroboree dance; *garrambala* a slower dance; and in the *waguda* the performers kept their feet still while swaying and making other rhythmic movements with their bodies.

The onlookers produced a rhythmic beat by hitting a type of pillow made of kangaroo skin and stuffed with possum fur. In the early days this had been used as a drum; several people were able to beat it at the same time, using their hands. Boomerangs were clapped together simultaneously and this made an effective accompaniment. At other times the dancers kept the rhythm with the sound of their feet and a chant of 'wir-r, wir-r, wir-r'.

There was one special Muruwari dance which I remember well. It was called 'Milidi Bingga', which is also the name of a small stinging ant that camouflages itself by changing colour to blend into its surroundings. This ant is very aggressive, about half an inch long with an abdomen like a bee, and both stings and bites; its bite is irritable for many days and considerably worse than that of a bulldog ant. It prefers hot weather and has particularly good sight, and is remarkable in that it is always alone. It is usually found on sandy ground, and when disturbed by a stick, it stands upright and jumps from left to right and forward and backwards in a kind of hopping dance. The dance of the Milidi Bingga is based on the movements of this ant when standing erect, and is a *bagada:* or fast dance. The dancers appeared suddenly with boomerangs or *gudjurus* in their hands, and dust flew from their quickly moving feet. Then they stood in one place and made leg movements like those of the ant when disturbed (it appears to dance on bent legs). During the dance boomerangs were struck together and a special song accompanied it.

This was one of the most popular dances, as even the children could participate by shaking their heads and bending their arms. Calls of 'gai-jai-ai' were answered by cries of 'ju-ai'. The decoration used by the dancers was usually kopi and feathers.

When tracking through the bush, the men sometimes

danced on their way. The main tracker was in front, and he danced with his head down as he followed the trail. Younger men and boys danced behind him carrying their spears and boomerangs. They would pretend to hit the leading tracker, who fell and was surrounded by the others. Then they would pick him up by one leg and give him some rough treatment. When he recovered they again followed him, dancing, into the bush. My memories of these episodes go back to Mundiwa and the early days at Milroy: by 1910 this spontaneous feeling for dancing was beginning to disappear.

Old Maria and I often went out hunting. She had dogs which she had trained to catch an emu by the neck. This method was not approved by the old rules, but it was a lot of fun. We spoke Muruwari all the time and cooked the emu ourselves in the bush and had a feast. She was good in the bush and could catch porcupines in the sandhills. Sometimes we returned to Milroy with a large load of meat which included goanna, emu, porcupine or fish. She taught me to make a *murrka* of kurrajong bark, and we carried our loads in these nets. I suppose her age was between fifty and sixty years; she was very active but had the use of only one arm. The other arm just swung uselessly; she told me it had been injured in a fight and had never mended properly. Strangely enough, the lack of an arm never seemed to limit her activities, but as I look back it could have been why she found a small boy helpful. There were others who took me camping, but my happiest times were with Hippai and Maria.

Whether in her hut or in the bush, Maria always had stories to tell me. They were usually dramatic, and I enjoyed them. Old Bindji lived a few miles from Milroy and I had always been puzzled by the way he walked. One day I asked Maria the reason, and this is how she told me about it: 'Jimmie-boy, many years ago Bindji went out hunting. Great hunter he thought he was. This day he chased kangaroos. All day he chased them but could never get close enough to kill one. Poor Bindji, he couldn't find any food and had walked a long, long way from his camp. The sun was low, he was hungry and wanted to go home. As he trudged along he felt very tired, his head was sore and his bones ached. It was a long time after dark when he arrived and he was too tired to light a fire. Anyway, there was nothing to cook. He just lay on his back with his tomahawk in his hand and went to sleep. A dream came to him. He was hunting and hunting for food, a man was following him all the time and he could not lose him. As he moved this man was always behind him. He was a strange-looking man and had no hair on his head. Then he saw the man crawling through the little entrance to his camp. As he watched, the man came closer and closer. He felt he could be killed in his own hut; the man was very close, and seemed to move his head a little. Bindji was still lying on the floor, but he raised his tomahawk high in the air to defend himself; then he struck hard and deep with his blade. Poor, poor fellow! He struck his own knee; he had gone to sleep with his leg bent and upright. That is why Bindji can't walk properly.'

Apparently he had taken some time to recover from his accident, and after this he was always called Binjal Dundu (straight leg), or his shortened name of Bindji.

Maria had another story about a man who spent most of his time hunting for beehives. It seemed odd that he often claimed to have found hives but never brought honey back to the camp. In this camp there was a jealous old witch doctor or *gubi*, and he sent his special 'singer' or spirit to follow the man on one of his expeditions. The small singing spirit followed the man, and was behind him when he came to the first tree which had a hive and honey. The man had to climb the tree before opening the hive, then he put his hand through the hole to collect the honey. As he removed the honey he ate it, and this procedure was repeated at several trees. While he was up one tree and eating greedily the spirit started singing to the hole to become smaller; this puzzled the man, as each time he removed his hand it seemed as if he had to drag it through the opening. Soon it was necessary for him to put his hand much farther into the hole, and this time he could not free himself: his hand was stuck. He dropped his tomahawk and tried to escape, but without success. Some days later he was found dead hanging by his arm from the tree. Even today some old Aborigines might explain similar and other strange occurrences as being caused by the 'little fella' of a witch doctor.

When I was ten years old Hippai and Maria took me to

Weilmoringle for a visit which lasted for several weeks. That was when I met Robin Campbell for the first time. He was a quiet boy, and is still a quiet and easy-going man. During my visit in 1910 there were a large number of Aborigines living in the district; most were only part-Aboriginal, and some of them were employed at Weilmoringle Station. The majority of people gambled day and night with cards or dice — Weilmoringle has long been a haunt for gamblers.

It was on this visit that I had my first sight of people smoking opium. The pipe they used was a small clay pot with a hole bored in one side into which a bamboo stick was fitted. The men lay on their sides and the pipe was put over a small flame while they held the opium against the hole with a piece of wire. They spent many hours daily smoking opium, and it was not until 1912 that the authorities dealt with the Chinese who had been supplying it and the habit was stopped. It was known that supplies of opium came from Brewarrina, Goodooga and Cunnamulla. The smoking of opium was replaced by the drinking of Chlorodyne* in large quantities. At that time it could be bought from any store, but recently it has been removed from the shelves. The Aborigines would drink a bottle quickly, fall to the ground and remain in a coma all day. While the older people were gambling, smoking opium or drinking Chlorodyne, the children ran wild; they had little chance to lead a normal life. This situation could have applied to Robin Campbell, whose childhood was very different from mine. The old people on the Culgoa and at Milroy still lived in the traditional way when possible, and clung to their old customs and beliefs. They neither gambled nor experimented with drink and drugs, and a normal family life was maintained.

When I returned to Milroy I began to play more with the Wellington boys. They were never allowed near the homestead because their behaviour was bad and they were frequently nasty to us. I still have a scar on my head from a tin can one of them threw at me. I have forgiven them for all those unpleasant episodes. Tommy Wellington and I are the

* Chlorodyne consists of chloroform and morphine in an alcohol base.

only ones who are still living and can remember those old days at Milroy.

It was not long before I decided that games with the Wellingtons were not much fun, and as my playmates from the homestead had gone I had to find other ways to occupy myself. The blacksmith's shop interested me, and I often helped with odd jobs; occasionally I was given a sixpence, but I did not really worry about being paid as I felt it was very kind of Billy to have me there. He allowed me to use any of the tools, and I worked on various mechanical ideas there or in my own little workshop. I did not always finish an idea; new schemes seemed to push it away. I also did small jobs for the men on the station, including elementary repair work which involved soldering. Some people paid me and others said that I was just a silly kid with stupid ideas. It never worried me if people thought little of me, I just loved helping in any possible way and working on my own dreams and plans.

I had been working on carbide in various ways, and made a gas container. This blew up and knocked me out. Then I tried experimenting with a brass generator. It gave a really good light, but Mother thought it was too dangerous to have in the house, so it was banished to my little workshop. Another experiment with an old muzzle-loader rifle belonging to Hippai was not too successful: there was a tremendous explosion with masses of black smoke, and a melon shot high into the air. The melon landed on a horse and the rider fell off, as both of them got a fright. I think Tommy spoke to the boss about that and spared me serious trouble. He also restricted my supply of carbide.

Soon after this I was taken to Corella Station for a visit which lasted about twelve weeks. I had small jobs to do each day: watering the garden, sweeping paths, and cleaning shoes; there were also about fifty knives which had to be polished each morning. After doing these chores I used to go out into the buggy to open gates for the boss. There was a steam engine which pumped water from the dam. George Wright was in charge of the engine and pump, and taught me how to use both. We enjoyed pulling them to bits and putting them together again — there was lots of black smoke and hissing steam, which appealed to me.

Eventually Hippai and Maria came to take me back to Milroy. There was an extra load consisting of presents I had been given; these included toys, clothes, and a magic lantern. I had missed Billy a lot while I had been away, and he was pleased to see me when I returned. The magic lantern was enjoyed by us both. We collected cigarette cards and looked at them through the stereoscope. In those days the cards were real photographs, and cigarettes were only threepence a packet.

Billy and I had our greatest year together in 1911. We seemed to agree with one another's ideas and spent most of our time together. After this year Billy had more playmates and our interests began to differ. We spent a lot of time rabbiting, and were given a penny for each skin. We saved our money, and it was a great day for us when the Indian hawker made his visits to the camp. Liquorice was our favourite. We bought it by the yard and wore it as a belt, which we removed when we wanted a bite. We saw our first car during this year. It moved well coming down the sandhills, but all hands were needed to push it up again. I had many rides in it, as old Tommy was the driver. I met Tommy sixteen years later when he was working as a hawker and driving a small van; we joked about that first horseless buggy and agreed that cars had improved since then. That was the last time I ever saw Tommy, and I lost a good friend.

During the year that I was eleven years old I experimented with many more inventions. Amongst them was a glider which Billy and I flew from a platform in a tree — great fun. We produced perfumed soaps and powders, and also made a lot of jam from any edible wild fruit we could find. There were wild lemons, oranges, quandongs, and many native fruits. The jam did not taste too bad. We made a concoction from wild hops: this stuff must have been really potent, as it. gave me a dreadful headache every time I drank it. I made a machine that produced sparks; when I showed it to Tommy he talked about electric light, but when I asked him more questions he had little to tell me about electricity. It was surprising that I survived this period, as I was always the first to try out anything new. There is no doubt that my curiosity and those experiments helped me at work when I was older and had to handle station machinery.

It was always interesting at Milroy; many people visited us from other areas, and most of them were full-bloods. Not long after this period it was a rare occurrence to meet a true Aboriginal, and I remember those old people with great affection. The most notable visitor was Goodooga Billy. He was a very old man, and would wander through the bush from Goodooga. Bangate Charlie was another old man who had taken his name from his place of work. I was not allowed to call any of them by these names owing to my youth: they were all 'gaḏi', or 'uncle' to me. This is what I called Hippai, and my name for Maria was 'ana:bu', or 'aunt'.

Peter Flood visited us frequently, but his purpose was mainly to extract as much food as he could from the station provisions. Peter's misdeeds have been mentioned earlier; now some of them gradually became clearer to me, as I was older and people spoke more openly in front of me. He was reputed to have killed two men; one was Paddy Burns and the other was a man named Buckley. The latter was Eileen Wellington's brother, and I think he was burnt eight miles from Milroy. I was fishing with Hippai and Maria when I overheard them talking and pointing to a place where Peter had burnt Buckley.

There was also an unexplained incident connected with the death of Peter's wife. Many people thought he had murdered her, although I did not really believe it. She was an old woman, and Hippai and a couple of others went to Mundiwa to visit her when they heard she was ill. They heard noises from within the house (this was the one in which we had lived), but Peter firmly refused to let them see her and told them she was sound asleep. They stayed there for some time, but Peter kept them waiting outside. When it became late Hippai and his friends returned to Milroy. A few days later they went to visit the old woman again, and Peter told them that she had died and he had buried her.

I was involved in another incident with Peter, some months before his wife died. Hippai, Maria and I were going to Weilmoringle, and stopped to see Peter on our way. Just as we were about to leave, old Jimmy Wellington arrived. He was drunk, which was not unusual for him, and started an argument with Peter, who was coming to Weilmoringle with us. Peter had already loaded his swag into the buckboard; Jimmy picked it up and emptied everything out of it. Peter packed and replaced his swag. Once again Jimmy tipped everything out, then pushed Peter away and shouted, 'You are not going.' Hippai, Maria and I were just sitting and waiting when the two men started to fight and struggle with one another. Peter freed himself and ran to his swag, which was still on the ground, took out his tomahawk and chased Jimmy round and round the buggy in which we were sitting. Hippai and Maria got out. Jimmy bumped into one of them and fell over, then Peter immediately hacked into him with the tomahawk.

Eventually Jimmy staggered to where his horse was tied and rode to Milroy; from there he was taken to hospital in Brewarrina. Peter came with us and the three of us drove to Weilmoringle. When we arrived I developed sore eyes and had to stay in the tent while the others were rabbiting and fishing, as the sunlight hurt my eyes. It was almost sunset and I was waiting for them to return when the tent-flap opened and a large policeman walked in; behind him I could see a dark man in uniform and recognised Alec Barnes, who was a tracker in this district. The policeman asked where Peter could be found. I felt most embarrassed, as Peter had been quite good to me and had been singing me special songs and making some of his witch-doctor efforts to cure my eyes. I just mumbled to the policeman that I did not know where Peter was.

It was very late when Hippai and the others returned, and I did not hear until the next morning that Peter had been arrested and locked up in one of the sheds at Weilmoringle. I think the policeman had asked Hippai to take him into Brewarrina, but this was difficult to arrange so we took him back to Milroy with us; he was locked up there and taken to Brewarrina the following day. In a few weeks I visited Brewarrina for the first time and had to go into court as a witness, although I had very little idea of what I was saying. The policeman's name was Constable Wells; he was shot soon after this incident. Some said he was murdered and others said it was suicide. Peter was treated as a suspect, but I did not believe that he was responsible for the shooting.

Many people were frightened of Peter and would be very

careful to prevent him collecting any scraps of their hair, skin or sputum as they feared his magic. They believed that he might attach some part of his intended victim to a thigh or arm-bone of a human skeleton and then chant to the spirit asking him to carry out the curses on the person named. I did not really believe this could harm a man, but felt frequently that a person became ill by some natural cause and then believed that he had been 'caught by magic'. When this happened the man would probably die. The belief that magic was killing him was much stronger than any faith he had in a cure. Another witch doctor would have to be very convincing before the health of the patient improved.

In addition to the unexpected visitors at Milroy, Hippai and Maria always added variety to my life. They would get a sudden urge to go walkabout in the bush; their swags would be rolled up quickly and they would send me home to collect my little swag in order to go with them. We would just walk off into the bush, maybe looking for emu eggs, always enjoying our surroundings, hunting and cooking our food. Hippai had horses and a buggy and could have driven to gather these things in half the time, but that would not have been the same.

An emu's nest is just a hollow in the grass, and the mother covers the eggs with grass or sticks. As the eggs are bright green in colour this covering makes them hard to find unless one is trained to recognise the surrounding signs. Emu tracks give the clue, and the tracker walks in narrowing circles. Children were sent to look for these eggs, but were told they must never touch them: having found a nest they must return and tell one of the old men. Those old fellows were cunning and liked the best of everything, and a fresh egg was a delicacy. Porcupine was a popular meal, and Maria prayed for windy days which would clear away all the old tracks, knowing that when the wind dropped all tracks would be new.

The Aboriginal has an amazing ability to be silent in the bush; this means that he can get much closer to his quarry than a white man. His instinct tells him when and where to move, and added to this is his knowledge of the bush and the habits of animals.

Any wounded animal had to be followed and killed, as the

laws forbade torture. I have seen Hippai and Jimmy Kerrigan following wounded kangaroos; they would stab their spears in the tracks and chant special words which were believed to weaken the animal. If this was done to the track of a man or woman the old people were furious. Sometimes I did it for devilment, and the result was great displeasure. In the old days when trackers were following a man they would stab the track and speak to the surrounding spirits in an attempt to weaken the man.

When in the bush an Aboriginal has a particular way of thought which is difficult for anyone else to practise; it is associated with being surrounded by the bush and those things which are found in it. He has his own interpretation of plant growth and which animals can be expected to be close. The old people can tell exactly where possums, carpet snakes or goannas might be hidden. I had the opportunity to observe this, and acquired their feeling for the customs of the bush. Snakes were recognised as being deadly, but the native has some uncanny way of walking and is seldom bitten. They used to say to me: 'He hasn't done you any harm, don't kill him.'

When camping we were always aware of the bird sounds. The inland bellbird has an attractive call but is difficult to locate, as the sound appears to come from another direction. The Muruwari say his call is *'nhu gagara balga:bu'* which means 'porcupine come out from there'. When Maria was hunting for porcupine and heard this bird high in a tree she called to it loudly, believing it was a magic bird and was trying to lure her away from the porcupine. It was a rule that no one must imitate the call of a willie wagtail, and children were told that their teeth would become similar to those of a dog if they mocked these birds. We called the bowerbird a 'ghost bird', because quite often human bones were found in its playground; its ability to imitate various sounds added to its ghostly reputation. When several were seen together no one was worried, but we were uneasy if one was seen alone. The *darunj*, or message bird calls once or twice, and Maria would call back to him. If the bird did not reply to her call she would conclude that something was wrong at home and hurry back to Milroy.

The 'death bird' was another which brought bad news. It is

small and stands erect, with a small top-knot on its head which is very sharp when elevated. It has a very persistent call somewhat like a knock: 'ep . . . ep . . .' and continues with this for a long time. If it became silent the old people were convinced that some bad news would be heard shortly, or if someone was ill they believed that the bird was warning him of his approaching death. There were many stories and rules of behaviour concerning birds. No one must look at a bird flying towards the sunset: if he did, something horrible would happen during the night. When walking through the bush no one must look back at a bird; if they did they would see something else which could be very unpleasant. The native must always look straight ahead when travelling.

When camping in the bush with Jimmy Kerrigan or Hippai there was never a problem over the lack of water, they seemed to have some miraculous way of finding it. During 1911 I went on a long camping trip with Hippai; it was very hot and I had been thirsty for many hours. We came to a lagoon; this sight raised my spirits, but it was quite dry. The heat was intense and I just sat down and cried. Hippai patted me reassuringly and said, 'Dinama', which meant 'underfoot'. This surprised me; I could not imagine how he was going to find drinking water in this desolate area of dried mud. These lagoons are flooded when the river reaches a certain height, and during that time crayfish are found in most of them. With a tomahawk in his hand, Hippai walked over to a white mound. There were many similar mounds, and Hippai explained that these had been made by crayfish. When the lagoon or river flat is drying out the crayfish can be seen, but when the mud has completely dried they are hidden underground and their tails have made these mounds. The old man started digging a mound with his tomahawk and then used a sharp stick until he reached some moisture; at the same time he was enlarging the hole on the surface. I could hear mud dropping into water, and it was not long before I had a refreshing drink.

Sometimes these holes are three feet deep, having been made by crayfish when the lagoon is full. They burrow deeply and the result is a cavity about the size of a football; as the water level of the lagoon lowers, this hole remains full, and when the lagoon is dry the crayfish closes the hole and lives in a small tunnel which leads to his water supply. Sometimes there are several crayfish in a hole or tunnel and there could be a passage between holes. Most of this water is good for drinking, although in severe drought conditions the crayfish may be existing in thick mud. They wait until the lagoon is filled again and then burrow out into the water. Hippai had taught me a valuable lesson. This is an excellent way to find drinking water, and also to catch crayfish. When I was older I caught them in the dry lagoons and some were over a foot long.

Hippai and Maria taught me many methods for finding water or a substitute during our camping trips. The *mundiling* or *buga:* is a vine with potato-like roots. (The former name is more widely used by the Muruwari.) As it is necessary to dig deeply to reach the roots, it is easier when they grow in sandy soil. These plants are not easy to recognise, as some of the vines are small and others almost conceal trees. In the latter case it is essential to know the growth of the tree before the root of the *mundiling* can be located. There are usually two large and watery roots joined by a length of fibre, and the consistency is sufficiently liquid to quench thirst. The kurrajong is another source of water: its roots have large bulbs like potatoes which contain a useful quantity of moisture. The tree needs to be young, or the depth for digging is too great. There is also a small type of pig-weed which grows close to the ground and has a few red leaves. The roots are reasonably watery, and when cooked they are like potatoes. The *bambal* or wild orange is another substitute for water: although there are many large pips in the fruit there is also a lot of juice. The roots of gum-trees in dry creeks can be cut and sucked, or if the sap has risen in the tree a stick can be cut and stood in a possum-skin bag, which will catch the water as it gradually runs out.

During those early days the lessons were valuable to me, and before I had my twelfth birthday I was quite confident that I could exist in the bush without additional food or water. There are many grubs to eat. The *bidjula* or tree grub is edible. The *bilca* and *birica* are ground grubs which are eaten, although I could not call them a delicacy. Blue-grass seed and nuts from the coolibah are ground in the same way as *nardu* and make quite a good damper. The leaves of the small variety of pig-weed, wild spinach and young thistles help to balance the diet. The tar-vine, crowfoot and yams provide root vegetables, and taste quite good when they have been dipped in water, wrapped in grass, placed in hot ashes and finally covered with dirt. This method of cooking is similar to steaming, and is also used when cooking fish. Quandong, *mandalinja* and many others are edible fruit. *Mandalinja* is the Muruwari name for a fruit resembling a banana.

From an early age I had been taught how to make a fire in the Aboriginal way. It must always be small and safe. In other tribal areas large fires were lit to drive out the animals and make hunting easier, but this was never done in Muruwari country as fire was always treated with care and respect. Many years ago I saw people carrying firesticks. The gidgee root is the best for this: a length of one foot will burn all day. Quandong wood is the best for making a fire when the method of rubbing sticks together is used, as it is very dry and has no resin. The presence of resin seems to make the sticks drag when rubbed and they do not make good contact. The old people often carried two stones and some dried grass in their bags; these were probably flintstones or something harder than found in our area. When one is held rigid and the other is hit downwards on to it, a spark is made which drops on to the dried grass. If it is blown quickly there is soon a blaze. Jimmy Kerrigan always carried a special stone which was small and had a hole ground in the middle of it; this was attached to a length of possum-fur cord. He held the cord in his teeth and swung the button-like stone, which made a spark when it struck rock. There were many rules about the lighting of fires. They must never be lit without a reason, must be lit correctly and put out with care. Apart from safety, the people were afraid that the smoke or glow would show their position to an unwelcome visitor.

The days passed very happily at Milroy, with my collection of self-made toys and gadgets increasing rapidly. There were frequent visitors to our growing community of dark people, and there were often incidents of interest. Old Fred, an Aboriginal station hand, died, and once again I saw how deeply this affected those who still lived. The family gathered together some 'criers' who were almost professional, and the chorus of grief was led by the closest relatives. They all cried; then they might stop until a distant sob was heard, when they all continued again. If they could not manage to cry too easily they hit themselves with a bundi or tomahawk and the pain would start them again. This happened after Fred's death, and one old woman gave herself such a crack on the head with a tomahawk that she finally died from her injuries.

Death made those who remained completely hysterical in those days. It is possible that death in our community worried the older people because it was impossible to move camp. We were all put through the smoke, and special songs were sung to Bida-Ngulu asking him to take the spirit of the dead man soon. Despite all these precautions, one of the young Wellington children became very ill soon after Fred died, and his spirit was blamed. The nearest witch doctor was Muckerawa Jack and he had to be brought from Weilmoringle. He stayed with the child for several days until she recovered, and it was said that he had been able to regain possession of her spirit. My belief was not very strong and I felt then, as now, that the child had probably recovered naturally and that her illness had been coincidental.

Before returning to Weilmoringle, Muckerawa Jack and a friend visited Mother and asked her if they could take me into the bush and put me through the initiation ceremony. My age was eleven years at the time. The normal age for going through the *bora* was fourteen and Mother refused them firmly, saying that she considered I was too young. She told me about this a few years later; and assured me that I would not have enjoyed it; I would have been away from her for some time and when I returned I would have been covered with marks and scars like those of Jimmy Kerrigan. I wish she had allowed me to go, so that now I would know more about the ceremony.

At Milroy some of the old women told me a few of the secret names and details of a Muruwari initiation — it appears that when a man becomes old he is apt to tell his wife about the events of his early years. They talked about the arm of the initiate being cut and others drinking the blood. Then this procedure was reversed: blood would flow and the boy must drink it. Apparently they lived on blood for some time during their period in the bush. The cold might be intense, and there were many other discomforts to be endured. The *brena:di,* a type of ghostly and evil spirit, was brought near the initiate, and if he was frightened, that was his failure. The *brena:di* emanated from a fire burning human fat which had probably been acquired from dead people. During this time the boy lay on the ground and was unaware of the events which were to follow. Afterwards he returned to his family, having lost a front tooth and collected many scars and a new name. Many special ceremonies and initiations were performed at Caronga Peak, which is now a station near Byrock.

Shortly before Christmas 1911 Mother told us that we were leaving Milroy and going to live at a place called 'the Mission' at Brewarrina, where we would both be able to go to school. I hated the idea of leaving Milroy, and the thought of school did not please me either. It was not until I was a little older that I learnt that this move was compulsory for us, as the authorities were forcing all Aborigines who lived on stations or in the bush to move into reserves near towns if they had children of school age. This law brought a lot of unhappiness and hardship to many Aborigines, especially the full-bloods, as their whole way of life had to change. It was also the beginning of an unpleasant colony of fringe-dwellers who camped on river-banks or the outskirts of a town; they were forced to move close to schools, and this was the only alternative to a reserve.

We packed most of our toys and gave the rest to the Wellington boys. In the last few days Billy and I never left one another and stayed by ourselves. At night we talked of this new place and wondered what the people would be like. We were very sad at having to leave, and had more presents given to us that Christmas than ever before.

The day came when we had to say good-bye. We left Milroy at nine o'clock that night. That was New Year's Day, 1912.

3 The Mission

'The manager walked between us with a stockwhip in his hand'

ALTHOUGH our new home was to be at this place called 'the Mission', the name was not really official. Many government reserves and supervised settlements were called 'missions'; it was a type of Aboriginal slang term frequently used. It is probable that the number of preachers visiting these reserves in the early days caused the name to be given to many of them.

Soon after our arrival we were taken to an old hut and told that this was to be our home. It was made of timber slabs and had a tin roof and a dirt floor. There was an opening in one wall which served as a door, and there were no windows. It consisted of one room with a very poor fireplace in which it was almost impossible to light a fire. There was no chimney, smoke went everywhere; and this was where Mother had to do the cooking. The only furniture provided was two dreadful beds. I believe that they were old convict beds which had come from Goulburn; they were heavy and impossible to move. They might have been comfortable if we had had mattresses, but we had to sleep on a blanket or bags. When we were able to collect sufficient bags we stuffed them with straw or grass; this was the best we could do. It was the same for most of the other people. Children seem to be able to sleep anywhere, but I could see that this was difficult for Mother. I was eleven and had become aware of her difficulties and problems. Although there were a lot of curious people peering at us, we managed as well as we could for that first night.

Next morning Mother was moving around early and had

begged a little wood from somewhere to light the fire. She learnt how obstinate and difficult that fireplace could be.

Our first and only welcome came from an old man who had known Mother some years earlier. When he had finished talking to her, Bill and I followed him down to the river where he showed us how to fill cans with water. He also showed us where we might find some wood for ourselves. Both places were a long distance from our hut, but we were able to carry some water back, which enabled Mother to produce some sort of a breakfast. Because of the lack of table and chairs, we had to sit on the dirt floor to eat.

Some children came and stared at us through the hole in the wall; they were whispering and giggling and making rather unpleasant remarks about us. Mother asked them to leave, but this was useless and they only became worse. At last the old man became annoyed; he swore at them and they went away. A little later an older boy came to say that the manager wanted to see us. We went into the office and had to give our names, which were entered in two books; I think one was a ration book. He gave us half rations and told us to come again on Thursday when he would issue more.

Bill and I were given two days' leave before we were called up with the other boys for the daily muster. There were about fifty boys; we had to stand in two lines while the manager walked between us with a stockwhip in his hand. He had no hesitation in using this on us if he was in a bad mood. He told us to help the others carrying water from the river to the houses; this had to be done three times a week. Our job was to carry many buckets of water, which involved staggering up the steep river-bank and then walking for several hundred yards with our load. We had to fill casks, hundred-gallon tanks and numerous kerosene tins, and pour water on the manager's garden. It was during this first morning with the manager and the boys that I realised that something different and unpleasant had come into our lives. We had no freedom, things were not right.

For two years this carrying of water was a hard and monotonous job. I realised that a windmill or some mechanical means of collecting the water would make a great difference to everyone, but it was not until 1922 that a pipeline was installed. Wood had to be gathered too, and this was heavy work as it had to be carried for a long distance.

The line-up occurred at six o'clock every morning. We were often whipped by the manager, and then had to do whatever he ordered. This work continued for many hours each day. The name of the manager was Scott, and he ruled over all the people as an absolute dictator. When he rang the bell all the residents had to rush to see what he required — the response had to be immediate. If a person did not answer the call of the bell, his punishment could be expulsion from this mission and all others. The lesser punishment would be many lashes with the manager's stockwhip; he hit both adults and children indiscriminately when he was annoyed.

During those first days of work at the Mission we met some of the most tough and spiteful characters imaginable. They were vicious boys who cared for nothing, and were complete no-hopers. They were like lambs when the manager was near, but they had no self-discipline, and this attitude continued throughout their lives. I hate saying this, but it is true. The majority were fine boys. The Darcy brothers and some others became friends of ours. Gradually we met them all; some of the older families were kind and helped us in many ways. It was the minority who thrived on disturbance; somehow there was no love and mutual understanding, no give-and-take, no appreciation of nature and humanity. Their day-to-day life just seemed to be hopeless and disruptive, which made the environment very unpleasant for others. It was hard to live normally with this element in the community.

There was a weekly issue of rations on Thursdays. We called it 'two, eight and a quarter'. It was given to all families but not to the able-bodied single people, who had to work for three days before receiving any rations. For an adult the issue was two pounds of sugar, eight pounds of flour, a quarter of a pound of tea, and a little salt. There was no baking powder to mix with the flour, no vegetables, meat or milk. How pleased we were when there had been heavy rain and we could gather wild spinach and thistle tops, or perhaps find crowfoot stalks. We might catch fish, but that depended on our luck. It was a starvation diet, and as I look back I realise that we were all suffering from malnutrition. The orphans, who lived in a dormitory, were given a plate of oatmeal each morning and two slices of bread with a cup of tea. At midday they received some watery soup and at night their meal was bread and tea.

Some of the families managed a little better if one of them was working. Deserted wives, widows, and women with lazy husbands suffered most. There was no type of endowment or pension and only a small baby bonus. Blankets were issued, but only one to each family every winter. We had two blankets between the three of us; they had two red stripes down the centre with 'N.S.W. Aborigines' in large red letters. There was a small issue of clothing each year. A boy received one pair of pants, a shirt and a tunic with dark buttons. The men were given a coat, shirt and trousers. The women were given lengths of light cotton material to make their own clothes, and the girls in the dormitory were given the occasional dress which was ready-made. There was a small government store at the Mission which was supposed to be cheaper than the shops in town, but people seldom had money to buy anything.

The Mission had twenty-two family huts, each consisting of one room with a fireplace. There was a larger hut for all the single men, a dormitory for girls and another for young boys, the manager's house, and an overcrowded school. There were no beds or mattresses for the boys, they just slept on the floor. I do not know how the girls fared. All the huts were about twenty feet by ten and the walls were just over six feet high. None of them were painted, and timber shrinkage made a gap of about one inch between slats. Some of the people lined their rooms with calico painted with Kalsomine. The existing fireplaces were only a hole in the wall: we all had to build and shape our own. This was done with mud. A couple of bars were put across the opening, and then we painted them with kopi, which was called *madinda* in Muruwari. When the kopi was mixed with water it made a type of whitewash, which improved the look of the mud. Mother managed to make our hut look reasonable, and we existed on the minimum of food.

Although the huts were overcrowded, most people tried to keep theirs as clean as possible. Others did not care what they looked like. The community lavatories were in a shocking condition and no disinfectant was ever used. The whole place was germ-infested, and I am sure that most of the deaths of the old or very young people were caused by vermin infestation rather than natural causes. Hardly anyone realised that germs are carried by dirt. I had learnt a certain amount about hygiene from Mother early in life and was aware of some of those things to which the human body should not be exposed.

A stable and a shed for sheep-shearing were a few hundred yards from the school, and the slaughteryard was also close. A storehouse was part of the boys' dormitory. The manager's house and office stood slightly apart from the rest. This was the extent of our small community.

School started early in February, and I shall never forget my first day. Billy and I sat together, both feeling very nervous. It was on this day that I learnt how unacceptable Aborigines are to other people. The manager told us straight out that we were just 'nothing'. He continued at some length, telling us that Australian blacks were recognised as the lowest type of humanity living today. He said that it was not much use trying to teach us and that he wanted to make it clear that it was a complete waste of time. I had never before encountered the cruelty and brutality which surrounded us here, and it was a shock to find that this could occur.

Mr Scott had left the Mission soon after we arrived, and this manager-teacher was a man named Keogh. To be told that we were all low in the social and mental scale caused me to worry, and was also hard to understand. At Mundiwa and Milroy I had never imagined anything like this. As we were told many times daily that white people despised the Aborigines, it had to be believed. I had to accept what Mr Keogh and his assistant, who was a preacher-schoolteacher, told us. Mr Keogh used to say that he could speak Hindustani and another foreign language but he never wanted to hear a word of any Aboriginal language: they were all too dirty. This manager was the same as most of them, he was tough and never showed any kindness to us. Mr Foster, the preacher, was there mainly for his preaching, but it meant that we had these two men hammering our inferiority into us all day and every day.

During my first lessons from these men I learnt that as I

was black, or partly coloured, there was no place in Australia for me. I learnt that anyone of my colour would always be an outcast and different from a white person. It gave me the firm idea that an Aboriginal, even if he was only slightly coloured, was mentally and physically inferior to all others. He was the lowest class known in the world, he was little better than an animal; in fact, dogs were sometimes to be preferred. As I was less than twelve years old it was impossible to disbelieve men of authority who were much older. I tried to stop their remarks from bothering me too much, but it was hard to adjust to being treated with such cruelty and contempt.

To return to that first day at school in the little schoolhouse (which was also used as a church): we were given a slate and a pencil and told to copy the figures from 1 to 10 and also to work on the alphabet. I had neither seen nor thought of these things before, but was quite quick at copying them and then sat very still until I was told to take my slate to the teacher. He asked me if I had been to school before; when I replied that I had not, he gruffly said that my work was not bad. Not much work was done that day; we copied a little from the blackboard and had a couple of songs and stories. Although we had to remain in the classroom all day, Mr Foster only came in for tne occasional half-hour and the rest of the time we were just left to occupy ourselves. That night I asked an older friend of mine to write out the complete alphabet and the figures up to 20. I sat up for many hours after my normal bedtime writing and learning the letters and figures. By the next day I knew them all, and in a short time I was beginning to build words. I was interested and looked forward keenly to being able to read eventually. I learnt a lot of spelling from jam tins: the labels on them and other containers were helpful. Newspapers were seldom seen near the Mission, but were precious if I could find any. By April, two months after my first lessons, I was able to read. I remember reading about the sinking of the *Titanic* and other news when I had been fortunate enough to find a discarded newspaper.

Mr Keogh used a heavy length of bush timber as a cane when we were in school. Outside he always used the stockwhip. He was unmerciful to both boys and girls, sometimes he would lift a child off its feet by the ear. One girl's ear was so badly injured that she had to be sent to hospital. Our ears were boxed as well, and we had many other unpleasant punishments. There were quite a number of backward children, and they were the ones to suffer most. I had my share of the cane for errors in my work, but not the severe thrashings that some of the others had. I shed many a silent tear for some of those poor children; maybe they were naughty outside but they did not deserve that treatment in school. I felt the injustice deeply. Those two men were really tough, and most of their successors were the same. It was hard to face such unpleasantness when young; those incidents have left their mark on me.

Our games were limited to marbles and foot races. I loved reading, and read anything I could find; also I liked doing sums and practising my writing. I learnt while the others played, and tried my hardest to gain the top place in the class. As the weeks passed the lessons remained the same; I was learning more out of school than during the hours I was supposed to be having tuition. In June a lady teacher came and everything changed in a very short time. The cane was not used much, she was kind and sympathetic, and she was also a good teacher. We were all much happier; the whole atmosphere was one of encouragement. The lessons were different, there were talks on new subjects, and it was not long before my position in the class was much higher. A number of the children were older and they called me all sorts of names because I had been at school for such a short time and my standard was higher than theirs. We learnt a lot more about English, and Muruwari was seldom spoken.

During those first few months we were in the same old broken-down hut on a near-starvation diet. The diet remained unchanged, but towards the middle of 1912 we were moved into an identical hut which was in a very much better condition. It had a dirt floor still, but we were able to cover it with bags and it looked and felt better. During this time Mother was working for a Mrs English for three days a week. This meant walking six miles on her working days, as her place of employment was three miles from the Mission. The money she earned was all we had, and payment for domestic work was low in those days. Mrs English was very kind and would often give Mother scraps of food to bring home. She helped us with food for many years.

During those first months at the Mission various preachers visited us and we were forced to listen to them. I remember one man who started his sermon by saying: 'I do not want to be thought a good fellow by you people. I have just come here to teach you heathens the way of Christ.' He taught us little, and the example he set was not Christian. Before hearing what all these men said to us I had always thought the world was wonderful; I had had no idea that we were lower and worse than everyone else. At Milroy I had been quite unaware of any discrimination; there may have been some but I did not notice it. Now that I was able to read I found that the *Bulletin* and newspapers were full of derogatory stories about blacks and 'Jacky Jacky'. Some of them were in the form of jokes, but the joke was always on Jacky, who never knew as much as the other fellows.

Later in the year there was a measles epidemic and the whole station was in quarantine. During this time there were approximately thirty deaths. The fullbloods suffered severely and many of them died. Billy and I had the measles; Mother escaped. I think we were better off than the others during this time. Mother had been able to buy sheets and cared for us well. We had three weeks of deaths and illness before any help was given. There was no medical assistance, medicine or additional rations. Eventually a doctor and a nurse visited us and the Board supplied some milk and cod-liver oil. Actually there was only one tin of cod-liver oil between us all. It is probable that more had been sent, but I expect the manager kept it for himself. During this time our rations were very low and there was little we could gather from the bush as sheep and cattle were gradually destroying the natural growth. During all this sickness and trouble our lady teacher went away and never returned. It was a miserable time for Mother, Billy and me, but for others there was acute suffering. There was one family named Howell with five children aged between five and eleven years; all the children died within three weeks of one another. There was another tragic story in the Wellington family: they had six children and three of them died of measles; then only a few days later their father, Jimmy Wellington, and his wife both died during the night. Measles and malnutrition were a bad combination, and the suffering during this period was horrible.

There were other incidents which resulted in the deaths of children. A family named Colless lived in a tent on the other side of the river; the mother was mentally retarded. The father went out to his job every day, a walk of seven miles. One day their child, who was four years old, must have followed him and not been noticed. When he returned in the evening and saw his wife alone he asked where their son had gone. She replied that she thought Willy had gone to work with his father. Dick Colless became very worried, and called and searched for some distance around their tent without success. Early next morning he wrote a note saying they needed help and gave it to his wife. He asked her to cross the river in the boat and take the note to the Mission while he was at work. She stayed all day and part of the next night at the Mission, until Mrs Howell pressed her for the reason for her visit, as she was worried that Willy might be alone in the tent while his father was at work. Eventually the mother replied, 'Oh yes, Dick sent me; little Willy is lost,' and showed Mrs Howell the note. By then it was dark, and although many people came out to help there was little that could be done until daylight. The following day they looked frantically, but it was not until the third day of searching that they had any success. Albert Wiley found the little boy dead on an ant-bed and covered with ants. Soon after Willy's death a ten-year-old boy was drowned in the river. His parents had left fishing lines set, and the child rushed to see them before his parents were out of bed. Apparently he fell into the water and was drowned. Those two were among the large number of children buried in the burial ground at the Mission.

My schooling was never more than part-time after my twelfth birthday in July 1912. The various managers said that I was too old and should be working. Most of my time was spent outside doing such jobs as chopping wood, sheep work, fence repairs, general cleaning, and that loathsome job of carting water. In addition to every week-day we had to work all day on Saturday. Sunday school lasted until midday, so I had very little free time. Despite that, reading had opened a new world for me and it was wonderfully exciting when I could find an old magazine or book. Later in 1912 we moved into Brewarrina for three months. I do not know the reason for the move, but it could have been the unpleasantness of the manager and our lack of food at the Mission. Mother worked and we had a little schooling. I found more reading material, and it was interesting to see something more of the town.

My first view of the Fisheries at Brewarrina had been when I was ten years old and Maria had shown them to me. At that time the river was high and muddy and it was difficult to see the yards. They are in Ngemba territory but the Muruwari used them frequently, although this was done only after permission had been obtained from some older Ngemba person. This custom continued until just before 1920. Maria had told me how it was possible to drive the fish into the larger yards, then through a labyrinth into smaller pens where they could be speared or caught by hand.

During this later visit I had a much better view, as the water was low and clear. The old people at the Mission kept the yards in good order by replacing the smaller fallen rocks and by diverting water to cut away the silt. At certain times the fish travel upstream in great numbers. The stone traps had their open ends towards the approaching fish, and the natives would guard the entrances to make escape impossible. The best description of the Fisheries is given by R. H. Mathews in *The Aboriginal Fisheries of Brewarrina*, although it is surprising that he does not mention the two large footprints which were to be seen on either side of the river. These footprints were on flat surfaces of rock and some distance above the yards. Maria showed me one of them during my first visit, and some of the old people promised to show me the other. Somehow that did not happen, and by the time I looked for both of them myself they must have been covered by silt. One footprint was about 400 yards downstream and on the town side of the Barwon River; the other footprint was directly opposite the large rock described by R. H. Mathews. The print near the town could have gone by now, as most of the rocks have crumbled. The footprints are believed to have been made by Baiame, the god of the Ngemba and several other tribes. Mrs

Langloh Parker has written a lot about the importance of Baiame in her books of legends and in *The Euahlayi Tribe*.

Some Ngemba people told me that Baiame once travelled from west to east accompanied by his pack of Mirijula or 'spirit dogs'. As he walked, one dog would move away from him and run in a slightly easterly direction. A little later another dog would run off on its own. All but four dogs went on their separate ways and moved towards the east. The remaining four dogs always stayed together and accompanied Baiame to his destination. When they were approaching the sea they all rested and waited for the return of the other dogs. Various stories have come from this legendary journey by Baiame and his Mirijula. It is believed that the path that Baiame trod is now the valley of the Darling River and the route that the four dogs travelled is now the winding Barwon River. The tracks of the dogs who moved separately are the tributaries of the Darling and Barwon Rivers respectively.

Some of the Ngemba people believed that Baiame stayed for a while with the Aborigines and showed them how to construct the Fisheries at Brewarrina. It was during this time that he made the footprints near the yards. The footprints of Baiame have also been seen at Cobar, Gundabooka Mountain, Byrock, and near Narran Lake. The dogs were believed to have camped beside the Narran Lake when returning to Baiame, and it was in this area that Mrs Langloh Parker referred to similar legends. Between Cumborah and Walgett it was believed that Baiame lit a large fire and cooked a giant carpet snake as a feast for the people. The burnt area is still visible.

The old Ngemba people from the Mission often camped on the river-bank near the Fisheries. There were frequently a lot of children in the group, and I joined them on occasion. They would go to the entrance of the great yard, which is downstream, and jab the fish with sharp-pointed sticks. These tactics were especially good for catching cod. The farther up the yards one progressed the smaller the fish became, although a lot depended on the height of the water. For the best results the water should be almost running over the yards and just a little of the rocks should be exposed. If the river was running too fast no fishing could be done. The fish we caught were usually catfish, cod, perch and bream. Crayfish and shrimps could also be found under the rocks near the yards. At that time no one was allowed to touch any of the rocks; the present disintegration has been caused by people rolling rocks aside and disturbing the formation. Since two large floods in the 1950s most of the yards have been deeply covered by silt; if it was removed the foundations would still be there. There are many rocks on the river-bank showing marks made by the sharpening of stone tomahawks and spearheads. For many miles on both sides of the river there are middens and an accumulation of shells which reach a depth of many feet. I have found nardu stones, also the smaller stones which were always carried for sharpening spears. Mill stones can still be seen in this area. The lower stone was always made of the hardest type of sandstone, and it could be that the slightly concave surface was shaped intentionally and not worn down from use.

During those early years our favourite place for fishing was the part of the Fisheries known as the 'wing'. This wing was in the shape of half an apple, with the stalk end facing the run of the fish. The fish came to the small opening which resembled the stalk. A few of us were placed near this entrance, and our job was to disturb the fish and prevent them from going back. The others followed the fish into the yards.

I was sorry when our time in Brewarrina came to an end. The police came and ordered us back to the Mission. There were very few Aboriginal children going to the school in town, as mixing with white children was not encouraged; so we were forced back to the Mission. During our absence the manager, Mr Keogh, had died, and this was a relief to us all. He had turned out to be worse than Scott; he was always armed with a gun, and threatened us with it. He hit and whipped both adults and children and had caused many horrible injuries. He had been ill frequently, which gave us some respite. Once during the hot weather he had ordered some of the men to dig a large pit so that he could cool off underground; however, he died before it was finished. I think all the people on the Mission would have enjoyed pushing him into that hole.

The vacancy caused by the death of Keogh was filled by a local man named Arnold. He was only an acting manager and we had relief from brutality during this period as he was good to us all, especially the children. Unfortunately he was only at the Mission for a short time. The name of his successor was Evans.

Mr Evans was a cruel and dishonest man. The managers were armed with a baton, handcuffs and a revolver. These were supposed to be used if there was trouble, but Evans used them for his own amusement. This applied to most of the managers; they did not give the Aborigines a chance, and we were always in trouble.

I found it harder to learn at school during this year; our teaching was very spasmodic and none of the others were interested. Also, I was now thirteen and, being considered too old to study, was kept busy with outside jobs during most days of the week. At this time I tried to study after work or school when the others were playing games. During my occasional days at school it was hard to concentrate; Evans had little to teach us and punishing the children was his main occupation. His favourite weapon was a piece of bush timber about three feet long and two inches in diameter. He was not fussy about how or where he hit us, and after about five hits with this lump of wood a child could be quite badly injured. I have seen boys trying to protect their heads with their hands; he would then hit them in other places and they would fall to the ground with blood streaming from them. Sometimes the children were unable to sit or lie down for many days. The crime the child had committed might have been to smudge his book, not to do his work to the teacher's satisfaction, or just to be generally irritating. At times the punishment was so brutal that the child's injuries prevented him from attending school for some days. When he returned to school the manager would often give him a few more cuts to follow up his previous punishment.

I have seen the master moving amongst the children where they had heavy ink-wells on their desks. The teacher, without provocation, would pick up an ink-well and bang the child on the ear with it. The poor children would shiver and cry; if they cried they were liable to have a few extra hits with the stick. Evans was one of the worst; it was horrible to have to sit still and just watch his cruelty to those children. As I was quite good at school-work I did not have so much ill-treatment. My most painful punishment was when I had my ears boxed because I had told him that I could not sing. I was always shy and nervous and did not like doing things in front of the others. One day Evans ordered me to come out to the front of the class and sing. I was shivering and terrified, but managed to sing 'Onward, Christian Soldiers'. I had trouble starting but once I had begun I was all right; I have always been like that. When I had finished he said: 'You told me you could not sing. That was a lie, you are the best singer in the class.' At the end of that he hit me and boxed my ears as a punishment.

He was a dreadful man, and the only thing he seemed to enjoy was making us march and drill outside the classroom. If our marching was not perfect, the result was a bang with the stick. He had an inhaler which he used frequently: he kept telling us he needed this as we stank like polecats.

Evans was also tough on the adults, and used to move around the Mission at night with a gun. He did not actually shoot anyone, but I remember when he fired some warning shots very close to one of the girls. At night, soon after dark, he would ring the bell and everyone had to go to their own houses immediately. One of the girls, aged about nineteen, had been sitting on some steps with a friend of mine. As she was slow returning to the dormitory, he rang the bell a second time and fired several shots close to her feet. Even in our own homes we could never be certain of privacy or freedom from the manager. He had the authority to enter any of the houses whenever he wished and he did this frequently. I suppose he found it amusing. Suddenly the door would open; Evans would walk inside and peer at us. Then he would examine some of our belongings, make a few unpleasant remarks and stamp out.

It was early in 1913 that old Hippai died. He came to visit us, and after a couple of days became ill and died very suddenly. He was buried in the cemetery at the Mission. We were very sad, and worried about Maria. There was little we could do for her as it was a constant battle to keep ourselves reasonably healthy.

The food position was always grim. We dived for mussels, which were quite good to eat when fried. We also supplemented our diet with crayfish when possible. They only appear during certain seasons, and there were none in the winter when we really needed additional food. Some of the people ran out of food before the weekly rations were handed out. Children eat a lot — even more than adults in some cases. When no food was left, the father might ask the manager for extra rations; the request was always refused. The father might plead and argue, and if this annoyed the manager, the man might find himself removed from the Mission: the manager had this authority. When the father of a family had problems over food the result was frequently a term in jail, following his having tried to steal something for his children. This misbehaviour could cause the man to be banned from all reserves in New South Wales when he was released. When this ban had been put on a man he was not allowed to come within twelve miles of the Mission. He might get a good job and want his wife and children to move closer to him, but the authorities would never release them. This made the father a complete outcast. He was told to send money to his family but was not allowed to visit them. This situation continued for many years.

I have mentioned the small government store at the Mission. This was presumed to be for the benefit of the Aborigines: the goods were supposed to be sold to us at reduced prices. The contents of the store included groceries and other basic requirements. I had suspected for a long time that the prices were unduly high. Much later I found out the reason. The managers used two docket books, one showing the correct price and the other a much higher price. We were charged the latter price, paid our money and probably threw away the docket. Most of the Aborigines could not read, and they were never allowed to argue. This was how the books were faked and why similar purchases would have been considerably cheaper in town; the profit was in the manager's pocket. We had no choice, there was no transport into the shops and eight miles was a long way to walk. There was an old sulky, but that was for emergencies only. If someone had been into town and brought out a couple of loaves of bread for friends, he ran the risk of being sent off the Mission by the manager. There was no way in which we could comfortably avoid the high prices of this store.

We were not allowed to grow any vegetables. This seemed peculiar, but it was impressed on us that we could not grow them because it was a government station and not our own land. If we had been able to grow fruit and vegetables we might have been able to sell them and make a little money. Also, it would have benefited our diet. The manager had a large garden of his own; Aborigines had to carry the water from the river and water it for him. He would sell us some tomatoes or other vegetables if we had the money to buy them. We were not allowed to keep poultry, although the manager kept hens and sold the eggs. All these things were sold by him to the people on the Mission, and the prices were very high. This situation had existed since the beginning of the century. There may have been better managers somewhere, but I spent twenty years at the Mission before meeting one who was kind and helpful. The public had no idea of the way we were forced to live.

In 1920 the Board decided to provide vegetables for the dormitory children, but the manager used them for his own family. The orphans never had more than the occasional outer leaves of cabbage or a little turnip. There were other incidents. Hundreds of yards of flannelette were issued and supposed to be made into pyjamas for the children. The flannelette never reached them; they still had to sleep in their clothes, and the material was sold in the stores in town. The manager probably collected the full value or a little less from the transaction. In later years clothing was sent to the Mission ready-made. The blue or grey serge we wore had the distinctive red stripes on it: this stripe seemed to brand us as outcasts.

As I said before, many types of preachers came around to convert us. There were evangelists, Inland Mission and every other type of missionary. They did not try to teach us carefully and gently; there was no discussion and we had to accept everything they told us. Our own religious beliefs were a subject for ridicule, and we were told that we were useless humans and must forget our Aboriginal religion and learn all they taught us. This was confusing, as there were a great number of preachers and it was seldom that two men would preach alike. We were forced to attend all services and listen to every preacher; if we did not our rations were stopped. We were willing to accept Christianity, but few of the preachers set an example of kindness; it was confusing to both the young and the old people. The preachers knew nothing of our beliefs or our religion. We had never worshipped an image or idol, yet the evils of idolatry were drummed into us.

This was not a pleasant introduction to Christianity, although it became an important part of my life eventually. I was young enough to adjust, but the older people only listened because force was used. There was a conflict all the time; the Aborigines were robbed of their own religion and the presentation of this new religion was very poor.

Through the years my thoughts have been with Bida-Ngulu and also with Jesus Christ: there is a similarity. Why can they not be the same God? In my opinion the Aborigines carried out the principles of their religion better than many Christians. I am still divided in my thoughts where religion is concerned. There are still many living in this area who remember and partly believe in their Aboriginal religion. My attitude bothers me, I feel I must be wrong to believe strongly in two religions, but it is a fact that cannot be altered. It is possible that it applies only to the Aborigines who have been pushed into missions or reserves after having lived a natural life.

During those years at the Mission there was some relief from unpleasantness and misery. For me this relief came from friends who were either my age or very much older. There were some quaint characters, and all the customs and beliefs had not been completely lost — they were just pushed under the surface. Steve Shaw lived on the Mission; he was known as Old Bugi (bugi means 'grey'). He was a Ngemba man and was recognised as a witch doctor. In 1913 there were still several men who were believed to have special powers, although Old Bugi was not one of the smartest. Quite often he would wander out in the mornings with two boomerangs which he would clap together. Then he would walk up and down our only Mission street talking loudly in Ngemba. He would reprove the people for drifting away from their old laws and tribal ways.

Old Bugi and I were quite good friends, and I was able to help him in various ways. Owing to his importance he was allowed to use a small plot of ground on the river-bank for growing vegetables. They could not be sold and it was a special privilege for him. He was the only man permitted to eat the vegetables he grew. The watering was heavy for the old man, and we had rigged up a windlass by which he could lower a bucket into the river and then wind it up on to the bank again. Even with this assistance it was quite a heavy job, and he needed help with the watering of his few cabbages and other plants. Quite often people sneaked into his garden at night and took his vegetables. One day he came up to see me and said, 'You are a smart boy, and I want you to work out something that will knock people over when they open my garden gate.' I found some long tubular springs lying about which were heavy and a few feet long. I rigged up a mechanical gadget which was set in motion when anyone pulled out the gate plug. The thing would swing around and hit the intruder on the chest. Old Bugi thought this was a great idea, and set his trap every night. One morning he forgot about this contraption and was knocked flat as he opened the gate. After this the poor old man lost his enthusiasm for the garden.

Jack Shepherd was another old full-blood on the Mission who was reputed to be a witch doctor, though I never saw him doing anything particularly clever.

In my opinion, Muckerawa Jack was the only true witch doctor living in this area. Most of the time he lived at Goodooga. If anything was seriously wrong in Weilmoringle or Brewarrina the first thought was to get Jack to come and deal with it. He was only part-Aboriginal but he had been through the *bora*. He did not die until 1927; after that there was no one left in this district who had special powers. I still believe that a witch doctor had some extra knowledge which is hard to explain. Despite our miserable condition at the Mission many of the old people clung to their beliefs. These had to be kept secret when white people were around, but talking among ourselves gave us some comfort.

One day Muckerawa Jack asked me to go with him to visit a man who was sick. He cut a strip of bark from a tree with his tomahawk, let it curl a little and then took it to his camp where he shaped some sort of a handle. When I asked what he was going to do his only response was a grunt. We visited the old man and I helped Jack to carry him out to some open ground, where we placed him on a blanket. Muckerawa Jack kept hitting the ground with great force within inches of the patient's head; he was almost breaking the bark. In due course we took the sick man back to his humpy. Later I asked Bill Campbell if he knew what it had meant. He could only suggest that Jack must have been more frightening than curative, as the patient died a few days later.

White people find telepathy hard to explain but probably recognise that it exists. The *gurungu* of the Muruwari seems similar. *Gura* means string, and the literal meaning of *gurungu* is 'magic string'. This communication of thought was used and discussed frequently during my first years at the Mission. I still believe in it and expect other Aborigines of my age to have strong feelings about it. Men and women talked about getting news from others who were far away: it might be of an impending visitor, or of a death. This *gurungu* was the magic way in which a message could be sent to another camp. It might be sent to disturb a person who had done wrong, and might come in the form of a bird, thought or dream. My first experience of it was when I was about eight years old and we were camping in the bush. In those days we often moved some distance from the Culgoa River to where there was a lot of scrub — it was before the Chinese had ring-barked most of the trees. On this occasion the old men said we must return immediately: a young child had died and the men were needed. These old people seemed to know when a friend or relative had arrived at home, or if someone was ill or in trouble. It has happened so often that it has been difficult to believe that it was coincidence. When we returned in this way some unusual event had always occurred. I am sure these messages were genuine.

When in the bush I lay awake for hours, perhaps listening to the people talking, or just to the sounds from the trees and the night birds. I always had thoughts of tomorrow, which is unusual for an Aborigine. I suppose my German father must have had some influence on my mental processes. One night I was awake and the old people were talking, when they were interrupted by a loud grunt from Jack Murray. Immediately there was complete silence. In due course they started talking again, but only in whispers. I heard one man saying, 'Things are not right at home, we had better return in the morning.' It worried me that we were many miles from home, as I had heard a muttered comment that someone was sick. The next morning Jack Murray said, 'We are going back to the camp, Gambu.' (I was often called by this Aboriginal name). When I asked the reason for our return he just said something was wrong at home. It was not the custom to tell details to the children. It took a day of fast walking, and it was very late when we arrived. I went home and asked Mother if something was wrong. She told me that an old woman — we all called her Grannie — had died. After this event I had more respect for the old people when similar incidents occurred.

There was another occasion when we were out in the bush some distance from Milroy. We had been camping for a week and were gathered around the fire one evening. I overheard an old man saying, 'um-um' and a moment later 'er-er'. I had learnt that these sounds were frequently the indication that a message had been received. Then the old man turned to a friend and said, 'Billy will be here to-morrow.' The following afternoon Goodooga Billy arrived. He had walked from Goodooga to Milroy and then the additional eight miles to find us in the bush.

They had an uncanny way of communicating with one another, and they had definite knowledge when someone dear to them had died or was in trouble. On most occasions it was impossible for them to have known of an impending visitor or event. They were just ordinary Aborigines and not reputed to be witch doctors or clever men. It was amazing how they could communicate by *gurungu* and surprising how all their predictions came true. In Ngemba it was called *gura:*, and they all made the same sound when a message was received, then pondered for a little while before speaking. They also made this sound if they were sitting near the fire in the morning and the shadow of someone passing fell on them; they would be very cross with the owner of the shadow. I had learnt this when I was very young, and always bent when passing them in the mornings, as a shadow caused them great distress. In some way it seemed to disturb the spirit, and the old men would say that 'a man's shadow goes right through you', and that it gave them the same sensation as when receiving a message by *gurungu*. The Muruwari call this type of shadow *gamingara*.

Unusual sounds or dreams caused concern to those old people, also the appearance of an unexpected bird, as these could be omens of trouble or indicate that something was wrong at home. One night when we were camping there was an exceedingly loud noise: it sounded as if a tree had crashed and fallen. There had been loud talk, and when this happened there was an eerie silence. In the morning the men walked round and round our camping area, gradually enlarging their circles. When they came back there was real concern, as no fallen tree could be seen. Within minutes we were on the move and returning to the Mission. When we arrived we learnt that a young child had died and there was great distress. This event remained in my mind for a long time. When an unusual or unexplained noise occurred like this the Muruwari called it Dinagunda, meaning 'a visitor from afar'. This also referred to an evil spirit which could appear in the form of a bird or animal: it might just be a solitary emu or kangaroo running across the plain. The indication that one of these was a Dinagunda was that the bird or animal would stop and look at a person. The natives would be very careful that this animal was not killed. Any obscure form in the bush could also be believed to be a Dinagunda.

During those early years at the Mission, from 1912 to 1914, there were a reasonable number of old people who still respected the old customs and were interested when stories were told of the past. Quite a few Muruwari still spoke the language when the manager could not hear them. They also used it when they did not want the Ngemba people to know what was being discussed. The greater number of Aboriginal speakers were Ngemba, and there were also some Waljwan. These two languages are very similar and have many words which are identical. However, it is only the words which are similar, the meaning is quite different. There were also a few Juwalarai and Kamilaroi people living in our small community.

When we arrived at the Mission one of the most important

old people was 'King' Billy. When a king was chosen it was important that he should have various attributes. He may be a good tracker or hunter, possibly a part witch doctor; certainly he had to be a man of authority and a good type. He was not really elected by votes, but there had to be some obvious respect from the white authorities and the members of the tribe before he was likely to attain this position. Age could also be an asset; young men wanted to be elected but it seldom happened. The word 'king' came from the white men and in the old days a man would be given this title and a brass breastplate. Peter Flood was self-elected, but this was unusual. A magistrate or some white person of importance was the usual one to make the appointment.

I have mentioned Billy Kerrigan before; he was a younger brother of Jimmy Kerrigan and later changed his name to Billy McCann. In those days natives often adopted the name of their employer, and this is what Billy had done. He had come to live at the Mission in 1900, and was aged eighty-seven when he died there in 1914. He was made a king and presented with a breastplate inscribed 'King Billy of the Barwon Blacks'. Although a Muruwari man, he was 'king' of the Ngemba tribe. Before arriving at the Mission Billy had lived an eventful life; he had even committed a murder. Some years earlier I had heard this story from Uncle Jack, who had not wanted to be involved and had refrained from reporting it. When I arrived at the Mission in 1912 and met King Billy I was curious about his story and decided to ask him about it. He was startled that I had heard of it. However, he admitted that it was true when I told him that Uncle Jack had been my informant. This is the story as he told it to me:

Billy went out one day with his digging-stick and tomahawk looking for porcupines. He was about half a mile from Enngonia and wandering around the sandhills when he was approached by a white man with a gun. This man followed Billy for a while and then asked what he was doing. Billy told him, then walked quickly away. The man continued to follow him, until they came to a large hole in the ground. The white man asked what animal could have made it. Billy told him it would be a bilbi, which is a marsupial and a cat-like animal. Bilbis are rare and good to eat, and their hole is similar to a large rabbit burrow. The man pushed Billy's ribs with the gun and said, 'You dig him out, you black.' (That is a more polite way of phrasing it than the words actually used.) Billy refused, and told the man it was not worth digging to the required depth. The man continued threatening with his gun, and rather than continue with this uncertain situation Billy started to dig into the hole. The white man kept moving around him in circles while he was digging; it was hard work and occasionally Billy had a brief rest. As he looked around him he saw that a horse was tethered about a hundred yards away and the saddle was leaning against a tree.

Billy continued digging, and as the hole became larger he had the horrible sensation that he might be digging his own grave. As he was enlarging the hole he poured loose sand into it, which could be removed quickly if necessary. Then the white man fired a shot which grazed Billy on the arm. As this happened Billy jumped at him and hit him with his tomahawk, which he had been using when digging. He thought he had killed the man with the first blow, but hit him a couple more times to make certain he was dead. Then he pushed him into the hole, together with his gun, a small quart pot, a swag and bridle. After that he covered him with sand; and it is probable that he is still there. Billy erased all marks and tracks by brushing the ground with a branch. Then he looked for extra covering to hide the grave. It was a windy day and round, grassy roly polys were blowing across the plains. Billy collected a few of these and put them on top of the grave. To stop them blowing away he placed the branch on top of them; then he walked off in a circle so that he could approach the small township of Enngonia from a different direction.

When Billy reached his camp his friends asked for a share of the porcupines he had caught. Billy replied with a story about a large ghost cat who had attacked him and prevented any hunting. The natives are always superstitious, and they believed him. For the next few days Billy persistently told people about this cat, saying that it was coming to him in dreams and worrying him so much that he was going away. One day he disappeared, and some time later was reported to be in Bourke. After that he went to Wilcannia, where he stayed for some years. Many more years passed before he returned to Enngonia, and it was on this occasion that he told Uncle Jack his story. We guessed that the incident probably happened in 1850. In recent years I went out and identified two large trees near Enngonia which had been mentioned in the story. I was not able to locate the exact place where the man was supposed to be buried.

The last 'king' on the Mission and in our area was King Clyde. Like King Billy, he was a Muruwari man but was proclaimed king of the Ngemba tribe. His breastplate is still in my possession; he had always wanted me to have it, and I treasured it for many years. His wife was Polly Marshall; she was reputed to be something of a witch doctor. When she was very young she had been wounded in the Hospital Creek massacre of Aborigines. Polly had been hit by two shots in the thigh while her mother was carrying her and trying to run away. There must have been a slight lull in the shooting, and as Polly became very heavy to carry her mother put her under a large log and continued running. Later that night she sneaked back, collected Polly and took her in the direction of Cumborah. They lived there, hidden in the bush, until Polly became older and married Clyde Marshall who later became 'king'. Ever since the massacre she had been unable to walk.

I was involved in one incident with Polly; it impressed me greatly and I shall never forget it. It happened when I was thirteen. I felt very ill and also had a headache which was absolutely unbearable. This condition continued for several days without respite; my head ached so much that I felt delirious and did not want to live. Mother and some of her friends talked about it and decided that a visit to Polly might help. With Mother's help I staggered down to her humpy. When we were inside she asked Mother to leave, explaining that she wanted to be alone with me. She made me lie down with my head on her lap, and then she sang to me in a very low voice for some time. This put me to sleep, and Mother had to waken me when she came to take me home. In the morning I woke up feeling completely normal, in fact even more lively than usual.

That afternoon Mother and I went down to see Polly and thanked her for curing me. The old woman was pleased that

I was well again, then she said: 'You had been chasing wagtails and they made you sick.' Owing to her crippled condition she could never move from her humpy, and I cannot imagine how she guessed what I had been doing the day before I became ill. A couple of boys had been with me in the bush several miles from the Mission. We had really been giving the wagtails a bad time, chasing them for hours. It was not my normal behaviour, but I had been very cruel to those birds. It was highly unlikely that anyone had seen us, and seemed impossible for her to have heard about it. It was a fact that she had cured me, and during all the rest of my life I have never experienced such pain as when I had that headache.

Charlie Cobbera was another old Muruwari man who lived at the Mission and claimed to be a witch doctor. He was talking to his wife one day, and as they spoke in Muruwari I could understand it. Charlie was complaining that someone had caught a lot of fish and had not given him any. King Clyde and the other old people would always share their fish with everyone if they had a good catch. Charlie went on talking to his wife and said, 'He did not give us any fish; as a punishment I shall catch him.' By that use of the word 'catch' he indicated his intention to make the fisherman ill in the way of a witch doctor. I watched the proposed victim's health for some days and he seemed to remain quite healthy and well. Poor old Charlie was quite blind and I used to lead him to the lavatory or wherever he wanted to go. I had always been very interested in his witch doctor's dilly bag, which was tied up with string. One day I managed to pull the string and open the bag. In it were bones and something that looked like glass. There were also other things that looked very greasy, and a bundle of hair. It has always been said that while the *gubi* held hair or bones of a person he would remain very ill. While I was examining the contents, the glassy material made a noise and the old man heard it. He was furious and swung his stick at me. I told him that I had just bumped the bag, but when Charlie grabbed it and found that it was open he became very angry. That was enough for me, and I did not go near Charlie again for a very long time.

Billy Campbell was some years older than I was. He was

also Muruwari, and lived at the Mission. He was rather argumentative and hot-tempered. When annoyed he would grab his tomahawk and rush at the culprit; this usually ended the argument. There were other families living on the Mission who were much more quarrelsome, especially the Coombs. They are members of the family still living in Brewarrina. They were not entirely to blame, as others seemed to take some pleasure in provoking them. Doreen Wright* was one of the Coombs family and lives at 'Dodge City', near Brewarrina. She can speak quite forcefully when dealing with our Aboriginal problems.

It was hard to compare all those families. Certainly some were a lot worse than others. They were all alike in having fights and arguments, but on the other hand a lot of them were fine people and could be well behaved most of the time. On occasion I have had arguments with men who have accused me of poisoning their dog or doing something similar. These were things which I had not done, and I would speak up and defend myself firmly. The next time I saw the man he would be more pleasant than usual, and an onlooker would think that I was his dearest friend. A few days later he would start the same old argument all over again. This type of thing occurred during all the years I was at the Mission.

Some of the children were badly neglected: they were obviously dirty and underfed. Although most of us suffered from malnutrition, these children were pathetic. If an outsider tried to touch or help one of them a fight could start. They were in the same category as dogs: a man might push a dog out of the way and find himself being attacked by the owner. Small fights often grew into large ones as friends of the combatants joined the fray. Fish, kangaroo or emu might be the cause of a fight. The part-Aboriginal knew most of the old customs of sharing and distributing food; however, he might bring home a large emu, give a little to someone and his family would eat the remainder. Then the older people would start grumbling that they should have had a share, and the result would be a fight. These old people had been

* Has recorded Ngemba/Juwalarai for the A.I.A.S.

brought up in the tradition that everything should be shared. If there was not sufficient for everyone, the donor must be the first to relinquish his portion.

The frequent fights on the Culgoa, at Weilmoringle and at the Mission were a constant problem. Some were between individuals and others involved groups. Frequently the women would manage to prevent a fight from becoming too serious. Their method was usually to get in the way of the combatants. This might quieten the men, but later the women would start fighting over the same issue. When women began lashing out with yam-sticks and pulling their opponents' hair, the men did not interfere.

When men were fighting, the old people were often able to control the situation. They would interrupt proceedings and talk to the apparent victor. They would talk about his dead mother and his long-dead ancestors. It was a sad story, and the victor would be almost weeping and would have forgotten his victim. If the loser in a fight was incapacitated the victor would have to feed him, carry his wood and care for him until he recovered. Most of the fights at the Mission were amongst the Ngemba people. The Muruwari were less aggressive; this attitude went back to their early days. In those days there were large tribal fights, but the Muruwari are not known to have been involved in many of them. The only large battle which is remembered was the one at Goombalie, where the opponents were believed to be the Badjiri and Galali. This was a great fight, and many Muruwari were killed and buried there. No one seems to know who was the victor or what caused the battle.

The tribes in this area were more likely to join one another for a corroboree than for a fight. The last big meeting or corroboree of all the surrounding tribes was the Gurilmuku in 1880. The Muruwari had close and friendly relationships with the Ngemba, Juwalarai and Baranbinja tribes. There might be occasional skirmishes between those who lived near a tribal boundary, and they usually started when one of the adjoining tribes tried to encroach on neighbouring territory. In individual fights there was always a spirit of fair play; this applied to early tribal fights and also at the Mission. If a man broke his spear or weapon his opponent would not take advantage of his helplessness. If he did attack a man who had fallen he would probably find himself injured by the onlookers.

I remember many old men and women who had scars on their arms and legs which had come from fighting incidents. With a large yam-stick it was easy to hit an arm and break it. Many of the old people on the Culgoa River had this type of scar. 'Hopping' Tommy Kerrigan, a brother of Jimmy and Billy, had lost a leg and was scarred in many places. Peter Flood had lost an eye in a fight. Jimmy Kerrigan was covered with scars, but had never been beaten in combat. He was very proud of his scars and would show them to all who were interested.

Mother told many stories of fights she had witnessed and other unpleasant incidents. Once she was camping in the bush with a group of Muruwari people. They were all asleep when they were attacked by another group of Muruwari, who threw boomerangs and other weapons, injuring many of the sleepers. The Aboriginal was well known for his sneaking way of attack, and Mother described those night raids as terrifying.

Muruwari weapons were similar to those used by other tribes. Wooden weapons were spread thickly with goanna fat and left in the sun for some time, then the wood was put into ashes until the fat was baked into it. When this procedure had been repeated the weapon was considered fit for use. Goanna fat penetrates better than emu fat and also acts as a preservative. Although stone axes were not used when I was a boy, many people owned them. Jimmy Kerrigan had four of them and they showed wonderful workmanship. They all had handles which appeared to be made of tea-tree, as the wood was so flexible. Certain climbing vines or willow would also be satisfactory for the handles. Old Jimmy was proud of those axes, and said that the spirits had given them to him in the night. When he died they disappeared. They could have been buried with him or thrown into the river in the customary way. Between Barwon Bridge and the Mission there is a ridge on which there are several large granite rocks. This is where the natives used to grind their axes, and the marks can still be seen.

In those early days with Jimmy Kerrigan I believed that a witch doctor had some special power. I still believe it, but there were a number of incidents at the Mission which created some doubt in my mind. In 1913 there were still some Ngemba who claimed to be witch doctors. Two of the old men persuaded a group of young lads to accompany them into the bush, telling them that when the party was sufficiently remote they would be taught the magic of the witch doctors. Six young men went with them, and George Brown told me about their experiences. They were taken to the river, where Tommy, one of the old men, tied three young men together on each side of him; he was firmly secured in the middle. They all sat on the ground, then he told the lads to lie down during the coming ceremony which, they were told, involved burning human fat. The other man had lit a fire, and kept putting fat into it. Each time he did this, there was a very loud sizzle as if there was water in the fat. George did not like the smell of the fat cooking. Then the lads heard a noise which sounded like drum beats; it made then uneasy and they tried to move. Old Tommy told them to remain still and assured them that they would all become witch doctors if they could endure this performance. There was another eerie sound even closer, and again the boys tried to move. One of the lads managed to turn over and then stand up. This enabled the others to struggle to their feet, and they all tore off into the bush. They were still tied to Tommy, and the lads were young and strong. As they ran Tommy was dragged along in the middle, and he was not sufficiently clever to save himself from having a very rough time. Eventually those on the outside were able to untie the rope and they were all free. After this episode the old men refrained from trying to teach their secrets to the younger ones.

This appeared to be a transition period. Most of the true knowledge was lost but some of those old men still had some queer belief in their powers. At the Mission the hut for single men stood several hundred yards from the family houses. Two very old men were camped outside this hut; one was supposed to be a witch doctor or *gubi*. The old men had two large tins and usually sat under them; when in a hut or house they also sat under their tins. The reason was not clear to me, but they said it was something to do with their older ways and customs. One afternoon I stopped to have a chat with them and it was apparent that a bad storm was approaching. Billy, the blind man, said, 'This is a bad storm, we shall have to stop it coming here.' I was pleased with this idea as I have always been frightened of lightning. Bill waved his stick in the air and chanted at the same time. This action made me feel safe: despite his lack of sight he seemed confident that the storm could be turned in another direction. The storm came closer and closer, while he waved his stick frantically. Then he held his stick with both hands and chanted very loudly. After a few minutes he told the other old man that he could not stop it alone and needed help.

They had a little fire burning and Percy, the man who could see, walked over and collected two large stones. He put them in the fire and when they were warm started chanting and throwing them up high. He threw one after the other, while the blind man waved his stick and they both shouted their chants at the approaching storm. Then it seemed as if the storm was too much for the blind man: he appeared to have to drag his stick from side to side, and he was shaking. There was a great flash of lightning and a clap of thunder. Both men were still chanting, the rocks were flying high, and while one was in the air there was an even brighter flash of lightning. The stone-thrower ducked and the stone hit him on the shoulder; it bounced from there and hit the blind man on the forehead. That stopped the stone-throwing and other antics, as Bill's face was bleeding copiously and Percy was almost crying from the pain in his shoulder. When the storm had eased slightly I took them up to the manager, who also acted as a doctor. The blind man had to have five stitches in his forehead without anaesthetic, and the other man's arm was put in a sling. This episode had seriously interrupted their magic performance. The poor old men suffered and the storm continued as anticipated. If it had altered course the old men would have claimed the credit. This was often the way 'clever men' gained their reputations.

Apart from these isolated incidents of interest, 1914 was a busy year for me as I did a lot of outside work on the Mission and attended school a couple of days each week. With the other older boys (my age was then fourteen), I had to chop and cart wood for all the houses. We had a tip-dray and a couple of horses to help us with this work. Whatever the manager ordered had to be done, and we never had any spare time for ourselves. Although I still spent some of my time at school, the manager did not add to my knowledge during this year. The extent of our schooling was to learn to read and write a little and add up some simple figures; anything more than that the pupil had to do for himself. We were an uneducated minority, and our ambitions had to be confined to being hired out to squatters for two shillings a week. The only alternatives were to become pick-and-shovel men or fencers. With a good education I am sure that most of us could have done better. The Aborigines' Protection Board had a lot of power and could move an Aborigine to any place or State. They did very little for us, and we all needed help, education and a better way of life. Although the teacher-managers did not have to work very hard around the station, they did not set aside regular times for teaching us. When in the classroom they might mark our books or leave the job to an older boy or girl. Very often they were under the influence of liquor; but, drunk or sober, their treatment of both adults and children was always unpleasant.

George Brown was doing repair work on the Mission, and later in this year of 1914 I was selected to help him. I do not know how he became a repair man, as he knew nothing about carpentry or general repairs. He could not read or write and had never had any education. He was kind and we became good friends. I was strictly forbidden to receive any money for my work, but had many extra jobs which I did in my spare time. Several people had phonographs, and I repaired them when necessary; in most cases they had been overwound and only needed lubrication. Most of the people had no money at all, and how they managed to own a phonograph was a mystery to me; they must have been able to buy them very cheaply. Other jobs involved soldering and carpentry. In this way I could earn a few pence, although I usually had to wait for my money. George collected the money for me, and I shall always remember how he would come to me and say: 'That job you did, mate, was worth ten bob. I could only get a few pence for you.'

George kept all my money in a tin which he had hidden in his room. When Mother or I needed it we went to George. In this way nobody knew that I was receiving money.

Conditions were so bad and food so scarce that this small amount was precious to us.

We had another small source of income. Whenever possible George and I went fishing and sold our catch to anyone who could afford to buy it. We received more money for the fish than for our other jobs. As the proper lines and equipment were expensive to buy, we used the old methods which I had learnt from Hippai and Maria. We made small nets from kurrajong bark and dragged them in the river or waterholes. We also dived into the river. It was necessary to dive very deeply to where logs or rocks were on the sand and the fish were hiding under the shelves. To catch the fish in this way we used small, short spears. The water was very cold at the required depth, and I was not one of the best divers. Some of the old men could remain below the water for two minutes.

Sometimes we put branches and a large roly poly in the river. When these were removed a number of shrimps and small fish would be entangled. Another method of fishing was done by using the pituri* tree. We broke off branches carefully so that the tree would not be destroyed. After the branches had been on the ground for a couple of days we would place them in a waterhole. When they had been there a day we would disturb the water and the fish would rise to the surface in a drugged condition: they were easily caught by hand. When we had collected sufficient fish we removed the branches.

We also made a little money by selling the eggs of turtles. They could be found along the river-banks during summer: in the winter the turtle hibernates under the mud. The eggs are easily found if recently laid, but are harder to locate after several days. Between twelve and twenty eggs can be found in one hole. The turtle lays her eggs and soon afterwards covers them with mud, which she flattens. The outer edges of the flattened mud are thin, and when this dries out a small circular crack is left; we knew how to recognise this crack.

---

* The leaves of the pituri tree (Duboisia myoporoids) are known to have been chewed by Aborigines as a mild narcotic. They were also placed in waterholes to induce a drugged state in kangaroos and emus that drank the water, thus facilitating their capture.

There was another way to find the eggs when they had been buried on the high and level part of the river-bank. If we walked along the water's edge and made a noise, the turtle immediately ran down to inspect the source of the disturbance. Where she had come from was obvious to us and we could collect her eggs. I did not enjoy taking those eggs, but when food and money were so scarce we had to do these things. Turtle eggs are very good to eat when cooked in the ashes.

George and I also used the old method of catching ducks. Before catching them, we fed and fattened them with mussels, cockles and a type of snail found near the river: we would throw this food amongst them in the afternoons when they gathered on the water. When they had become used to being fed, we spread their food on the river-bank. As they appreciated their evening meal, the next move was easy. In the old days there had been a way of making small snares with human hair; this was placed in the food and the ducks became entangled in it. We used a similar but more modern method. Two feet of fishing line would be pegged to the ground, a hook was baited and the ducks were easily caught. This was probably illegal, but our need for food was so great that it was not the time to have scruples. The eggs of frilled lizards were also good to eat; these were found in sandy places where trees had been burnt. The eggs were buried where the ground is soft, and we knew how to recognise the small ridge which indicated where they were hidden.

Although sheep and cattle had damaged the bush surrounding the Mission, we were still able to catch this additional food and also extract some medicine. We had no medical attention unless we were sufficiently ill to be sent to the hospital in Brewarrina; consequently remedies for minor ailments were gathered from the bush. Bark from the leopard-wood tree solved the problem of aching teeth: a small container was made of this bark and water put into it for several hours, then the water was held in the mouth for as long as possible and usually the soreness of the tooth improved rapidly. If the tooth had a cavity, it was filled temporarily with beeswax. If the aching persisted the tooth would need more treatment. In the later days leopard-wood bark and water were boiled together until the quantity reduced; this is a method that I have used frequently and with success. Another cure for toothache is to heat some of the root of leopard-wood until it becomes black. A small amount of this is applied to the tooth when hot. This stings and hurts until it cools, and then all pain has gone from the tooth. Other applications can be made with a small piece of the root when cold. This is rather drastic treatment, as it is not long before the leopard-wood rots the tooth and neither pain nor tooth remain. The gum of leopard-wood is a cure for gastric trouble: mixed with a little honey and water and taken as medicine, it is very effective.

Quinine and wilga bark were soaked or boiled and taken to prevent pregnancy. For many years the natives had considered that this treatment was successful, but I have no proof that it was effective. Whitewood gum was a cure for diarrhoea. There is a small plant that grows everywhere and cures gastric trouble like magic. People were often in agony with stomach pains and if they chewed and swallowed a couple of its leaves they were completely well in several minutes.

Dogwood has a long, thin leaf which when broken smells of turpentine. A bundle of these leaves can be collected, boiled in a tin and then rubbed on any festering sores. No scar is ever left, which has often amazed me. This is also a cure for chilblains, boils or sores on the head.

Our cure for burns was the best I have ever encountered. First we had to catch a fat young pelican and cook it in a camp oven. During this cooking process a large amount of fishy oil can be collected; the oil is very strong owing to the great number of fish eaten by the bird. When this oil was applied to burns the healing process was rapid and no scar was left.

The beefwood tree has two varieties of gum, one is coloured red and is used as an adhesive. At a certain time of the year there is some white gum, which is soft and feels like a sponge. This was kept and used when needed for snake bite. When I was very young Mother took some from a tree and gave it to me. She insisted that I should always carry some of it with me, and I did this for many years. She explained that if it was swallowed it gave the victim some extra time if a tourniquet was not immediately available.

Apparently it deadened pain and shock; there must also have been some slight antidote to the poison. The victim would be able to return to his camp and have a tourniquet applied: in the old days these were made of kangaroo sinew.

There is a type of drug which is found in any of the acacia trees which grow in the north-west of New South Wales. The Muruwari call it *bidjiri,* and it is similar to tobacco. This was used a lot in the old days, and strangely enough, it is still mixed with ash and chewed. I have chewed it frequently and find it a good substitute for a cigarette. There is another type of wattle which we call *ma:bu.* This must have contained some sort of a drug, as people craved for it and would walk many miles to gather it. The leaves were dried and then burnt; the result was a white ash. The ashes were chewed and when the chewing became a habit the result was magnificent white teeth which did not decay.

These remedies were used by us all at the Mission; some of them we had also used at Milroy. There were some other types of treatment that were based on superstition and did not appeal to me. Old Maria strongly believed that threading possum sinew through the lips would extract all ills from the patient. The lips bled and the blood lost was supposed to remove the ailment. Maria did it to herself, and I have often seen her with very sore lips. During these early years at the Mission there were still some strange customs. A lot of the old men collected honeycomb when it was at a certain stage; this was squeezed in their hands and then eaten, in the strong belief that it prolonged youth.

It was good to have a friend like George Brown. We worked together and spent most of our free time together fishing, hunting for food or collecting medical aids. George lived on his own in a small hut and spent many hours at night making children's toys by the light of a hurricane lamp. If possible he would sell them for a few pence each. One night I suggested that we should try to make a steamboat. I thought we should attempt a model of the old paddle steamer, the *Wandering Jew,* which used to travel up and down the Barwon and Darling Rivers. The remains of this old boat can be seen upstream from the Fisheries at Brewarrina. We made our boat four feet long, and the driving power came from an old steam engine I had made a couple of years before. It worked well and we could make it sail in circles or travel straight down the river.

George and I worked together on the Mission until the end of 1914, when he moved to another job in the country. In the meantime war had been declared. We knew little about what was happening overseas, but everyone was talking about it. Suddenly it made a difference to us; people bought newspapers and there was more knowledge of world events. Even the school children became aware of other places and of the importance of such occurrences as the sinking of the *Emden* and the fighting at Gallipoli.

It was early in 1915 that the manager ordered me to do different work on the Mission, as well as going to school once or twice a week. I was nearly fifteen years old and considered fit for the heaviest work. I worked long hours and missed my friend George a lot. Food was very scarce, but we supplemented our rations with fish and the usual additions from the bush.

In March there were new developments in my life. Mr Evans, the manager, told me that he had found an excellent job for me. He said I ought to be apprenticed and have the opportunity to learn all about machinery and electricity. In fact I could gain some knowledge of engineering, and he had made the arrangements with great care knowing my preference for this type of work. I shall never forget the smile on his face when he told me all this. He said that I was to leave the Mission in two weeks and that I had a great future ahead of me. I believed him and was overjoyed at the prospect of learning about these things.

I told Mother about it: my greatest worry was the thought of leaving her. She reassured me and told me that young people had to make their own way in life and this was my great opportunity. She told me that Aborigines had few opportunities and that I must prove myself capable of learning and working well. I knew in my heart that love and kindness to others, one's own standards of behaviour and doing the right thing were the essentials needed when going through life. And yet, I was concerned about Mother and wondered how she would manage without me; she seemed to have aged and her health had deteriorated.

A week before I was due to leave, the manager told me I

was not to do any more work: I must be free to see my friends or to stay at home. When I look back I cannot imagine how I was stupid enough to believe all he said and to suddenly feel that the world had changed into such a wonderful place.

I had about twenty-six shillings in my treacle-tin money box. The only boots I owned were a pair that had been issued to me for work on the Mission. They were white from lack of blacking, hard and rough-looking. I felt too embarrassed to go away in them, so decided to go into town and try to buy a better and lighter pair. The only way to get to Brewarrina was to walk the eight miles. My poor old boots had practically fallen apart by the time I reached the general store. The cheapest boots were on a table and they were all odd. I managed to find two that were almost the same: the price was two and sixpence, and this included a tin of boot polish. I bought a shirt, some socks and braces. There was sufficient money left to buy a packet of cigarettes, some sweets for Billy and some bread for Mother. Then I started the long walk home. These last few days passed very quickly. My excitement was intense, but I was also worrying about Mother and Billy.

The day before my departure the manager was still full of kindness. I decided that I must have misjudged Mr Evans, since my wonderful future and career were all due to his efforts. He told me to be ready very early the next morning as I had to catch the train at Brewarrina. He told me that he had everything organised and was also providing food for me, which I would need when travelling. Then he gave me a coat and trousers from the store. They were made of navy-blue serge; all boys received this issue once a year. That night Mother removed the large brass buttons and sewed on some ordinary ones. She insisted on making me some little cakes to eat on the journey.

The next morning we were all up very early. This was near the end of March 1915; in four months I would be fifteen years old. All my dreams were coming true, the opportunity to learn many things was ahead of me and if I worked hard I might become an engineer. I was too excited to eat any breakfast. As I was leaving, Mother put a small text of St John's Gospel into my pocket. I still have this little book.

I kissed Mother and Billy goodbye and walked slowly towards the waiting sulky. The manager handed me a letter of reference addressed 'To whom it may concern'. 'Here you are, Jim,' he said, 'give it to a train guard, station master or policeman if you get lost. They like to help young coloured lads going out into the world for the first time. You have a great future ahead of you, and nothing to worry about.' He handed me a sugar bag and said there was enough food for several meals in it. As we left I saw Mother and Bill standing near our hut. We waved to each other several times as I slowly moved away.

We arrived at the station and Dick, the handy man who drove the sulky, gave me my ticket. He asked me if I had any money and I told him I had three shillings; he gave me half a crown. The train drew out of the station. My excitement was mounting: there were wonderful experiences ahead of me. It was hard to believe that I could be so fortunate, and I resolved to work and study to the best of my ability. I thought about the day when I would become a man with special training and be of use to the community. My days of making models were over, much larger things were ahead of me. I was an Aboriginal, but why should my colour make any difference when I was willing to learn and work? The opportunity to succeed had been given to me and my hopes for the future were high.

The only other passenger in the carriage was an old Chinaman. He did not look at me and was very busy rolling cigarettes. At last he spoke to me and asked: 'Where you go?' I had not looked at my ticket and he was rather surprised when I told him that I did not know. He asked to see my ticket, then he said he did not know Kadungle, the place marked on it. He commented that it must be a long way and said that I ought to look at the names of the stations when the train stopped. After that he was quite talkative and told me that he was going somewhere past Dubbo. He smoked many cigarettes and it was a long time before I plucked up sufficient courage to ask him for one. He said: 'Aha, little boys don't smoke.' I told him that I did and he gave me some Chinese cigarette papers and his old tobacco pouch. I was able to buy some for myself when we reached Nyngan. By this time I was hungry and I opened the sugar bag the manager had given me, hoping I would find some good sandwiches. There were only six slices of dry bread with a scrape of raspberry jam on them. I ate half of Mother's cakes instead.

During my years at the Mission it had been made quite clear that Aborigines were unacceptable. At Dubbo I had my first experience of real discrimination; it proved that what we had been told must be true. The train had stopped for refreshments and we were in our carriage when a woman came to the door. She looked at us and then called the guard and asked him to remove the old Chinaman and the black boy immediately. The guard replied that our seats were all right and our money was as good as hers; she was furious and moved on to another carriage.

As the guard moved away I hurried after him and handed him my ticket and letter of reference. He was very puzzled and said that I was either on the wrong train or had gone past the station. He told me to return to the carriage and that I would be notified later. He kept the letter, and I felt that I had no more worries about getting to the correct place; someone would look after me. Very soon I fell asleep.

It was dark when we reached Orange. A policeman collected me from the train and took me to a hotel, where I slept until early in the morning. Another policeman woke me and put me on a train bound for Molong. He told me that I need not worry, the police would see that I reached my destination. I went to Bogan Gate and was then told to change to the Tullamore line. This was the terminus at that time and the small village of Kadungle was between Bogan Gate and Tullamore. A new ticket was issued for me and again the police came to my rescue at Tullamore. They placed me in the care of a very nice man who took me to his home where I had a warm bath before having tea.

It had been a horribly mixed up journey and was caused by the wrong ticket being issued at Brewarrina, or it may have been the fault of the manager. My ticket should have been to Cathundral, a small siding between Trangie and Nevertire. I spent the next day with the police at Tullamore and eventually a man arrived with a motor bike and sidecar; he was to drive me to my place of employment. This was some distance away and it was late in the evening before we arrived. I had been travelling for thirty-eight hours, had eaten very little food and felt very tired and confused. Mother, Billy and the Mission seemed hundreds of miles away. I tried to forget them and made myself concentrate on the work ahead of me and my success in the future.

4 Apprenticeship

'I must not raise my hands, even in self-defence'

I WAS relieved when I was taken into the kitchen and told to sit down. The meal did not look exciting, but as this was the place where I was to be employed, the situation was sure to improve. On the wooden table was a tin of jam, a knife and fork, a tin mug and about five pieces of bread. There was also a tin of Glauber salts. A young woman came in and gave me a plate with a little meat on it. When I said 'Thank you', she made some remark about being surprised that I should have any manners. Then a man appeared and introduced himself as my boss. He was carrying a hurricane lamp, and asked if I had brought any blankets. I had not, so I just picked up the small basket Mother had given me and the manager's sugar bag and followed the boss. After about two hundred yards he opened the door of a large building, gave me the lamp and disappeared into the darkness. He had not given me much time to eat my meal, and I was still hungry and confused.

I found myself in a very large room. It was packed with chaff bags, which were stacked against the walls; there were many seed boxes, and some horses were feeding. There was something that resembled a bed, so I sat down on it and wondered about the type of work they were going to expect me to do. There did not appear to be any machinery and it seemed an odd place to be commencing my engineering career. I felt this must be a large wheat farm, because of the number of draught-horses feeding. None of this agreed with the manager's story that I would be going to a large engineering firm and would be given a good home. My dreams were shattered, and I just sat on the bed and wept. It eased me when I thought of Jesus in the lowly manger. I tried to sleep, but the chewing and bumping noises of the horses got on my nerves. In the darkness mice and rats came out in dozens. They raced everywhere, and I felt that I could not stand it much longer. I had no matches to relight my lamp, so struggled in the darkness and moved my bed about forty feet away from the building. I had no blankets, several sugar bags were the mattress and the bed was dreadfully uncomfortable. At dawn I replaced it in the building and sat there until it became lighter.

There was little else to do, so I went and sat on the doorstep waiting for instructions. A young man came in to feed the horses, and he invited me to go to the kitchen for a cup of tea. I was given the tin mug which I had used the previous night. We did not talk much and I thought he might be the son of the boss, Mr Lindsay. I wandered around for a while until I was called for breakfast. The food was exactly the same as had been given to me the previous evening. Someone came into the kitchen and told me to go to the dining room and clear everything from the table, then I must wash and dry all the dirty dishes. I had learnt a little about washing up from Mother but was not too keen on the job. I was half-way through it when I had a visit from Mrs Lindsay, the wife of the boss. She watched me and then told me that from now on I would be doing all the washing up and would also be given additional jobs around the house during the day.

That night when I had finished the washing up Mr Lindsay said he wanted to talk to me. He took me into a room where his wife was sitting and then closed the door behind us. He started by saying that his name was Jimmie, the same as mine. We could not have two people with this name on the station, so I was to be called Joe. He told me that I was apprenticed to him for four years and I must never try to run away. If I did I should most certainly be brought back again each time, or be sent to jail if I tried it too often. I must not address anyone by their Christian name, and must do everything I was asked to do. Any refusal or rudeness would be dealt with by him. He stressed that I must not raise my hands to anyone; even in self-defence. If any black touched a white man he would be shot down. He told me that I would be fed and clothed by him and my pay would be two shillings a week. This money would be banked for me. He gave me a paper to sign and then sent me back to the stable. Once again I moved the bed into the open; I did this every night until it became too cold. As I had no blankets I had to use discarded chaff bags when I needed additional warmth.

During that second night I lay on the bed and looked at the bright stars. I was thinking of everything Mr Lindsay had said to me. I did not like the warning that I must not raise my hands; I was not aggressive and had only occasionally hit back when badly treated. Here I was all alone, and if anyone hit or hurt me I could not strike back. While thinking of this I remembered my resolutions for the New Year. They were that I should never become drunk or keep bad company, that I should do my work well and try to be kind and helpful to those around me. The four years ahead seemed an eternity when all these conditions were forced on me by the boss. It was all so contrary to what I had been led to expect, and I felt dreadful. The hopes for my successful future were worthless, I should never be an engineer and my training was directed towards housework. I thought of walking off this property near Tottenham: they might tire of me if I did it frequently. Then I thought that I might win eventually if I did my best with work and behaviour. There was little choice.

My work was constant: washing up, fixing fires, scrubbing and polishing floors, peeling potatoes, chopping wood, and numerous other dreary jobs. In a little while I had learnt to ride and was allowed to bring in the cows and milk them. I also fed the pigs and horses. I preferred the outside jobs, but most of my days were spent inside or around the house. In that first year I can remember having only two Sunday afternoons off. On one of those days I was allowed to ride four miles to a bush church meeting. I sat alone on a long form. People moved away from me and all the congregation stared at me. I suspected it must be because of my dark skin. Several weeks later I went to my second meeting, and I realised then that it was not a place for someone of my colour. There was only one class of people and I was unwelcome.

After living in the chaff room for eight months I was given a small room adjoining the kitchen. It was not much of a room: there was no floor-covering and the boards were an inch apart, which meant that it was draughty. However, this was a palace compared with the mice-ridden chaff room and the smelly horse stable, and it made me feel more contented. The stretcher and straw mattress were an improvement and I was able to rest and sleep better. I made a table and seat from two packing cases and began to enjoy life more.

A week before Christmas, the two brothers of the boss and the women of the family went away for a holiday. This left only the boss, an assistant for the outside work and me on the property. I did the cooking as well as helping in the paddocks. There was a lot to do, but it was better than working for women who stood over me all the time.

During the morning of Christmas Eve the boss told me that he and the other man were going away too. He said that they would be away for a week, and he told me that I was to be in charge of the place during that time. They were just getting into the car when the boss said, 'Here, Joe, I nearly forgot to give you this,' and handed me a small tin of Christmas pudding. As they drove away they called out: 'Merry Christmas, Joe.' I remembered this the next morning, Christmas Day 1915. There was no sound of children, no voices, nothing but the chirping of a few birds. While eating my breakfast alone I thought of Mother and Bill. I felt sure that Billy would be playing with other children and enjoying himself. I felt down-hearted and depressed. I was still only fifteen years old, and Mother had always managed to produce something special for Christmas Day. We made our own presents for one another, saved our rations and tried to make it a happy day. The boss had said that I need not work on this day. That fact did not cheer me up; just sitting around made me feel lonelier. During the months I had been at the property I had been missing companionship more than I can express.

Suddenly I thought of the large room near the laundry which I always called the Haunted Room. To my knowledge no one ever went in there, and on the door was a large lock with a chain and staple. It had always appeared firmly locked, but when I investigated I was surprised to find that no key was necessary. I opened the door and found the accumulation of years. There were books, magazines, glass, crockery, old saucepans — everything one could imagine. Some of the shelves had collapsed under the weight and many things were scattered on the floor. I looked at the books and read a couple of magazines. There was a book in the corner; it seemed as if someone had left it partly open and upright. For the first time in my life I saw the golden letters saying 'Holy Bible'. I had never seen the complete book before. I took it out on the veranda and read it for a little while. Then I looked up and noticed some smoke along the tree-tops. It looked like a bush fire about a mile from the homestead. I put the book in my room and rode out to investigate.

Some grass was alight in a five-hundred-acre paddock. I rode quickly back to the homestead and telephoned our nearest neighbour and asked for help. It was not long before people were arriving from all directions. We used fire-beaters and fought the fire all day and well into the night. Someone had told the boss, for he arrived during the night. By the next day the fire had swept through several large paddocks and had moved away up into the hills. It was impossible to put it out completely, and it rushed through the adjoining properties. When we returned to the homestead we were very tired and weary; there was nothing more we could do. What a Christmas that was! Nothing to eat all day and night, and then it was Boxing Day and there was no time for more than a cup of tea. The boss and I went to assess the damage. A lot of fences were down but there was no loss of stock. A wide road had separated the fire from the stock paddocks, and a change of wind had moved it away from the animals.

We returned to the house late in the afternoon, and as we walked along the veranda the boss noticed all the old books and magazines which I had left there when I saw the fire. He asked me where I had found them. When I told him he became very nasty, swearing and calling me all the bad names he knew. He looked inside the old room and then came towards me with some menace: I really thought he was going to knock me down. He told me that my punishment was to make things tidy in the old room, and I must clean up all the mess as soon as I had finished my dinner. The shelves were to be repaired that night and the room must look perfect before I went to bed. That Boxing Day was not much fun; I was about to have my first meal for two days and had missed going to bed on the previous night. I was very tired, but it was no use arguing. Before the boss went to bed he came in to see me. It was obvious that I would be spending most of my night in there. He asked if I had removed anything, and I told him that I had put the Bible in my room. He told me to bring it to him immediately. When I gave it to him he turned over a couple of pages and then asked if I really wanted to read it. When I assured him that I did, he said I could borrow it provided I read some of it every day while I was working on his property. Somehow, from that day onwards he treated me a little better. We worked together in the new year of 1916 as there was a lot to be done repairing fire damage.

It was mid-February when all the holiday-makers returned. I was not pleased to see them back, because it meant that I had to start doing housework again. One good result from the holiday was the marriage of the younger brother of the boss: he brought his wife back to live on the station. I shall always remember her; she treated me as a human and made it quite clear that the others should give me more consideration. In a very short time she disposed of my old tin mug, plates and shoddy cutlery. She insisted that I should use the same china and cutlery as everyone else. She said we all had to be on the same level, and allowed me to read books from their large collection. They had a Webster's Dictionary which I studied at every opportunity. Ever since my first day at school I had appreciated what education meant and had been struggling to add to my knowledge. Her kindness to me made her unpopular with the others, but it made a great difference to me and my attitude to the life at Tottenham. During the year I had been on the property there had always been unkindness, which was sometimes close to cruelty. No one had ever spoken a friendly word to me and I was very miserable when living in that atmosphere. Mrs Bob Lindsay's understanding helped me through the remaining years.

Some time after her arrival she said to me: 'Look, Joe, there are thousands of rabbits on this place. Why don't you catch some of them for their skins?' I explained that this was difficult as I had no traps or rifle. Mrs Bob promised to see her husband and try to get something for me. In a very short time she gave me a new 22-calibre Winchester rifle and cartridges. She also produced eighteen rabbit traps. The boss gave me a firm lecture about the use of the rifle but he did not prevent me from using it. Each afternoon when I went out to fetch the cows I would set the traps and possibly shoot some rabbits. At about nine o'clock in the evening I would go out again with my hurricane lantern and collect the rabbits from the traps. I did not reset them then as there was never time to go around them again in the mornings. Sometimes it would be midnight before I had finished with the skins. It was hard work and long hours, but it gave me about five shillings a week during that year. This was more than twice what I was getting for slaving on the property. By the end of the year I had saved ten pounds, and nothing would persuade me to spend it. If I had been as careful with money in later life I might possibly have been almost rich today.

During that year I was allowed to muster sheep with the men, do yard work and ride around the fences. There was also ploughing and wheat sowing as well as the usual carting and chopping of wood. The floors still had to be scrubbed and the washing up done. There was never any time off, and the days passed with eighteen hours out of every twenty-four spent in hard work. I had to work fast to get it all done, and was becoming a man of many jobs. At this time I was learning more about stock, but I have always hated that type of work because I dislike sheep, cattle and horses. Whatever work I did out on the property I had to be back in time to bring in the milking cows. My days began before those of the others, as the fuel stove had to be alight when they appeared. Some days I was unable to leave the house because there was so much to be done for the women. The job was incessant for seven days of the week. Most of the time I hated it, as there was so much unpleasantness from the boss and general discomfort. I had made a vow to myself that I would never run away, but when I look back at those days I wonder how I managed to endure the life.

The following year, 1917, I was still doing the same type of work. In May the boss called me into the office and said: 'Joe, there has been no rain for a long time, no feed for the cattle, and the paddocks are becoming bare. I want you to take on a new job. We shall move the cattle and horses eight miles out to the big tank, and I want you to look after them out there.' I had to accept, there was no choice. Then he continued to tell me in an unusually pleasant voice that I would have to live in a tent and cook for myself. He said I could take two rifles and an old shotgun so that I could shoot rabbits or pigeons in my slack time. There was nothing for me to say, I had to agree to it. He continued laughing and joking with me for a few minutes. I had a nasty idea that his apparent kindness and agreeable manner indicated that a bad time was coming for me. He said that I could take the old phonograph and some records from the store-room.

Within a week all my camping gear was taken out to the big tank by spring cart. I rode: the horse would be needed when I was moving around the paddocks. They were all very large paddocks, and it seemed remote from everything. When I arrived at the tank the driver of the cart was waiting; he was supposed to help me cut rails and pitch the tents. One tent was for me and the other was for storing chaff and equipment. The driver was no help, he just sat on the ground and smoked while I did the work. As he drove away he called: 'You want to look out tonight, Joe, there are a lot of ghosts at this tank. They might get you, old fella! I wouldn't like your job.'

By the time the sun had set I had done all that was necessary, and that first night was horrible. My age was seventeen then, but I felt queer and frightened at being out there completely on my own. There was no sound other than foxes and night birds. I felt lonely, and my mind went back to the days when I had loved camping in the bush with Hippai, Maria, Jimmy Kerrigan and the other old people. I thought of their stories of ghosts and some of their legends of the bush. I told myself that I was too old to be worried by their story of Gambil Gambil, the female spirit of the bush. Surely I need have no fear of her. Even so, I felt that she was close.

Gambil Gambil was the spirit who was reputed to lure inexperienced people or children who were foolish enough to stray into the bush. She had the power to form edible fruit on trees when it was out of season. There would be a little fruit on one tree, perhaps none on the next, then more fruit would be visible in the distance. Her victims would have to move from tree to tree: in this way she lured them farther into the bush. She had other powers, and could cause fungi of beautiful colours to appear on the sides of decaying logs. This fungus would be seen in varying shapes; it may be in the shape of male or female sex organs. It could also resemble the cutting edge of a tomahawk. The children would collect the fungus and joke about the obvious resemblance to sex organs. Then they would run towards another log and find some more which was completely different. They would run farther and farther into the bush, where they would see fruit in abundance which was not edible. This fruit looked beautiful and the smell was delicious; it was impossible for the children to resist tasting it. The fruit was created by Gambil Gambil, and the children would continue running and looking for more. Later, having handled the fungi and tasted the inedible fruit, they would develop hallucinations. They would imagine they heard voices calling them: the voices sounded like their parents. There would be confusion about the direction from which the voices came, and they would run towards the sound. This was the voice of Gambil Gambil drawing them towards her. Eventually, seemingly by chance, they came out of the bush into more open country. They would see water, but it was only a mirage caused by the spirit of the bush, and as they ran to drink it the water would disappear. Then it would reappear farther away. As they ran towards it they might look back and see water behind them. Finally they would collapse from exhaustion and thirst. If they were not found in time they would die.

This was Jimmy Kerrigan's version of the story. Other stories which are somewhat similar have been told. The chase may have been after birds of beautiful plumage, or other attractive lures. Flowers frequently drew the inexperienced person towards them: they became bigger and more beautiful as the searcher moved deeper into the bush. In some cases adults who lacked experience became lost when following a false track or trail of a wandering animal. They would also be confused by mirages, and the pattern was the same as for the children. The Muruwari always believed that Gambil Gambil caused these incidents.

As darkness fell during that first evening on my own, I saw

strange shadows and movements. It was eerie and I was tempted to investigate, but I knew it was unwise to leave my camp. There was one reassuring thought: I had two rifles which, when combined, meant twenty-five shots. There was also the old shutgun. And there was the knowledge that I had been trained in the Aboriginal way when camping in the bush; this gave me some confidence.

After a few days I was not worried about being alone. When I went to bed at night there was one thing I never forgot: that was to secure the tent door. The firearms were always in their special position near my bed. Day or night, I never went outside without a rifle. When I left the tent I hid the rifle that was not in use. I never used the old phonograph after dark: someone might approach unheard if I was listening to it. Eventually I had no fear of the bush, the night or the spirits. I had lined my tent with hessian so that strangers could not see my shadow when the lamp was alight. When lighting a fire I did it in the Aboriginal way, which meant that there was very little smoke or glow from it. My knowledge of animals and plant life was helpful: if I was short of food there were always rabbits to be eaten, and I could catch goannas without much extra trouble. Hippai had taught me how to drive stock in a special way. When an animal's foot sinks into a hole, this indicates that a goanna is underground. At Milroy Hippai would tell the women and children when he was moving a mob of sheep; they would follow the tracks and collect as many goannas as they required. I used this technique on my own and found it very satisfactory. I had always suspected that the old people looked after themselves by taking the best part of the meat and I was able to prove this when eating goanna. All my life I had been told that no child could eat the tail, which has red streaks of flesh through it. We were told that we would be struck by lightning if we swallowed any of this meat. When I was alone near the big tank I tasted the tail, and it is certainly the best part of a goanna.

Most weekends someone visited me; this meant that I usually had a reasonable supply of food. When the supplies came there was always a parcel of papers and magazines from Mrs Bob Lindsay. Sometimes she came out with her husband and brought me tobacco and cigarettes. She had a saying: 'A man must have his smokes.' I was always very pleased to see her, as she was my only friend during those years.

There was always a lot of work to be done, so the days were busy. I had to cut scrub for a number of cattle, and the horses had to be fed and given regular attention. The tank was surrounded by wire-netting which had to be kept in repair. I was allowed to use a couple of coils of wire for the netting of rabbits. I was supposed to kill all the rabbits each night, but I only killed the larger ones and let the small ones survive. Quite often I caught a hundred in a day, but it was hardly worth the work for me. Each month the skins were taken and sent by rail to the market. I received very little money from the transactions: I think someone else made the profit. Later I collected the skins and tried to sell them privately.

Every night I read until very late. Mrs Bob Lindsay had given me a large dictionary, which I studied for hours. She also lent me an encyclopaedia. I read every word of it. During this time alone I felt that I was able to add to the small amount of schooling and education I had received. I had found an old telescope at the station, and spent many nights star-gazing. The telescope had needed some attention before I could make it work, but the lens was powerful enough for the purpose. I made a tripod for it, and on the still, clear nights spent hours studying the sky. The stars had fascinated me when I was a child and had heard about them from the old Aborigines. With the help of the encyclopaedia I learnt a lot about the sky at night.

Some good rain fell in November which filled the tank. There were other good falls in December. Christmas Day 1917 I remember well. I had brought out on horseback the scraps of food I had been given for my Christmas dinner. I rode out to a mountain about a mile from my tent and spent most of the day there surrounded by storm clouds, with rain falling in the distance. It was another lonely Christmas, and my only enjoyment was to observe the weather and the bush.

At the beginning of 1918 I returned to the station. I had spent eight months at the tank by myself; I had quite enjoyed it, and returned with some regret. It had been lonely, but I found that I preferred the solitary life to the unpredictable treatment I received at the station. When I was alone the days passed peacefully with no one to worry me.

Nineteen-eighteen was a busy year, as many improvements were being made at the station. I did not do so much housework after my return; the boss said I was becoming too old to do the inside work. As I was almost eighteen years old I found this a great relief. My first big job was making six 2000-gallon galvanised-iron water tanks. It was through my earlier experience with this type of work at the Mission that I was able to make the tanks. We erected two new windmills and tank-stands. A new house was to be built, and I cut and carted all the wooden blocks required. The carting was done in a horse-drawn wagon and involved a trip of forty miles each way. The boss and I had many rows on those trips. His nastiness was frequently unbearable.

One day a carpenter arrived and a start was made on the building, which was to be half a mile from the old homestead. The carpenter's age was seventy and he was a very frail old man. He was very slow with his work and had an abominable temper which resulted in dreadful language. I was told to spend most of my time helping him. On our first day we sank holes for the blocks; he cursed me all day. All our days together were like this, or worse. He was a terrible old man, and I felt like knocking him out many times daily.

Four months later, when we had to line only a couple more rooms, the old man was up on a scaffold; I was holding one end of a particularly long piece of timber. Somehow his feet slipped and he fell down on top of several tins of paint. He had some broken ribs, and was taken to hospital and did not return for further work. The boss knew quite a lot about carpentry and I had learnt a little from the old man. Between us we completed the new house, which contained four bedrooms, dining room, living room, kitchen and bathroom, and was completely surrounded by a veranda. I felt satisfied that the standard of building had been reasonably good. I had done most of the interior painting, and the rooms looked good. For a long time I had worked during days and nights on this house, even on Sundays. Soon after they moved into it the boss asked me to draw up a plan for the laundry, an office and a room for me.

I enjoyed having some freedom in the design of this small

building. Since childhood I had disliked gable-topped houses and felt they would be better with a flat roof. I drew up a plan and listed the materials required. As it was weatherboard it did not take long to complete. It was the first flat roof in the district and many people came to look at it. Some praised it; others condemned it on account of the low roof and said it would be too hot in summer. Later I built another building: it was a gauzed meat-shop. By the end of August all was completed. We had built a fence surrounding everything; cement paths led to the various gates. The last job was to plant flowers and trees.

The result of this work was an improvement in the attitude of the boss and his wife to me. I was allowed more freedom and could eat the same food as they did. Most of the plans for my work were my own and they allowed me to go about it in my own way. Even Mrs Lindsay spoke to me occasionally when she was in the garden. My life was much more pleasant until it was spoilt by one incident. It was the worst and last event to upset me when dealing with the boss.

The argument started in the meat-shop one Sunday morning. I was busy cutting up the meat for the day when I noticed that two chops had fallen from the table to the floor. At that moment the boss came in and shouted: 'What's the idea of having chops on the floor?' Before I could explain he had picked them up and thrown them in my face. I still have the scar near my nose which was made by the bone as it entered my flesh. I was dazed for some moments, and dropped the knife which had been in my hand. Perhaps someone else might have picked it up and used it on him; it was fortunate that the idea did not enter my head. I just opened the door and tried to go outside to escape from him. He pushed my shoulders and kicked me. On the floor was a large piece of cypress wood, and I picked that up and went for him. He took to his heels and I chased him right through the house until he disappeared around the corner of an outbuilding.

I stood still for a little while and started mopping up the blood that was pouring from my face. Then I walked off to the old homestead where Mrs Bob Lindsay, my very good friend, lived. I told her what had happened and she said: 'I'm glad you didn't hit him with the stick, Joe. The next time he starts banging you it would be better to use your fists, boy. At your age you're old enough and big enough to give the old bully a hiding.' Then she dressed my wound, gave me some breakfast and kept me at her house during the day.

I was near the gate of the old homestead just after sunset when the boss came along in his car. 'Well, you'd better get into the car with me, Joe,' he said. I got into the car and sat in the back seat as we drove back to the house. When we were there he said: 'You'd best get your tea now, Joe. When you've finished, come into the sitting room. I want to talk to you.' When I went into the kitchen I noticed that the table was set for me. This had never happened before. I sat for a while just thinking. Queer thoughts came into my mind: could this food be poisoned? Two years earlier the boss had been annoyed with me and had said: 'I could put some strychnine in your tea.' These words came back into my mind, and as I sat at the table I did not dare touch anything. I made a lot of noise with my knife and fork on the plate. Occasionally I banged the cup on the saucer and tried to make sounds which would indicate that I was enjoying my meal. I allowed myself the usual time at the table, then I took all the food and tea outside and threw it over the fence.

After I had washed up the utensils I knocked on the sitting-room door and was told to come in. I opened the door and just stood and waited. The boss said: 'Close the door and come closer, Joe.' He was standing by the fire, and his expression was less menacing than usual. He placed two chairs near the fire and told me to sit down. We sat silently for a moment until he said: 'Now, Joe, I want to apologise for all that happened today. It was entirely my fault and you have no apologies to make. You have always been a good boy and have done your work well during your time here. I want you to forget all that has happened between us; you and I are going to be friends from now on.' He grabbed my hand; I was silent and stunned. Then he said: 'This is a gentlemen's agreement, Joe.' He took a box of Havana cigars from the mantelpiece and offered me one. I accepted it and bit off the end. He laughed a little and said: 'I can see that you're an old hand with cigars.' The unpleasant incident of earlier in the day was forgotten, and we talked about various things for over an hour. He told me that he was getting someone for the housework, which would make conditions easier for me. He also told me that I might become manager of the place if I stayed there long enough. He suggested that I should save some money, because I might want to build myself a house and get married. He said that I might eventually become the owner of a station property if I tried hard enough. That night he was very nice to me, and I might have done better in life if I had taken more notice of his words. I had never been interested in stock or station work, and his proposals did not appeal to me. There were no more quarrels after that and I was treated well until I left in August of the following year.

It was in the later part of this year, 1918, that a girl aged about seventeen arrived to do the domestic work. Before her arrival I had not had much to do with girls. In fact, since I had left the Mission I had not had any friends or companionship of any sort. Jean was the name of the new girl working at the homestead, and from the first day of her arrival I liked her immensely. She was white, but did not seem to mind my colour. Her face appeared lovely to me; she always seemed to be smiling, and I found her captivating. I could not help admiring her from that first moment I saw her. There was a lot of work to do in the house and I helped her as much as I could. It was certainly unusual that I should voluntarily work in the house! In the evenings I helped her wash the dishes, then we sat down and talked.

As the days passed I found that I was thinking only of Jean; she was always in my thoughts. One night I told her that my real name was Jim and that I was only called Joe because the boss had insisted on it. After that she always called me Joe when others were present but used the name of James when we were alone. Before Jean's arrival I had bought an old hand-operated projector: in those days one could get a collection of films on loan for several shillings. Most of them were slapstick comedies, and on those rare occasions when new ones arrived we called it our picture night. If I had no films we just looked at photographs I had taken and made into slides. They were usually local scenes taken with a small camera I had bought for five shillings. It was my first camera, and I managed to do all my own developing and printing.

As the time passed I came to love Jean more and more. During my working hours I thought about her all the time, and when I had any leisure I spent it with her. I had never known happiness such as this. From the day I left Milroy my life had been tough and miserable; Jean brought something very special into it. On our picture nights she would sit very close to me while I turned the handle of the ancient projector. My thoughts would wander, and I kept pretending we were somewhere else. Each day I wanted to tell her how much I loved her, but somehow I could never pluck up sufficient courage. Quite often we visited Mrs Bob Lindsay at the old homestead; we enjoyed the evenings with her. Sunday nights were memorable because Jean often played the organ and sang hymns. It was on one of those nights that Jean put her arms around me and told me that she loved me. In those few moments my world was made complete, for I knew then that we loved one another. We stood together for some minutes; there in the stillness of the night the gates of paradise had opened for me. I was eighteen years of age, and shall never forget my happiness. From then on Jean was all I wanted, and we both enjoyed our secret for some weeks.

Each time I called at the old homestead Mrs Bob would say: 'Well, Joe, how are you and the girl getting along? Have you kissed her yet?' My reply was always in the negative. Then she would say: 'What? A beautiful girl like Jean . . . oh, Joe you *are* slow. What's wrong with you?' I could not keep hiding my happiness from this good friend for long. I had some discussion with Jean and then told Mrs Bob that Jean and I were in love with one another. Her reply was unexpected:

'I'm not blind, Joe. I knew all the time, but you wouldn't admit it. I'm very happy to know about this — and would you ask Jean to come and see me?'

It was some time later that the boss started asking me questions about Jean. Eventually I admitted our love for one another, and he said he was pleased to know of it. After that he started giving me a lot of fatherly advice about girls. I thanked him, but did not bother mentioning that I had heard it all before. My knowledge had come from the old people in my very young days, also from my own studying of life. One sets standards, not only for one's own good, but also for those one loves. As for Jean, I loved her more than I could ever express.

Christmas was over and it was January 1919. One night when Jean and I were talking I told her that I had only another eight weeks of my apprenticeship to serve. After that I would be leaving Tottenham and going home to the Mission at Brewarrina. She did not want me to leave, and suggested that I ask the boss to keep me after my time had finished. She wanted me to stay until she was ready to leave herself, and I promised to stay if the boss would keep me at a certain wage. I kept wondering about the best way to approach him, and the weeks passed quickly. He solved my problem when he called me to his office and said: 'Well, Joe, your term of four years is over in a few days. What are you going to do? Are you going to stay or leave?' I was surprised when he suggested that I might stay, but wanted to get in my word about wages before committing myself. He spoke first and said: 'Now, Joe, you're talking about going away. You are young. You're not nineteen yet, and if you leave here you'll have to find a new job. Why not stay on here? I shall give you thirty shillings per week for a start.' The wage was more than I was going to suggest, so I told him that I would be pleased to stay. Then he started speaking in an unusually gentle voice: 'You've been away from home for four years and have not seen your family at all. Why not take a trip to Brewarrina next week and see them for a few days? Your wages will still be paid while you're away.' I was thinking of Jean when I said I preferred to make the trip later in the year. The boss agreed and said that I could do whatever I liked. We both sat in silence for a while, then he said: 'During the four years you've been here I haven't given you anything. You've done your work very well and your conduct has always been excellent.' Then he took his silver watch and chain from his pocket and put them in my hands, saying: 'I want you to have these for your own, and I hope you will always look after them.' In the excitement of receiving this present I trembled and could hardly speak when I tried to thank him; I held back tears with difficulty. He could see that I was feeling emotional and only said: 'All right, Joe, just look after the watch.'

That night I showed the watch to Jean and told her of my

interview with the boss. She was very pleased that I was staying longer at the station, and asked if she could come with me when I made my trip to Brewarrina. I promised her that we would go there together. Although we were both very busy every day we were able to spend a lot of time together during the next five months. We discussed many things and made our plans for the future. I have seldom been happier, and those days were a landmark in my life. One day we set off for a long walk together. We enjoyed these walks when we had the spare time. That day I was carrying a hammer and chisel, and Jean wanted to know what I was going to do with them. I told her to wait and see. When we came to a sturdy tree I cleared the bark and chiselled our initials. It is probable that this reminder of our walk is still there.

Early in June the boss told me that his wife would be away for several weeks. During that time Jean would be sent back to her parents and, as all the women would be absent, I would be the cook. A couple of days later I was asked to have the car ready for their departure on the following morning. I hated the thought of Jean leaving, but she reassured me that on the next trip we should be together.

The next morning we were all moving early; it was dark and bitterly cold. I lit the fire in the kitchen and Jean prepared the table in the dining room. I remember that Jean did not eat much breakfast, probably because she was to leave immediately. It was not long before the boss came and told me that he would also be away for a few days and was leaving me in charge of everything until he returned. He walked out to the car, while Jean and I stood beside the stove whispering our farewells. I could see that she was trying to be brave. Then I heard the mistress calling her. Jean asked me if I was coming out to see them off; I pressed her to me and shook my head. She embraced me once more and said: 'I'll be back. I'll be back.' We kissed and said goodbye. I listened to her footsteps as she walked along the veranda and then down the pathway to the car. The door of the car closed and I stood listening until the sound of the engine had died away. I felt horribly sad and lonely during that day. I was not very busy, and seemed to be worrying and thinking about Jean all the time. Her words 'I'll be back, I'll be back' were in my mind constantly.

Three letters came from Jean, and I enjoyed answering them. She had been away for two weeks and I was looking forward to her return quite soon. It was during the period that the great influenza epidemic was sweeping across Australia; I read about it in the newspapers, but we seemed very secluded at the station. Just as I was making preparations to welcome Jean, a telegram came saying that she was seriously ill with influenza. Two days later another one came saying that she had died.

Jean's death was such a great shock to me that I became ill, mentally and physically. It was early in my life, I was nineteen, but this was my first experience of really great sorrow. I imagined that I could see her wherever I looked. Sometimes I seemed to hear her voice saying 'I'll be back, I'll be back.' The nights were long, I could not sleep, and I spent hours just sitting in a chair. All the people at the station were sympathetic and I was told to forget, otherwise I could finish up in hospital. One cannot forget easily in those circumstances. All my dreams were shattered. I had adored Jean, and there seemed to be little happiness for me without her.

Has one to lose love to find love? I found love some years later, only to lose that again in a few short years. Their love will always live in my memory, and the sweetness of Jean still lingers and inspires me to be kind and helpful to those who may need it. In memory I frequently relive the happiness we had together. I visit the tree where we carved our initials, see the place where we said goodbye, and still hear those footsteps as Jean walked away. It was all so long ago, but I shall never forget it.

5 Return to the Mission

'I am about to leave you and want to say goodbye'

IT WAS in August, six weeks after Jean's death, that I left the property at Tottenham. I promised to return if possible, but I felt strongly that it would be better if I did not go back there. I arrived in Brewarrina on the night of 4 August 1919. It was quite late; the train had no particular time-table in those days and no one could ever estimate its movements. Leaving my heaviest luggage at the station I took my small hamper and started walking the eight miles out to the Mission. When I was about two miles along the track the Mission sulky appeared with two men in it. I knew them both well and they insisted that I should get in with them. If I had continued walking I would have reached home much sooner. They were both shockingly drunk, and kept stopping to talk and drink some more. It was a dreadful trip and I did not reach the Mission until early in the morning.

I hurried across to Mother's house and knocked several times on the door. When she called asking who was there my reply was: 'Come and see.' When she opened the door she stood amazed and could not speak for a few minutes. It was more than four years since we had seen one another, and I realised how much I had missed her. We talked for some time and then I rested. I felt incredibly tired, but it was good to be home again.

It was about midday before I left Mother's house for a stroll around the Mission. It was in a shocking condition and I was horrified by the sight of it. There were dozens of pigs running around, rubbish was scattered everywhere and the whole place looked filthy. The manager was too drunk to come out and see me. I spoke to his wife for a moment and then continued my walk. The children were ragged and dirty and showed all the signs of malnutrition. The dormitory children received the worst treatment; their condition was pitiful. Later I learnt that school lessons were given only occasionally when it pleased the manager, which was seldom more than once a month. Most of the families that I had known had left; now only nine families lived there. Some were new to the Mission, and this group included people of all ages. Most of the houses were without doors and parts of the walls were missing. Where once there had been yards around the houses, now there was only partly buried wire netting; all the posts had been burnt for firewood. This Mission was a paradise for gamblers and drunks, and the manager took part in it all. Head Office should have dealt with this shocking situation.

My brother Billy had been apprenticed for a couple of years before my return to the Mission. When he went away Mother took a job at the Post Office in Brewarrina; later she worked at the local hospital. Owing to ill health she had to leave her job and return to the Mission, where she was now living in a small two-roomed hut. It was obvious that her health had deteriorated considerably. She kept her hut clean and tidy, pictures from magazines decorated the walls and she was good at folding paper in various patterns which covered the shelves. Apart from hers, there was only one other hut which was kept in a reasonable state of cleanliness.

It was also disappointing to find that my work at Tottenham had not produced as much money as I expected. When Aborigines were apprenticed, their earnings were paid into the Aborigines' Protection Board and the money was banked at the Board's headquarters. When the Board received an application signed by the Aboriginal concerned they sent a cheque to the manager of the nearest Mission; this had happened in my case. In those days the cheque was made payable to the manager, and in some cases the Aborigines never received their cheques. Every three months Mr Lindsay had presumably sent my wages to the Protection Board. I had to pay for everything I broke, and I always seemed clumsy with the crockery. Sometimes I wondered if the correct amount had been sent to the Board; it would have been simple to deduct an excessive amount for my breakages. I was allowed sixpence a week for myself, but it had never been paid to me. After four and a half years of hard work my earnings were apparently thirty pounds. When I commenced work the normal payment was two shillings weekly; the payment for girls was one and sixpence. Each year there was supposed to be an increase in wages, but I think someone had been dishonest with my money. It was no use writing to the Board and asking for an explanation; their reply would always be to the manager, who would not show it to me unless it suited him. He would just say that no more money was due to me, then he would punish me in every possible way for taking action with the Board. It was much too easy for managers to be dishonest during those years before the system was changed and money was paid directly to the person who had earned it.

The manager at the Mission at this time was not really a nasty man. His greatest fault was that he spent most of his time drinking with the worst type of Aborigines. He was not doing his job, and everything was suffering from neglect. His name was Jones, and his best trait was that he neither hit nor hurt the children. Certainly there was only school for about one hour a month and the children of that period learnt nothing. Jones was always loafing or drinking somewhere, and I was horrified at the miserable condition of the very old people. As soon as I had recovered from my weariness I asked permission to borrow the old dray so that I could bring in some loads of wood for Mother and the other elderly people. This seemed the best way to help them.

After spending five days with Mother I started in a job outside Brewarrina. We were mustering sheep for shearing, and I was earning seventy shillings a week. When that job was finished I spent four weeks acting as a cook for a drover. During that time we had several dry storms with lightning and thunder. I have always hated them, and when I drove the slow-moving buckboard I expected to be struck at any minute. When the job ended I vowed that I would never go droving again. I returned to the Mission and stayed with Mother and tried to help her as much as possible. Once again I spent a lot of time carting wood for the old people. One day when I was bringing in a load the manager stopped me and ordered me to get some wood for another Aboriginal. I refused, saying that he was quite capable of cutting wood for himself. I knew that this man spent most of his time playing cards and drinking with the manager, and I did not see why I should do his work for him. I might have been willing to cart the wood in the dray if it had been already cut; however I was being asked to do the whole job for an able-bodied man.

The manager said: 'You refuse?' I replied: 'Yes, I do. I am willing to get wood for any elderly person here, but not for a man who is young and capable of getting it for himself.' Mr Jones was furious, and told me that I must leave the Mission if I did not do as he ordered. We had some heated words and I reiterated that I was not prepared to cut wood for young people. Also, I told him he was not fit to be a manager. I thought he was going to strike me; I just walked away, knowing I could not hit back. Whether right or wrong, or for self-defence, I would be put in jail if I struck a person of authority. In those days we had no say in any matter relating to the Missions. I had been banned from the Mission and there was nothing more I could do about it.

I went to see Mother and gathered a few belongings together, then I started the long walk to Brewarrina. The police were quite a good crowd at that time, so I went to see them. Sergeant Brandon was in charge of the station, and another officer named Dowd was helpful. Dowd said there was little they could do, but he suggested that he should write a letter for me to copy and sign and then post to the Board. This was very good of him, as the police were not supposed to help in this way. I had to refuse his offer. I knew it was useless because the letter would be returned to the manager for his verification. He would deny everything and I would be called an agitator and be served with a formal expulsion order preventing me from entering any of the Board's stations. During the afternoon I saw one of the members of the local Aborigines' committee and gave him all the facts of the incident. I stressed the dreadful condition of the Mission and suggested that some of their members make a surprise visit there and investigate the situation.

The following day I started in a job which involved pumping water out of a creek for stock. It was all very easy and I did it for sixteen weeks. Probably I should have done it for longer, but it was a lonely sort of a job and got on my nerves. It reminded me too much of 1917 when I had spent eight months alone in the bush at Tottenham. In February 1920 I gave notice and left.

When I returned to Brewarrina I stayed at one of the hotels. The next day I met a man who had just arrived in the town. He told me that he wanted to go out and have a look at the Mission, and asked where he could hire a horse and sulky. I found the transport for him and he suggested that I should go out there with him. I told him that the manager would not allow me on the place, but this man was firm in his request that I should accompany him. I kept on refusing until he told me that the existing manager had been sacked and that probably he would be taking over the management himself. His name was Burns; he was Scottish and seemed a good type. Eventually he persuaded me to go with him, and during the slow drive asked me many questions. He told me that he wanted to make certain that this position of manager was one that he would like.

When we arrived at the Mission I was greeted by Mr Jones yelling at me to get away from the place immediately. Mr Burns managed to calm him a little and I was allowed stay for a short time. While they were talking I went over to see Mother and spent a couple of hours with her. I gave her most of my money; she had been unable to work and the conditions were very difficult for her. On our way back to town Mr Burns remarked on the squalor and untidiness of the place and said he was undecided about taking the job there. He said he would stay in Brewarrina for a few days before making a decision.

The following day I accepted a job scrub-cutting at a station forty miles out of Brewarrina. There were usually eight of us in the camp, although most of the men did not stay long. I stayed there until June, when heavy rain started to fall.

When I returned to Brewarrina I heard that a new man was in charge of the Mission; this meant that it was probably safe for me to visit Mother. When I went out there I found that the man I had met five months earlier was fully in charge. The whole place had been cleaned up, including the drunks. Several families had been asked to leave and some of the old inhabitants had returned. School lessons were handled better and all the people seemed much brighter and happier. I was pleased to see Mr Burns again; we got on quite well together. He grumbled all the time, lost his temper on occasions and could be difficult, but despite those characteristics he was not very unreasonable.

During my first two weeks back at the Mission fifteen inches of rain fell. We were warned of the approach of a big flood and everyone was moved to the Red Hill in Brewarrina. Billy had come back for a visit and we camped together in a tent. We quite enjoyed helping in every way possible during this crisis; water police had been sent to the town and a state of emergency existed. It was about two o'clock one morning when we heard shouting and cries of 'Fire, fire!' I woke Billy and we rushed into the town, where several shops were blazing. The rain was pouring down but the fire was out of control. I remember the old chemist wandering around in his nightshirt asking everyone to save his microscope. Several attempts were made, but it was useless. There was no fire brigade at that time and it was impossible to save anything. Although the fire was surrounded by flood waters, the buildings and their contents were a total loss.

Billy and I had a few pounds, probably enough for a couple of weeks. Mother had forgotten her steel money-box which she kept under the floor boards in her hut at the Mission. This box contained my bank book, some bank notes and a cheque for thirty-seven pounds which I had forgotten to cash. I was worried about the box and was very keen to go and collect it. That night I met an old friend who asked if I would help him row a boat to a place about three miles above the Mission, a distance of eleven miles. I agreed to tackle the journey and we started rowing the next morning. There were three others in the boat who were supposed to help with the rowing. They did nothing and were just a dead weight for us to pull along. Perhaps others would have thrown them overboard into the swirling waters; they certainly deserved it. We cut across streams and followed the calmer backwaters whenever possible, but it was five hours of hard work before we reached our destination. I collected the money-box and we rowed back to Brewarrina. Although the flood was not as high as some we have had in more recent years, it was probably the most devastating. The year of 1920 will be remembered by all who were there.

When the water receded I took a job with my old friend Stuart Gordon; it was sheep work, which I have never liked. It was not long before I was able to get another job repairing flood damage. There were six of us working, and we all received forty-eight shillings weekly. Most of the others, who were older men, took their money to the town on Saturday and could not be found on Monday morning. They drank a lot and took many days to recover. Despite their drinking habits I liked being with them. I must admit that we loafed. Sometimes we put up a post and then sat down and told yarns, or went shooting. The boss was very easy-going, but I think he was tired of us in the end.

That Christmas Mother and I were pleased to have Billy with us. It was the last time he saw Mother. He left for the North Coast in the New Year and was away for three years. Everything seemed very slack in January 1921; there was no work of any kind, and I stayed at the Mission with Mother. Burns had improved our conditions, and he had daughters who mixed with the dark people and came to our dances and church meetings. One of his sons became quite a good friend of mine, and the general atmosphere was much happier. Burns was very loyal to the Aborigines; he would not listen to anything that was said against us. He helped us in many ways, but in other respects he was less pleasant. He became infuriated if he made a request and it was not dealt with immediately: it was sufficient provocation for him to expel a man from the Mission. I remember how he banished two brothers one morning and I had to drive him into town that afternoon. The brothers were standing near a street corner. Burns told me to stop, and then mumbled: 'Where can they go?' He thought for a couple of minutes, then suddenly said to me: 'Put them in the truck; we can take them back with us.' Basically he was reasonably kind and had some sympathy for the Aborigines, but he also made a profit when dealing with them. Any money owned by Aborigines was in the care of the manager; when people needed money they had to ask Burns for it. He filled in the necessary form and usually had his hand covering the required amount. He gave the Aboriginal the money he had requested, but the total written on the form was often twice as much. Burns kept the remainder for himself. Most of the dark people could neither read nor understand figures, so they did not know what was happening to their money. I saw Burns doing this many times, but if I had mentioned it to him he would have made my life unbearable. The best I could do was to insist on filling in my own forms and cheques.

One evening I was chatting with a few men, who said they were taking their swags and walking to Walgett. As I had no job at this time I decided to go with them. I told Mother of our plans, and we left a few days later with our swags on our backs. That day we walked about fifteen miles, then we camped and fished in the Barwon River. It took us five more days to reach Walgett, where we spent three weeks camping on the river-bank near the town. I did not tell the others that I had a little money with me, it seemed better to work and earn some more. One of the men agreed to work and we did small cleaning jobs in the town. With the money we earned we were able to buy some food. It was very little, and on some days we had nothing to eat. The other men were lazy, so lazy that they would never even help make a fire to boil the billy. It was a tough town for Aborigines, work was hard to find; so the two of us decided to leave our lazy mates to look after themselves. We rolled our swags and set off for Coonamble at ten o'clock one night. I often wondered how the other men managed without us. I have never met them since those days; they belonged to the North Coast, and probably returned there.

For about three months my friend and I wandered. We tramped at night and slept during the day. Sometimes we had to move during the day if we were seeking a place where food or work was available. The large stations usually handed out food to us, but around the wheat belt the situation was different and the farmers would never part with a crumb of bread. They were equally mean with jobs, and almost expected us to pay them for the honour of doing their work. We visited Gilgandra, Warren and Dubbo; it was just as well that I had a few shillings to buy bread at those towns or we might have starved. In due course I arrived back at the Mission. It had been a long walk, and I cannot imagine why I tackled it. I have always loved camping under the stars at night, but I had proved that carrying a swag did not appeal to me.

When I saw Mother again she was not at all well; she seemed considerably worse than when I had seen her several months earlier. I had intended to get a job somewhere in the district, but now felt that I should wait until she was better before I left her alone. I had been at the Mission for about ten days when the manager asked me to repair some windows at the school and at his house. I did not know too much about windows, but finished them in a week and was paid a fair price for the work. During the next few days I was idle and the manager was trying to find a job for me in the vicinity of the Mission. One morning he called me into his office and asked if I would take the position of handyman at the Mission. I asked for time to consider his offer, as I felt I must see the man who had done this work previously. When I found Bill Martin he was no longer keen about the job and was hoping a replacement could be found.

I returned to the manager and told him that I was prepared to work for him. The pay was not good, but as I wanted to be near Mother constantly this seemed the best decision. The only transport to Brewarrina was by sulky and I had to make the trip four times weekly, collecting mail and other necessities. The main stores were brought out to us by contractors. There were only three ancient horses on the Mission and they were kept busy most of the time; we owned only one dray, which was in constant use bringing in wood supplies. There were five hundred sheep in the surrounding paddocks; we killed four of them weekly for meat. Most of the people had to exist on a fish diet. Sometimes I suspected that the poor diet was the reason for most of the adults and children becoming pot-bellied.

A small amount of water was pumped up from the river into a very old 400-gallon tank. The pump was on a stand at the river-bank and the water had to be lifted for many feet. This was a tough job for two men and quite impossible for one man. Later I made some improvements to the pump and conditions were easier. There were several able-bodied men on the station and they had to do two and a half days of work weekly to entitle them to rations; this meant that I could occasionally find helpers. In many ways the Mission had improved, although there were still some people who did not care about their surroundings and who caused disturbances. They upset the more peaceful residents who had to tolerate their bad behaviour.

Towards the end of the year Mother became bed-ridden. Before I could leave for work I had to prepare everything she might need during the day. It was a rare event for an adult to visit her but I shall never forget some of the children, especially the dormitory children. They tried to help her in every way. There were two lads who were particularly good to her and stayed with her at night when I had to go into town. I gave them a few shillings weekly and did my best to bring them food and sweets from Brewarrina. In spite of her illness Mother never complained; she told the children stories and was always interested in the activities of other people. I knew she could not last long, and occasionally managed to get someone to do my work so that I could stay with her. It was late in the afternoon of 2 February 1922 that a message was delivered to me as I was pumping water from the river: Mother wanted me immediately. I hurried to her room. She was sitting up in bed as I entered and went to stand beside her. She looked at me and said: 'I am glad you came, son, for I am about to leave you and want to say goodbye.' She just took my hand in hers and lay back and died. I often think of her now, and of the great love she had for Billy and me. Her life had been one of unselfishness and effort on our behalf.

Billy did not return to the Mission until the following year, when his apprenticeship was finished. He told me about one night when he was camping out in the bush alone. It was about eight o'clock and he was eating his evening meal beside the fire. He said: I was stooping a little as I was pouring out some tea, then I sat back with my mug in my hand. I happened to look towards the side of the fire and in the glow I saw a vision of Mother. She was standing. This lasted for some seconds and then she slowly disappeared. I could not sleep that night, nor could I work the next morning. I made several attempts but felt that I had to go back to the station as I knew some news would come for me. It was almost eleven o'clock that morning when one of the station hands brought me your telegram. I knew what it would say: it told me of Mother's death. I had not been frightened during the previous night, but I was horribly worried and knew there was trouble at home.'

After Mother's death I considered leaving the Mission, but there were only station jobs offering. I had never liked that kind of work and it seemed better to stay where I was. I had always felt at home at the Mission; I liked being amongst my own people and had suffered enough because of the colour of my skin when I worked in other places. During those years it was a constant fight with the white people to get any type of job. The only work available to an Aboriginal was on stations or roads. In those days there was no mechanical equipment on the large stations; this type of work might have appealed to me if machinery had been involved. I tried to get work in a local garage, but when they saw my colour I was not wanted.

It was not possible for an Aboriginal to have any ambition or to make much progress in the world. My wish was for a little security and freedom from trouble with white people. During those years country towns usually had a group of white men waiting to beat up a dark man: the latter always had to fight a mob. I am not a fighter, and it was better to stay at the Mission living the life that was familiar to me. This decision was the beginning of twenty years' work on the Mission.

Although I was still young — my twenty-second birthday was approaching — I found the attitude of white people to my colour a constant strain. Even a visit to the café or a shop was an effort. When a dark person entered he would usually have to listen to comments on his colour and low social position and would probably have to wait a long time before being served. It was not what they said to me about my colour that worried me, it was having to listen to it so often. In the course of a day in town I heard unpleasant remarks and jokes countless times. If there were two men behind the counter when I went into a shop they would probably start their conversation by saying, 'What does this blackfellow want? There are other places for him.' One gets used to being called 'Abo', 'buck-toothed nigger', 'Jacky', 'boong',

'Charcoal', and 'no-good dirty nigger'. To the people who called us these things it was all good fun; for us it was depressing and horrible.

Even when accompanied by white friends it was always an effort to enter a public place. I remember one incident with a white friend who suggested that we should go into a hotel for dinner. There were two dining rooms, and as we walked through the first I saw a couple of whites, ordinary working men, eating their meal. I told my friend that this was where I should eat, but he insisted that I must eat with him in the better dining room. Reluctantly I followed him and we sat down. Then one man called out to another that there was a blackfellow in the room, and a lot of noisy unpleasantness was the result. My friend told the diners that they were despicable and went to see the manager. When he returned he was accompanied by the manager, who insisted that we should continue to eat our dinner and threatened to remove the other people. There was no more trouble, but it was the type of incident that dark people have to endure frequently.

Since the age of fourteen I had suffered many unpleasant episodes; they continued when I went into Brewarrina, but less frequently. To be settled in a job at the Mission would spare me having to listen to those remarks about blackfellows. I feel that early this century, or even before that, the whites must have been encouraged to hate the Aborigines. Mr Lindsay, my boss at Tottenham, used to say: 'All nations have a flag, but the blacks have not. A blanket would be good enough for you.' Many of these incidents are still in my memory, and they hurt when I was young. I remember trying to find a place which was some distance from Brewarrina; I saw a white man near the road and asked him for directions. His reply was: 'Find out for yourself; I don't tell blacks anything.' These occurrences were very embarrassing to the dark person, and also to any decent white man who happened to be present. Despite the aggravations, the Aboriginal had a dislike only for the individual who was rude to him. It did not affect our opinion of the majority of white people. We have often discussed the subject. We have never had any prejudice against skin of any colour. From the early days we have had to depend on the whites for many things, and if they were fair to us it was appreciated. If they were rude it was something that had to be suffered, but it did not influence our opinion of white people as a whole.

The white people have neither encouraged nor discouraged us in our liking for our legends. They have been largely responsible for the disappearance of speakers of Aboriginal languages. I have noticed that when people were talking to one another in Muruwari or Ngemba the white man who heard them would immediately jeer at 'old Jacky-Jacky speaking in his dirty lingo'. On many occasions I have noticed that the dark people would just stop talking when a white person approached, as they did not want to appear foolish.

During the last century the situation was not a happy one for Aborigines living in this district, and no estimate can be given of the number massacred by white people. At the Mission and on the Culgoa many old people told me stories they had heard from survivors, and most of them were similar. Nobody seemed to know exactly when the worst shooting occurred, but it must have been close to 1860. In those days there was no law to protect Aborigines and they could be shot at any time. It was some years later that missions, reserves and Aboriginal protection were introduced. The first time I heard about the massacres near Brewarrina was in 1912, and the stories were told by people who had been alive at that time.

There was a path from Barwon Bridge to the Mission; it had been in use for many years before the Mission was established. Along this path, three miles from the Mission, stood the Butcher's Tree. The tree was given this name after the massacre had taken place. This tree had heavy limbs and the lower branches were almost horizontal. I saw it first in 1912 after it had been ring-barked; however, it gave the impression that it must have had very heavy foliage, and on both sides of the trunk notches had been cut. These started about one foot from the ground and there were thirteen slits at regular intervals to make climbing easy. It was from the area surrounding this tree that all the trouble began. I can tell only the Aboriginal version of the story:

A cattle owner had lived close to where the Mission was later established. All accounts indicate that his treatment of the natives was bad. He owned some cattle, although there were probably not as many as credited to him by the white people. The Aborigines killed some of his cattle, and this caused the trouble. Their method was to wait until the animals came close to the Butcher's Tree, where several men were concealed in the branches. Other men would gently urge the beasts towards the tree, where they settled in the shade. When this happened the men jumped from the tree and hamstrung a couple of them. The herd was then driven towards the river, half a mile away. Here in the twilight or moonlight more natives gathered and indulged in further slaughter or distribution of the meat. This must have happened during summer months, as cattle do not seek shade in the winter and tend to scatter when driven. It was said that runners carrying beef fat were sent out to more distant natives and that other Aborigines were invited to the river to share the meat. After this had happened several times the owner of the cattle declared war on the offenders and enlisted the help of other white men. The killing of cattle at the Butcher's Tree was the cause of the deaths of many Aborigines.

Only a few natives were killed at the Butcher's Tree, as not many were there at the time. The largest massacre was at Hospital Creek, which is eleven miles from Brewarrina on the Goodooga road. Many natives were camped there, and early one morning the white men rode in from two directions. There was a lot of shooting and a great number of Aborigines were killed. Shooting was the main cause of death, but many people were also injured by the stirrup irons carried by the white men. The fire-arms used at that time were muzzle-loaders shooting lead balls. Groups of Aborigines either lived or met near the water, and it is thought that a number of those killed at Hospital Creek may have had nothing to do with the slaughter of cattle at the Butcher's Tree. It is said that some men escaped being killed near the tree and ran to join the group at Hospital Creek. The country is open there and it was difficult for the Aborigines to hide or escape. Very few survived. Skeletons and bones can still be seen there today, although I saw many more in 1928. The bones must have been there for a long time, and their quantity indicated that a large number of natives had been left dead or dying.

The massacre occurred at a time when there was a movement amongst the whites to kill all Aborigines when found in a group, or even separately. There is no doubt that the hamstringing of the cattle was the cause of the murder of so many of the dark people. Killings took place also in Brewarrina, along the Barwon and Narran Rivers and as far away as Walgett. In 1920 I found a number of lead musket balls and skeletons on the northern side of Brewarrina. The bones were embedded in hard soil, and there were also a lot of teeth which appeared to belong to children. It has been said that this area was an Aboriginal burial ground. This could not be true, as some skeletons were overlying others, and this method of burial is contrary to the native custom.

Although the Hospital Creek massacre was the worst in the district, there was another occurrence, on the northern bank of the Barwon about four miles above the Fisheries. On this occasion a lot of Aborigines were killed without warning. There were a couple of survivors who hid in the reeds and escaped to the west during the night. In addition to this, many isolated groups of natives were killed on the banks of the river where they usually camped. Skeletons can be found at most of the bends of the Barwon River as it moves towards Walgett. While recording this story I am living near the river, and have found human bones at the bend just below the house. There is little doubt that the white people tried to eradicate all blacks from the district. There were some survivors, and it is from them that this information has been acquired. The last Aboriginal known to be shot was returning home carrying fish he had caught. It happened approximately ten years after the events at Hospital Creek, and was very close to where I am living now.

After the massacres, the Aborigines disappeared into the bush and most of them moved towards the west. Those who survived warned the others who lived near the Culgoa and Birrie Rivers, and they disappeared also. It was not until some years later that they dared to return. I am not too sure when the Mission was actually established, but I think it was near the end of the last century; this encouraged the Aborigines to return. They felt that there would be some sort of a sanctuary for them, and the issue of food was an attraction. The advent of cattle and sheep had disturbed the bush's natural balance and existence had become more difficult. It was at this time that most of the Muruwari drifted back. Other people came in from Byrock, which was part of the Ngemba territory, and they were the nucleus of the original settlement at the Mission.

Another small item of interest dates back to the years between 1850 and 1860. Mother and the old people frequently discussed the importance of the Culgoa River to the Muruwari tribe. They also spoke about thirteen completely hairless Aborigines who lived near the river during those years. I have noticed that all the natives who came from this area have less facial hair than others.

In addition to the Butcher's Tree there were several other trees which were considered important. The Chinaman's Tree was a mile from the Mission; a Chinaman was reputed to have hanged himself from the branches, and was buried close to it. The Muruwari had a great aversion to suicide, so this area was avoided; we believed that a small mound near the tree was the grave. There was another tree with special associations; this was at Little Bend, not far from the Mission. It was large and had a very smooth trunk. It was said that the witch doctors held their secret meetings there and that the hollow part of the trunk contained human bones and various other belongings of the *gubi*, or clever men. It seemed odd that the tree appeared to have been burnt near the lower branches and in the centre of the trunk. The fire had not damaged the outside part of the tree in any way, and the burnt part never healed although the remainder was extremely healthy. There was always some superstition about this tree; people would not go near it alone when fishing or approach it at night.

Another tree which had special significance to the Muruwari was approximately forty miles from Brewarrina. Their legend of the two eagles or spirit birds was believed to have emanated from this tree. In the very early days this was such a tall tree that it was impossible for anyone to climb it; it grew right up into the sky. The trunk was too large to be chopped or burnt. At the top of the tree one limb grew out in the shape of an S, and this was where the eagles had their nest. These eagles were supernatural, and controlled the people who lived below them. If the tribe was hunting and one man walked apart from the others, an eagle would swoop and carry his victim up to the nest. Many people were disappearing, and it was imperative that the tribe remain in a group. This was not a good arrangement as it meant that the old people and children had to accompany a hunting party, the crowd made a lot of noise and the hunting was not very successful. The tribe tried in every way to remove the eagles or destroy the tree. When they cut into the trunk it would continually heal itself; the same healing process occurred when they tried to burn it. The local witch doctors tried everything they knew, but could harm neither the tree nor the eagles.

The people had given up all hope of removing the menace of these birds, until they heard about two very special witch doctors who lived far to the south, close to the Murray River. Messengers were sent to plead with the witch doctors, asking them to come north and solve the problem. In due course the messengers led the witch doctors to the Muruwari country. When these clever men arrived they studied the tree for some time. It had a long, straight trunk and when people tried to climb it something invisible would knock them to the ground. On other occasions they climbed for a short distance and then suddenly felt dizzy; their noses bled and they were unable to continue.

The witch doctors listened to the stories and then told the people what should be done. They were told to move in a large group towards the tree, then a couple of men were to stray a short distance from the crowd. When this was done an eagle flew towards the two men, who returned quickly to the shelter of the crowd. This happened many times and both eagles were kept occupied while the witch doctors started their work. They were close to the tree and had made themselves invisible so that the eagles were unaware of what was happening. They chanted songs which gave them strength to bore a hole into the centre of the tree. Then they put many firesticks into the hole and sang louder and louder. The clever men also caused a wind to blow which encouraged the fire to burn more strongly. They had reached the hollow part of the trunk, and they stoked the blaze with many branches and dead leaves. They told the people to come closer and to keep the attention of the eagles while the fire was gaining a hold on the tree. The fire burnt more and more strongly and when a great inferno was raging inside the trunk there was a tremendous cracking sound and the tree fell to the ground, bringing the nest with it. For some time afterwards the trunk continued to burn along its full length.

This eagle tree lay between the Barwon River and a place the Aborigines called Gurdi Springs, meaning Bitter Springs, and later called Cuddy Springs by the white people. In more recent years bones have been found at Cuddy Springs which are reputed to be those of Aborigines who had been taken into the nest of the eagles. The old people say that the glow of the burning trunk has been seen at night ever since this event, but more realistic stories explain that this is a place where there are many glow-worms.

Several other places have some legendary significance to us. There is a large, evil-looking bend in the river four miles above Brewarrina; the water is extremely deep and the bend is called Miriga:na by the Aborigines. This name was given to it many years ago as it had some association with the Jugi, or spirit dogs. However, people have also spoken about this unpleasant stretch of water as the home of the rainbow serpent, or water snake. These snakes are reputed to be enormous, close to the size of a large prehistoric animal. The Muruwari called them *gabuda ga:n* and the Ngemba called them *wa:wi*. It is still believed today that this is where the monsters lived and that one could be there even now.

Another place of great interest to the old people was away from the Culgoa River and towards Enngonia. Mother, Jimmy Kerrigan and Hippai used to tell me about the little hairy men who lived there. It was believed that they lived in holes in the ground and could be seen only during the afternoon. Sometimes a hollow drumming sound was heard coming from their underground home.

When Mother died in 1922 the belief in these stories was strong. I still believe quite a lot of them, but people who are younger than I am are seldom interested. It was soon after Mother's death that I realised that many of the Muruwari customs were lost. During the influenza epidemic of 1919 there were many deaths amongst the old people, and most of the full-bloods died. Only the younger people were left at the

Mission, and some of them died later from the after-effects of the illness; others were left deaf or partly paralysed. It was amazing that King Clyde and Mother were able to survive. Old Maria died at this time: she was one of the twenty people who died at Weilmoringle.

Approximately thirty people died at the Mission during this epidemic. They were not given any help or medical attention; the only medicine available was Epsom salts or castor oil. The old people died and the dead had to be buried. King Clyde helped constantly as a grave digger. I do not think the graves were as deep as they should have been, and there were no coffins available at this time. The population of the Mission was considerably reduced by the epidemics of measles and influenza, and this hastened the loss of Aboriginal beliefs. At the time many people still believed in the use of smoke to confuse the spirit of the dead man. Although they could still use the smoke they could not move away from the place of death, which took some adjustment and caused fear and unhappiness. Until 1922 they destroyed all the possessions of the dead man — they were either burnt or thrown in the river. The manager did not know about this: he would never have condoned the destruction of clothes and blankets. Eventually Mr Burns found out what was happening and made trouble for all the people who had destroyed government property. He insisted that all the belongings of a dead person should be given to him, and indicated that he would have them fumigated before returning them to the relatives. Before this the people would chop up a sewing machine with an axe, or destroy other items of value in the same way. Plates and crockery were smashed, and a comfortable house would suddenly become a hovel.

When Mother died it is possible that I was responsible for the end of all customs relating to death at the Mission. I did not bother using the smoke of dogwood or sandalwood leaves, and I treasured her simple possessions. These were mainly photographs, china and linen. I had many visitors who asked when I was going to destroy her belongings. I told them that I was going to keep anything of value, and they were horrified. King Clyde disapproved strongly; he had helped Mother when she was ill and was a strong believer in the old ways. It almost created a scandal amongst the local Aborigines when nothing was burnt. I gave away her clothes, and told the people that they could burn them if they were not of use. Despite all the disapproval, I noticed that from this time onwards the relatives kept the possessions of a person who had died.

There is still a basic fear and mental disturbance amongst the Aborigines when a death occurs, even when the deceased was not a relative or friend. This attitude remains at the present time amongst dark people over the age of forty. Those who are younger seem to regard a death in the same way as white people. An incident occurred at the Mission in 1940 which showed the effect a death and burial can have even on people who knew the dead man only slightly. There were a lot of people from Weilmoringle visiting the Mission at the time, and one of the visitors died. The manager was new, but his idea of the correct procedure was to read the burial service and then praise the deceased at length. I warned him that any lengthy service was unwise, for both the Weilmoringle and the Mission people could cause some sort of a riot. Being the undertaker, I advised a very brief service and immediate burial afterwards. Despite this warning, the manager was extremely verbose and prolonged his words of praise. The people were becoming very restless, and I whispered to the preacher that it would be advisable to finish. He took no notice of me and continued speaking with even more enthusiasm. Suddenly all the listeners started to dance and rush around in circles; one man even jumped into the grave. The grave-digger and a number of the mourners, anticipating trouble, disappeared quickly. The manager hurriedly tried to get away but found himself surrounded by the dancers, and had some nasty moments when he thought that his funeral might be the next. Eventually I was the only one remaining after the riot, and there was nothing to be done but to deal with the body and cover the grave on my own.

The burial ground at the Mission is near the river, and we feel that it is one with special associations for our people. One of the managers who was there in the very early days wished to be buried in this place, and 'Hopkins, 1900' can be seen on his grave. There is supposed to be another grave dated about 1890, but this is hard to locate now. The man who caused the shooting of the natives at the Hospital Creek massacre is also supposed to have been buried there. Farther east is a place where a house and cellar had been; a depression in the ground is all that remains to indicate its position. It was said that a man kept young Aboriginal girls in the cellar, and stories are told of their voices being heard crying for help.

Unlike most Aborigines, I am not afraid of death or the dead. For that reason the job of undertaker was added to my duties at the Mission, and I made the coffins in my small workshop. Early in 1922 an old man died at the hospital in town. I made the coffin and then had to go into Brewarrina by dray and collect the body. The manager asked if I needed help and I replied that I would like someone to be with me. We asked many people and they all refused firmly. Eventually one man consented to come if he could ride a horse and keep well away from the dray. By the time I reached the hospital it was after sunset. We put the old man in the casket and then went into town to do a few other jobs. My assistant had been quite a help, and it was after eleven o'clock on a very dark night before the dray reached Barwon Bridge. My helper went into a state of panic, dug his heels into the horse and disappeared into the darkness. As I had to sit on the casket when driving the dray, I could not whistle or sing; all I could do was smoke cigarettes and plod on at our usual slow speed. It must have been 1 a.m. when I arrived at the Mission. All lights were out and everyone was asleep except some boys who always waited for the saveloys I brought for them. They helped me with the casket, which we put in the school until the time of the funeral. This was the usual practice, as the school building was also used as the chapel. Being the undertaker was far from pleasant; it was not long before I had another similar experience. I was in Brewarrina with the sulky when the manager sent a message saying that a man had died at the hospital and must be brought to the Mission that night. A wardsman helped me wrap the dead man in a couple of blankets and we put him in the sulky. It was an eerie drive, but someone had to do those jobs.

Burial customs differed according to the tribe. The

Muruwari and Ngemba people buried their dead in a horizontal position, and the angle of the grave was determined by the home of the person: if the dead man came from the west his head would point in that direction. It was the best that could be done for him when return to his own territory was impossible. In the early days the body was wrapped in bark. There are a number of recognised burial grounds in the Muruwari area; sandy places were preferable as digging was easier. Sometimes a body was carried for many miles to the appropriate place. There was a large burial ground at Nulty Station, on the northern side of the Darling River near Bourke. Goombalie is possibly the largest and oldest of our burial grounds. Another one is near Yarrawin. Many old bones have been found there, not only of humans but also of prehistoric animals, and various scientific people have visited the site, which is about forty miles from Brewarrina. These people found the remains of a giant lizard there, and a few miles downstream from Brewarrina they discovered the large incisors of a gigantic water rat. They took them away and I think they were put in one of the museums. There is another very old burial place at Culgoa Downs, a few miles from the old reserve. Near Cumborah are the old *bora* grounds and many marked trees; there are also marked trees along the Culgoa River. The only time the Muruwari marked a tree was when a particularly important man was buried close to it. The markings on the tree are similar to those on the body of the deceased.

During 1922 my job at the Mission gradually settled into some sort of routine. I had met Evelyn Wighton the previous year, and had enjoyed her company when we had our little dances or entertainments. We went for walks together, and it was good to have some companionship. Since Mother's death I had been lonely and had few people who shared my interests. It was at this time that I consolidated another friendship with a boy who had helped Mother greatly when she was alive. From my early days at the Mission I had liked this lad, whose name is Dudley Dennis. After Mother died he lived with me and we became very good friends. I had started a little school for children which we held at night or on Saturday afternoons. I had a large blackboard, and taught them the alphabet and elementary sums. Sometimes I read to them and tried to teach a little geography. On other occasions I showed them pictures from an old-type projector; I had made an amplifier so that there could be a musical accompaniment. The records played for only four minutes, and I found myself very busy on these picture nights. We had lots of fun and I felt some satisfaction in adding a little to the knowledge of the young people.

Dudley found it impossible to grasp reading or figures, but he seemed a natural carpenter and loved timber work. As he was willing to help me with those jobs, I appreciated his assistance and we both found it very satisfactory. He had a natural instinct for using a saw, and some years later he went to work at Pilliga and was extremely good on the saw bench at the mill. Later he started building houses, and it was amazing how well he did the job without any knowledge of figures or measurement. Also, without understanding the principles, he became an excellent mechanic. After all these years he is still my best friend, and often comes from Walgett to visit me.*

My job became less difficult with Dudley's help. The Board had installed a windmill and we were encouraged to make small gardens. Occasionally the manager suggested that something special should be done, but most of the time I felt that I was my own boss and the order of my work was left to my discretion. The majority of the people on the station were decent people; some of the families progressed well and their children now live in Brewarrina as respected people.

Our main entertainment consisted of games of cricket, rounders and football. We had small concerts and dances occasionally in the evenings. Most of the dances seemed to end with arguments, and it would be a couple of weeks before the participants spoke to one another again. Sometimes a few of us had a game of euchre. Apart from these activities our lives were very quiet. I read everything

* I met him in Walgett in 1973. J.M.

possible in the evenings and continued my efforts to add to my limited education. I bought myself a large dictionary and spent many hours a week studying it.

The drinking of alcohol is a dreadful problem amongst Aborigines. It was during 1922 and 1923 that I became aware of it. During those days the men worked on remote stations for several months without a break. I noticed how they descended on the town and were completely drunk until they returned to their outlying stations. This was apparent only in Brewarrina: no liquor was allowed at the Mission. Mr Burns adhered to this rule firmly, and if anyone was caught drinking he was banished immediately. This meant that the offender probably finished up in town where he joined the men who drank all day and night. I noticed also that a lot of methylated spirits was being drunk on the river-bank or in the park. The money these men earned was never spent on food or for the benefit of their families; always on drink. A situation arose where dark men were being arrested in the town whether they had been drinking or not. An Aboriginal who did not drink and was chatting to a white man near a hotel could find himself pushed into jail. Another equally innocent dark man might be walking past the hotel and be suddenly grabbed by a policeman and locked up. This situation was a reflection on the police system and showed discrimination. The feeling of injustice could make a man drink for the first time in his life when he was released. There is no doubt that when an Aboriginal drinks he is a nuisance; it is also true that too many Aborigines drink excessively. It is hard to guess when and how this situation will improve. In the early days drinking by women was not tolerated, but unfortunately this has changed in recent years.

Gambling was something I had noticed earlier in Weilmoringle, and since those days Aborigines have seldom stopped gambling with cards or dice. They played for money if they had any; otherwise the stakes were tobacco, clothes or other possessions. Sometimes a well-dressed man visited the Mission, then the word went around: 'Johnny Mann is here, he has a couple of pounds. Let's get up a game.' In a short time the poor fellow found that he was completely broke. I remember walking past them near the end of a game: Johnny had lost everything except the trousers in which he was sitting. Somebody won the trousers, which made it awkward. The problem was solved by the victor giving him an old pair of pants from the rubbish tip.

The use of and concern for money does not come easily to Aborigines, and it is seldom that they try to accumulate any savings. When they have money they might buy a few necessities; more often they squander it. They most certainly spend it very quickly and do not consider what might be needed for the future.

Sometimes a man comes home from work with a cheque for, say, one hundred dollars. He cashes the cheque at the first opportunity, spends some of it, gives away a lot more, and within hours it is all gone. He uses very little of it for himself. This attitude goes back to the basic Aboriginal tradition of sharing with one another and of having no thought for the future. Only a small number of dark people are careful with their earnings and so ensure that they have some money in reserve.

I have mentioned my friendship with Evelyn Wighton. I met her for the first time in October 1921, and she was so young and beautiful that I fell in love with her at our first meeting. During three months we spent many happy hours together; I found that I depended on her companionship, and dreaded the time when she would have to go out to work. During my earlier years at the Mission courtship was always done from some distance; this had been the Aboriginal custom for hundreds of years. I used to notice that a boy and girl would spend a lot of their time just looking at one another. The girl sat on the dormitory steps for hours daily while the boy strolled up and down about ten yards away from her. They did not speak to one another. This situation might continue for months. Often a manager would take action: bring them together and suggest that they get married. Having done that he would go ahead and make arrangements for the wedding. I remember at least six cases like this; the young couples had been hurried into marriage and had parted a few days after the wedding. They separated and neither could marry again.

Sometimes the girl found another man and just lived with him. Her husband would be in a similar situation and live with another girl. I was thankful that times had changed when I met Evelyn. We could spend time together, were able to get to know one another, and felt confident that we would be happy together for the rest of our lives.

As January 1922 approached Evelyn and I realised that we would have to be separated: the time had come for her to be sent out to work. We decided to wait until she had worked for a couple of years before we married. I knew that I would miss her greatly, and also worried about how her employers would treat her. She had reached the age when she must be placed on a station and work for a reasonable length of time. There had been a lot of unhappy cases and many of the young apprentices had suffered from shocking treatment. Two boys were apprenticed to a man who lived three miles out of Brewarrina. This man was continually hitting and bashing the boys, who kept escaping to the Mission. We saw them with black eyes, cuts, bruises and various horrible injuries. Their employer always forced them to return, and their lives were miserable. There was another case where two girls were employed about forty miles away. Early each morning their boss entered their bedroom and kicked them while they were still in bed. Eventually the girls retaliated and brought in a couple of logs. They arranged the logs and pillows, covered them with blankets and ran away. No doubt the boss kicked the logs when he came for his morning visit. There was another case at Walgett, where the employer kept hitting his Aboriginal apprentice with sticks. The injuries to the boy were shocking, and the scars can still be seen on his face. I felt that I had endured a lot during my apprenticeship, but it was not as bad as these other cases.

Evelyn's mother was always talking about New Zealand, and I guessed that her family was probably Maori. Their features did not seem the same as a true Aboriginal, although the colour of the skin was similar. I did not meet Evelyn's father, but he was either white or partly white. He was a brick-maker and spent most of his life at Nyngan. There were thirteen in the family, but only three of them are living now. Evelyn's younger sister died a few years ago; she was the grandmother of Evonne Goolagong, the tennis champion. The Wighton family were active and athletic. The eldest sister, Clara, is still living, now well into her eighties, and there is another sister who still lives in Brewarrina.

The time came when Evelyn had to leave the Mission. She was fifteen, and her job was on a station at Yantabulla. I was miserable without her and during the first few months we wrote to one another regularly, but after that no more letters arrived from her. I continued to write, but it hurt me when no letters came; it also made me worried. It was hard to believe that she could ignore my letters and forget me so quickly.

One day towards the end of 1922 four boys ran across to me and spoke about a new girl who had arrived at Mrs Barnes'. I asked all sorts of questions: 'Is she big? Is she pretty?' They replied that she was a big girl and just a little pretty. A couple of hours later I walked past Mrs Barnes' house and the new girl was sitting outside, surrounded by children. As I came closer I noticed her dormitory-type dress with the familiar red stripes. When I said 'Good morning' I could not help looking at her lovely face and jet-black hair. We talked for a few minutes until Mrs Barnes appeared in the doorway. She looked at me firmly and said: 'Now, Jimmie, don't you start talking to my girl, you know that you have a girl of your own working in the country. This is May Clements, she is in my care and I don't want you here.' Mrs Barnes always called me Brother Jim and treated me well when no girls were there. However, when she was looking after girls her smiles were not for me. I walked away thinking that I could have had a better introduction to the new girl whose lovely face attracted me.

A few nights later a dance was held at the old schoolhouse. Instead of reading I strolled over to the dance, wondering if May would be there. I saw her immediately; Mrs Barnes was close to her and looking very fierce. I had never learnt to dance, so I could not ask her to join me. Eventually I plucked up enough courage to walk over to May and try to talk to her. She nodded and hung her head. Mrs Barnes kept moving her away from me. It was hopeless, and it was many weeks before I could do more than greet her briefly.

In due course May was put in charge of the dormitory children; she was also their cook. This change gave me more opportunities to speak to her, but she always kept her eyes lowered and appeared to be very shy. When I delivered the milk in the mornings she started having a cup of tea ready for me. After that I usually separated the milk and helped her with the washing up. Gradually we became quite friendly. Every couple of weeks we went out for a picnic, played with the children or went fishing. We were never on our own, but I enjoyed her company. Ever Sunday night we had a little church service in the dormitory dining room; we sang hymns and read from the Bible. It was during one of these services that I realised how much I loved May. Evelyn had disappeared and forgotten me. May could not take her place, but I loved them both.

I owned an old cylinder-type phonograph. How well I remember May and the other girls coming to my little house in the evenings to listen: they had no hesitation in almost yelling their requests for their favourite music.

Time passed pleasantly and it was a year later, November 1923. I was talking to the girls on the dormitory veranda when the manager joined us and said: 'We have quite a lot of girls here, Jimmie. They will either have to get jobs or marry.' May commented that the man she married would have to be good and also have a lot of money. Everyone laughed at this remark, but it had a different meaning to me and rather put me off. I knew that I had no money, and her meaning seemed clear. I had never made love to her, so how was I to know whether she really meant this or not?

I wrote to a Sydney store and ordered an engagement ring. I asked for a single diamond, but when the ring arrived it had seven diamonds. Now that I had it I did not know what to do with it. An occasional letter had arrived from Evelyn, and I had written to her weekly ever since she had left the Mission. To which of these girls should I give the ring? I had a feeling, of insecurity with them both, and just hoped I could make up my mind eventually. In the meantime I hid the ring.

Christmas 1923 was a happy one; May and the dormitory girls had put up decorations and prepared a wonderful dinner. I had never seen May looking happier or more at ease; she seemed to have gained some confidence. It was early in 1924 that she told me of her intention to take a job in the country as the pay was better. I told her that I was not pleased about her imminent departure, but if she wanted the additional money there was nothing I could do to stop her. A week later, when I was in town, her new employer came and took her away. When I returned to the Mission and found that she had gone without any parting words or message for me I was very upset. For days I was in a horrid sort of dizzy dream, and it was some time before I felt able to live normally. Early in March I received my first letter from May, and it pleased me greatly. She said she was happy and liked her new job. I answered immediately, and after that we corresponded constantly. At this time I was very unhappy as I had not received any letters from Evelyn for months, but May's letters cheered me. During all the correspondence with May neither love nor our future was mentioned.

Evelyn arrived back at the Mission in May, but I did not speak to her for a couple of weeks. One day she came over to me and said: 'You don't speak to me now; why?' I told her that I had considered everything between us must be finished as she had not written for many months. She replied: 'I always loved you, Jim, and I always shall. All your letters were kept away from me after my first employers left the property; then my new employers would not allow me to write to you.' I believed this and gradually we began to see one another more often. She asked me if I loved anyone else. I told her that I did not actually love someone else but wrote to a girl who was a very dear friend. Although I was seeing a lot of Evelyn I promised her nothing, and eventually she asked if there was any chance of us returning to our old relationship. She forced me to answer, and I could only say that I needed time to think things over. She pressed me for a more definite answer and I replied that I did not have sufficient money to consider marriage. My mind was tangled and I had a terrible evening of indecision. At midnight I wrote a short letter to May; it was indefinite but I said that I might have more to tell her when I wrote next. Her answer arrived quickly, full of questions about what I had to tell her and requesting that I write to her immediately and tell her my news. Ten days later I wrote to her briefly and told her that I was thinking of making my peace with Evelyn and that it was possible that we would become engaged to be married. I asked for her opinion and urged that she answer me quickly. I realised later that this was wrong, and have regretted my letter ever since. I waited and waited but no answer came.

It was towards the end of July that May and her sister Margaret visited the Mission. Margaret was a lively girl, but May did not seem the same as she had been before. I was worried about her and thought that she must be in love with someone else. Occasionally I felt that she might be sad about the change in our friendship. I loved her so much but it was impossible to tell her, probably because of my feeling of inferiority and lack of money. I was noncommittal with Evelyn, and longed to escape from my state of mental chaos. I confided in Margaret, who suggested that I wait a little longer and the situation might become clearer. She knew that I had never confessed my love to May and that there was nothing more than friendship between us. I admitted that I was deeply in love with both May and Evelyn, had bought an engagement ring, and was in a state of utter confusion. Margaret suggested that it would be harder on Evelyn if I deserted her now, since we had known each other for such a long time. May had really known me only since we had been corresponding, and her worry could be caused by the possible loss of a friend.

Soon after this May and Margaret left the Mission. For five months I had been evading Evelyn's questions, and considered leaving the Mission myself. The confusion in my mind became worse. Sometimes I did not speak to Evelyn for days and volunteered for outside jobs so that I would not see her. When we did meet there was no quarrel, but I left all her pleas unanswered. Evelyn was patient; I suppose she had to be. I admired her forbearance, as my behaviour was enough to make any girl disgusted. May did not write, and some nights I just lay in bed and cried for hours. I had to find a solution. Finally, on the night of November the 25th, I asked Evelyn to marry me. She was happy, and I put the ring on her finger. I had to write to her father for his consent as she was not yet seventeen. When his reply came we made arrangements for our wedding: the date we chose was 17 December 1924.

The day came: 10.30 a.m. As I stood beside Evelyn my thoughts were of May. I had not given her a chance; I was leaving her for another and had not even asked her to come to the wedding. I hardly heard a word the preacher said, I only heard Evelyn's voice. As for me, I think the best man answered all the vows. There was no honeymoon; we just walked over to the small house in which I lived. There were no visitors, and it was known as the quietest wedding ever held at the Mission.

Two weeks after we were married May arrived at the Mission for a short visit. On New Year's Day I spoke to her for a few minutes; she had changed a lot and looked sad. I knew it was not wise to talk to her for long. I had intended to ask her to our house, but felt that would be unkind to both girls. When she was due to return to work I was asked to prepare the utility truck and drive her into town when I fetched the mail. I asked Evelyn if she would like to come for the drive, but she refused. Usually a crowd wanted to accompany me when I drove into town, but on this day no one else wanted to come.

May and I left fairly early in the morning. She seemed shy and kept her head turned away from me. When we stopped near the post office there was still an hour to wait until the mail was due. Suddenly she said: 'I'm so glad to be with you today. I wonder why we were never alone together like this before. I can't believe you are married, Gem.' She had always called me Gem. Then she covered her face with her hands and wept. After a little while I said: 'You really did care for me?' Her reply was: 'Always, always.' She struggled with her tears, and it was only then I realised that she loved me. We had a few quiet words together until she said that she must leave. I asked her when we would meet again; she answered that I would never see her again. I could only sit and watch a girl of medium height with black hair, wearing a light dustcoat, walk across the street and away from me. She was right: that was the last time I saw her. In 1925 I heard that she had married and was living in Victoria. It was not until 1960 that I heard more about her when I happened to pick up an old newspaper and saw a small item with the heading: 'Woman's Tragic Death'. I read more and realised that it was May who had been killed in a dreadful accident.

Evelyn seemed to understand my feelings for May. My love for Evelyn grew into something that was half worship,

Evelyn in their garden at the Mission, 1933

Jimmie near his house at the Mission, 1933

and I realised that my decision to marry her had been right. If I was away for a couple of days my heart seemed to ache and I longed for her to be near me. Nothing seemed to worry us; our life was simple, easy and happy. Evelyn handled our small amount of money and was a wonderful manager. If there was not enough money we lived frugally, and she never complained. Our little house had only three rooms; I had added a bathroom, and it was a pleasant little place. We made a garden around it, and our lives settled into a contented routine. Evelyn was not very dark, although her colouring could be noticed. She had suffered some unpleasant experiences because of her colour and was pleased to live at the Mission where we were free from discrimination. Being Maori she was not particularly interested in Aboriginal culture or customs. However, she worked to help the Aborigines and had strong religious beliefs.

Early in 1924 many people left the Mission, but for some reason they reappeared in 1925 and we became a reasonably large community. This was a good year and conditions improved considerably. During the year I built five new houses; they were small but quite solid. In addition to the windmill we were given a pump; when I installed it there was more water available for us. The only taps were a few along the line of houses, and our way of life was still rather primitive. The dray and sulky were seldom used and the Ford utility truck made my work easier. I made many more trips into town: sick people had to be transported, while others had to catch the train or be met at the station. In addition there were the regular trips to collect stores and mail.

One wet day I had to take a maternity case in to the hospital. The manager sent three men with me: their job was to push the truck if we were bogged. He did not think of sending a woman with us. All was well until about three miles from town when we became firmly bogged. We all looked for sticks, and were fixing them under the wheels when we heard a baby cry. As soon as the others heard it they tore off down the road and left me to deal with the problem. They did not go very far, but just stood around not knowing what to do. I had read a little about the birth of babies, and did my best to calm and help the woman. When she seemed more comfortable I called them back and we finally got the truck out of the bog. When we reached the maternity block the baby was crying loudly; both mother and son were well. On several occasions babies were nearly born on the way into town, but this was my most dramatic episode.

During this year the people seemed reasonably happy at the Mission, although medical help was not readily available. The patient had to be taken into town and often this was left too late. Quite a lot of people died of tuberculosis; others died of cancer which had been neglected. The death rate was highest amongst babies and children. We tried to keep some standard of cleanliness and did our best to prevent illness. All of the sheep had been sold and most of the cattle; I had to do the milking and separating required for the few remaining cows. As the little truck meant more work for me away from the place, another man was employed to help with jobs around the Mission. The boys and girls who left the dormitories for employment had to be driven to Walgett, Bourke or Byrock. I could be called at any hour of the night when a patient had to be taken to hospital. For various reasons I had to visit Angledool, Goodooga, Enngonia and Weilmoringle. I was still the undertaker, and occasionally had to read the burial service when the manager was away. The life was hard and food was scarce, but I quite enjoyed my work and was always happy at home with Evelyn.

Sometimes there were fights on the station and frequently I had to go out and stop them. The women used to fight as vigorously as the men: they punched, hit and scratched one another. Evelyn was not a person to fight, and was very good at controlling the women. Sometimes the manager appeared and stopped the fight — frequently only a temporary measure, as the combatants were apt to start again in some other place. The troubles and fights were always domestic: it might be an argument about children or between families. The only time we saw a drunken man was when one came from town. Aborigines were forbidden to buy or drink spirits: the men had to persuade a white friend to buy them an occasional bottle. There has been some deterioration in the Aboriginal drinking habits since the early days; during those years alcohol was no problem on the Mission itself, and was seldom the cause of fights.

A strange type of jealousy exists in Aboriginal society, often between men and their respective wives. The people did not meet one another in a particularly friendly way, because this jealousy was always close to the surface. They might play cards together for a short time without trouble, but this basic jealousy prevented friendly visits to the homes of other people. It was not possible to have a joke or chat with the wife of another man: it might be completely harmless, but the husband would not see it in that way and a bad fight could follow. This jealousy is something that has remained of the Aboriginal heritage. Marriage laws and beliefs have been broken, religion has been changed and customs lost. The result of this is confusion and jealousy, which is more apparent in those who still speak their Aboriginal language. Children tell tales about others and this results in trouble between the parents.

The attitude to the police among people living at the Mission was always one of fear. No Aborigines would ever go near the police station or a policeman. When help was needed the police would be the last people approached, probably because the normal words of greeting from a policeman were: 'What do *you* want, boong?' or 'Hey, Charcoal, come here.' In those days the police regarded the dark people as something worse than animals. They handcuffed men and hit them on their heads with batons for their amusement. The Aboriginal was frequently innocent. We had every reason to fear the police. One night, just as people were going into the picture show, they hit a man until he was unconscious; a few months later the man died. They were cruel and terrible to all Aborigines. In those days a dark man would run and hide if he saw a uniformed policeman approaching. This is not the case today: in all my years at Brewarrina we have never had a better police force than at the present time. There is no fear at all now: if an Aboriginal needs help he will happily go to a policeman. It is hard to say when this change for the better occurred; it could have been helped by pressure from white people who had some sympathy for the Aborigines.

The people living at the Mission included many types. Some were quite happy to take what was handed out to them and would make no further effort. Others wanted regular jobs and were willing to stay working at the same place for many years. These people might spend their entire life on a station and take their name from it. Bangate Charlie and Muckerawa Jack were in this category. Others remained in a group: these were lazy men who gambled and never worked. There was another type who might get a good job and collect his pay on Friday but would not turn up for work on the following Monday morning. Consequently another man would be given the job, and if it was another Aboriginal he might stay there only a week or two. On the whole, Aborigines will not stay in a job for any length of time and will not persevere. Then they apply for some form of social service and when the cheque arrives regularly they do not try to work again. Sometimes the police caught the offender for this, which is only right as the man would be quite capable of working. The problem with an Aboriginal is that when he gets some sort of a 'hand-out' he is well content to let it continue for ever. This situation was noticeable during my early married years at the Mission and has become much worse now. The attitude of women to the husband's money was probably much the same as that of white women. Some of them were honest and careful with it, while others gambled or spent it quickly. The women gambled too much and most of the men stopped trusting their wives with their pay.

In the early days the people at the Mission probably did not realise that white people had better houses and conditions than they had. Most of the dark people just stayed at home and saw nothing else. When they became aware of the difference they did not envy the white man living in a mansion and owning a car, and their feelings are still the same. The thoughts amongst themselves are different. If an Aboriginal owned a good house, a sewing machine and a car the others would resent it. It is only comparatively recently that Aborigines have realised that white people have better possessions. There has been some basic attitude amongst the dark people which has enabled them to take hard treatment from the whites without resentment. This attitude probably comes from their tendency to live entirely in the present with no worry about the past or the future. It did not really worry them unduly when they were told that they were low-grade and had no place in normal society. This happened so frequently in the old days that it was better to take very little notice of it. Although the dark people had known from the beginning that the whites had suppressed them, this was never discussed between themselves. It appeared to be a way of life that was both accepted and expected. This does not apply to the young people today: they are seeking something better. During my earlier years I knew that things were not right, but it was hard to diagnose what was wrong. I never blamed the whites, but accepted our bad times as a part of life that had to be endured. I did, however, blame the managers and controllers for their brutality and lack of kindness and understanding.

Before the Aboriginal marriage system was lost there was no immorality. The old laws forbade promiscuity and the penalty was death. The laws were broken occasionally, but the people involved had to escape and live with the fear of punishment for the rest of their lives. When I was a child I doubt if there was any immorality. We were all told the facts of life at a very early age, not necessarily by a parent; but the old people made certain that the children knew all about everything. Although I was not aware of any misbehaviour when I was young, there is no doubt that immorality largely appeared after 1850 when the old marriage laws were beginning to disappear. The part-Aboriginal was proof that the old laws had gone, and after 1910 there seemed to be a further deterioration of morals.

There was an Aboriginal called Dick Howell living at the Mission. He used to ill-treat his wife, and even used a stockwhip on her occasionally. One day I went to his house and took the whip, giving him a couple of cuts before I left him. His wife was quite a good woman, and the fights were caused by his bad behaviour with other women. He was not the only man to visit women when their husbands were away: a number of others behaved equally badly. One day Howell was in a house with a woman when her husband returned unexpectedly: the husband grabbed a hammer and practically killed Howell. The wife had been pleased with the visits from Howell, as were quite a number of other women. It was hard to blame the man entirely when these situations arose; the women were also at fault. This behaviour caused many fights, and it also meant that a lot of children were born as the result of these philanderings. One married couple at the Mission had four children; there were also three more children belonging to the mother: these children all had different fathers. In this case the husband did his best to support his wife, children and her additional children. It was more usual for a family to have one illegitimate child.

On another occasion there was a child born to an Aboriginal woman and the manager was the father. The girl is still living today and I am probably the only one who knows about her parentage. The morals of most managers were bad, and their power made it difficult for an Aboriginal woman to refuse. One day I was talking to Jessie, who lived in the girls' dormitory. She was laughing about something and I asked her to tell me the joke. After some persuasion she told me that on the previous night the manager had come in and slept with one of the girls. The managers did this type of thing frequently, and it continued until recent years. I recollect one incident when a manager went to some trouble to acquire a job for a married man which meant that he would be working in Walgett. His wife was a very nice woman, and it soon became obvious to us that she was the favourite of the manager: she was given many special provisions and concessions. We all knew of the relationship, but the manager's wife had no idea of what was happening. This sort of occurrence was common. If the manager's attentions were unwelcome there was nothing the woman could do about it. He had absolute power over us all.

I remember another incident when the manager had been seeing too much of a woman and the husband suspected that something was wrong. The man was away every day working on fences, and one evening he returned earlier than expected. The manager was in his house and appeared to be forcing his attentions on his wife. The husband almost went mad with fury. The next day he asked me if I would write a letter for him, as he could neither read nor write himself. I suggested that he ask Bill Murray, who was better educated and wrote good letters. I was with them when this letter was written to the Aborigines' Protection Board complaining that the manager was having an illicit affair with a married woman. According to the usual rule, when the Aboriginal wrote a letter of complaint a copy was sent back to the manager. The result of this letter was that the man was dismissed from the Mission. In this case the manager was a bad man and the husband quite a good fellow. The managers could say or do anything they wished and we were the only people who knew how badly they behaved.

During all the years I lived at the Mission there was never any rape or incest amongst the Aboriginal people. In this enclosed community it was impossible for anything to happen without others knowing about it. The Aboriginal has a way of watching his neighbours all the time. Also, they talk together and any unusual event will be known by everyone.

The girls' dormitory was frequently a problem. It was large and a lot of girls lived there. An inspector from the Board was visiting the Mission and I told him that I was not happy about the manager's son, who was practically living in there with the girls. We were good friends and this inspector trusted me more than the manager. It was not long after this that the dormitory was emptied. All the girls were sent to a home in Cootamundra and put in charge of a matron. This was in 1929 and Sid, the manager's son, was involved in another unpleasant episode. A girl was sent out to a domestic job in Queensland; although she was part-Aboriginal her colouring was quite fair. Sid was working on the same property and was responsible for her becoming pregnant. It was all kept very quiet; I knew about it because Sid had confided in me and hidden it from his father. Sid had a car of his own and took Molly to Warren, where she stayed until the baby was born. He told me later that he had paid all her expenses. I asked why he did not marry the girl; he replied that he was frightened of his father and did not know how to handle the situation. I told him that he should think of the girl and not worry about his father. Sid kept Molly in Warren for some time, but it became awkward as people were wondering what had happened to her. The matter was resolved when the baby died, and no one knew of Sid's responsibility. He escaped without trouble and the girl took another job farther south.

In the old days an Aboriginal covered himself with mud and then dived into the river to clean it off. He never wore clothes and did not take this mud bath very often as rain and grass are cleansing. When dealing with food he caught an emu or kangaroo, cooked it, then probably ate the whole lot. There were no dishes to wash or floors to sweep, they just moved on to a cleaner place when they felt like it. It has not suited the Aboriginal to stay in the same area and to be surrounded by modern possessions, he does not bother keeping everything clean. There is no doubt that many of the children at the Mission were neglected and brought up in dirty surroundings. The same thing occurred when families lived on the country stations. Many of the children died during their first year of life. Mothers breast-fed their babies, but frequently fed them this way for too long. Apart from the welfare of the child, the mother was seldom in a fit condition to be feeding a child at the breast. There was probably very little milk and the child was almost a skeleton. The part-Aboriginal managed better, but the little full-blood suffered. In those days the parents had no idea of what they should do to keep a child healthy. Also, they did not worry unduly when a child was sick. There seemed to be a complete lack of understanding of the needs of a child. The parents did not grudge him a share of their meagre supply of food, but he was given unsuitable food. The full-blood has been the worst problem, and on average it seems to me that if he had six children only one would survive.

My married life was wonderfully happy and free from worry. In 1926 I built another small house near the river; it was made of galvanised iron, and we lived there until 1930. By that time we had four children; they seemed to arrive very frequently. In those days children were born anywhere, and the mothers had to manage as well as they could. I was able to take Evelyn into the hospital for the arrival of Jack. Billy and Roy were born at the Mission. Bert, Margaret and Mary were born in hospital. During the births of Billy and Roy I helped as much as possible and some woman from the

Mission came to assist us. Having a baby never seemed to bother Evelyn; we loved them all, and did our best to keep them well fed and healthy. At this time I was also driving the mail; usually it took me two days to go through Weilmoringle and Goodooga and back to Brewarrina. Mr Burns, the manager, owned a car which he ran as a taxi, and I drove it for him when required.

After 1930 there were many changes at the Mission. Manager Burns left. Despite his faults we had got on well together and I was sorry to see him leave. However, I did not know that better times lay ahead. The name of the new manager was Danvers. He was a very fine man and the only really good manager at the Mission during all my years there. His wife was wonderful, and she bought presents and necessities for the children with her own money. They were both extraordinarily kind and we all appreciated it. He made the Board pay for a lot of improvements and was always pressing them to provide what he considered necessary. He was the first and only person to try to improve our conditions and to fight for us. He obtained seeds, plants and wire netting and established a community garden with fresh vegetables for those who wanted them. The people were helped and encouraged in every way. Prizes were given for the best-kept houses and gardens. There was wholesome food for all the dormitory children, and the schooling was good.

The improvement in the attitude of the residents to a manager who was really trying to help them was remarkable. A small element caused disturbances still, but it was mainly the younger people who fought one another. Frequently I had to interfere and sometimes wondered why I did not have my own head knocked off. I seemed to be able to reason with them, and they listened to me when I asked them to be careful when using a bundi or throwing stick. A number of people enjoyed looking at fights and encouraged the combatants. When Mr Danvers had to stop a fight he never used physical violence, and he did not drive anyone away from the Mission. He proved that the place could be run with decency and efficiency.

Mr Danvers delved into every aspect of our lives. Our rations were improved, and I had to go into town three times weekly to collect meat. This had to be carefully weighed and issued to each family. The children were given milk and a new lorry was bought. I was busier than ever as more work was needed to assist with these improvements. My wages did not increase, but it was rewarding to see happier and healthier people around us. A new pump was installed, new pipes were laid and several of the houses had taps. I did the pipe-laying and a lot of the plumbing, and made a number of new tanks. In 1933 an electricity plant was installed and I did all the wiring for the houses and streets. By this time I was responsible for a number of the mechanical improvements and was enjoying the additional work. The starvation diet of the earlier years appeared to be behind us. The children were given bread, butter and cocoa before starting school in the morning. Many of the earlier deaths had been caused by neglect and malnutrition; now we had a trained nurse living at the station and she did most of the necessary medical work. Most of the people had trachoma, and she treated them every morning. Overall there was a great improvement in the health of the community.

Although conditions were better for our family, with our own four children and one we had adopted our little house was very crowded. I felt that the time had come for us to move to something better. I had chosen a pleasant area which was some distance away from the other houses, and the manager gave me permission to build there. When Mr Danvers realised that I was really trying to make things better for my family he helped by making timber and fibro available for me. This was a very good little house and the best on the Mission. There were three bedrooms, a dining room, kitchen, bathroom and a large veranda. I planted a lawn around it and bought a lot of rose plants. Ever since my early days at Milroy I have always loved flowers. People used to come down to look at our house and garden.

The additional member of our family was George Kearney. We had not legally adopted him, but had reared him from the age of nine years. He was very small for his age and seemed neglected when he arrived at the Mission in 1926: he was just a miserable little boy. The manager must have brought him out to the Mission at night, and I did not see him until the next morning when I noticed a lot of boys teasing him. They made him so frightened and agitated that he ran away and hid in a large hole in the gutter which ran down to the river. His tormentors were waiting with sticks and stones for the moment the little boy came out of hiding. I went down to the gutter and had to crawl along until I found George. I told him that he need not be frightened and asked him to come back with me; we both crawled out and I took him home. Evelyn produced some food for him and I went off to see the manager about his future. Burns suggested that we care for him. Evelyn and I were happy to do this; our own two boys were small at the time and we were sorry for the little fellow. The result was that George stayed with us, calling Evelyn 'Mum' and me 'Joe'. He was a good little boy, but the other children did not seem to like him and he had a terrible time at school. He was quite bright and I was able to help him with his reading and sums.

George stayed with us until he was fifteen years old; we liked him and he liked us. He was always helping me with various jobs, and had learnt how to drive a car by the time he was twelve. There was no doubt that he was brighter and better than the children who were always nasty to him. In 1933 he told me that he wanted to get a job. I agreed that he could go if this was what he wanted: sooner or later he would have to make his way in the world.

George roped a little swag which held most of his belongings. I gave him some money and a couple of blankets, and he went off to Queensland. He did a lot of train-jumping there and became rather a hobo; his jobs were few and far between. By 1934 he was tired of this life and went to the Northern Territory, where he had a good job at a station called Lake Nash. He learnt to be a blacksmith and moved to Tennant Creek. By this time he had saved some money and was able to buy some land. Occasionally he returned to visit us: on one of these visits he told me that he had the deeds for his land and was going to give them to me, but this never happened. He wrote frequently and described various jobs in Alice Springs, Adelaide and Darwin.

Eventually George spent quite a long time working at Port Kembla, and in due course he was married and had two sons. He was not very dark: I guessed that he was probably three-quarters white. His letters described his wife and said she was always fighting and disagreeing with him. This worried us, as George was not a quarrelsome person. It was in 1939 that he wrote telling us of a tremendous row with his wife in which her father had interfered. George apparently knocked the old man down with a shovel, and for this he was sent to jail for three months. While in jail he enlisted and was allowed to leave for training with the 17th Battalion.

He went to Egypt, and during this time still wrote regularly. When on leave he visited Jerusalem, which was a great experience. He mentioned a bombardment and offensive, then there were no letters for some time. At last a letter came saying that he was in hospital with a wounded ankle. When he recovered he went to Tobruk and was one of the 'Rats'. During this time there were no letters and I was worried again. After the relief of Tobruk a letter arrived, and in due course he returned to us and was able to tell us about his experiences. His wounded ankle had left him with a limp, and a medical check would have made it easy for him to leave the army. I tried to persuade him to do this, but he was determined to fight the Japanese, who were close to Australia at that time. He was parachuted behind the Japanese lines and landed at Scarlet Bay in New Guinea. As the troops landed the Japanese mowed them down. George and many others were killed. It was some years later that my son Jack was in this area and went to the cemetery at Scarlet Bay, hoping to find George's grave. Just as he had given up hope of finding it and was returning to the entrance he saw 'G. W. Kearney' on a tombstone. Jack took a photograph, which I still have. Evelyn and I were very fond of George.

Life on the Mission was fairly normal. Friends invited us to their houses and we were happy to see them in ours. No one had any money to spare, but we could make some little effort to welcome friends and they did the same for us. Our best friends were probably the Sullivans, Howells and Murrays. There were other older people whom we liked: Evelyn visited them or they came down to see us. I cannot remember Evelyn having an argument with anyone; she mainly stayed in our house and we kept to ourselves most of the time. When I was out working or away Evelyn just carried on quietly at home. She was always interested in any church activity, and we both enjoyed the evenings when we sang hymns. The main games played at the Mission were euchre and rounders; she played until the children began to arrive, then she did not have the time. Evelyn really preferred her own home; she liked pottering in the garden and always liked the house to be kept in good order. Sometimes we went into town to the pictures, but this did not happen often. When I came home from work we might wander down to the river to fish; this was our main relaxation and helped provide extra food.

Our church meetings at night enabled quite a large number of our people to gather together. Occasionally some of the residents refused to come to the meetings; it interested me that they were only absent for a short time and then happily joined us again. It was unfortunate that there were some people living on the Mission whose behaviour was impossible to tolerate. All the children seemed to get on fairly well together and there were no more than a normal number of fights, which were ignored or probably forgotten. Sometimes the parents did not forget so quickly, and this was how a lot of the more serious arguments began.

Occasionally we had what we called a corroboree — nothing like those in the old days, but we enjoyed them. It was just a chance to get back into the bush, move away from buildings and sing and dance together. Sometimes we cooked an emu in the traditional way, or we ate goanna and porcupine. Somehow the spirit of the bush and the old customs stimulated us. Billy Campbell was always keen to leave our semi-civilised life behind and try to recapture some of the fun of the old days. I feel that a lot of nostalgia still exists in the Aboriginal mind for the earlier days in the bush. Quite a number of people, including myself, recall our old times of freedom with a mixture of pleasure and sadness.

At night I used to talk or read to the children. I tried to tell them about subjects they might not learn elsewhere. The result was that our children knew more than the others. Jack was a clever boy, and this annoyed his schoolmates. Poor Jack would come home crying because children had hit him; I did not take any notice because they all seemed to be friends again about an hour later. Bert was younger and had very little schooling: it was much the same for him as it had been for me in my youth. The children were in school, the teacher-manager was somewhere else, and the result was that the children played games and learnt nothing. Apart from our children, the others at the Mission all had the same attitude. As soon as they were released from school they wanted to play games, and they did not listen to the teacher on the rare occasions when lessons were given. After school if anyone wanted to tell them anything of interest or general knowledge they would not believe it. I remember trying to tell some of them about the new inventions of telephone and radio. They said I was mad; they could not use their minds sufficiently to visualise new developments. It was an unusual child who returned home from school showing some interest in what he had learnt during the day.

There was a reasonably good teacher between 1930 and 1940; he tried to be of assistance, but must often have felt discouraged. I did a lot for myself and our children with a dictionary and atlas. Also, I brought home newspapers and made them read to me without mistakes. Evelyn felt the same way about encouraging and helping the children to learn as much as possible. She could read and write herself, but had not had much schooling apart from a short time in Wellington (N.S.W.) when the family lived there. During all my years at the Mission I cannot remember one adult or child who knew how to open a dictionary and look for a word. I have always spent many hours reading and studying any books that I could acquire; this was considered unusual and peculiar.

The years when Mr Danvers was manager were the best we ever had at the Mission. Our home was happy and it was wonderful to have so many improvements for the people. The whole atmosphere had changed during Danvers' term. Unfortunately he left in 1934 and was followed by Marshall, a tough and hard man. We had several arguments, as he interfered with my work and swore at me. A white man was employed as assistant in the garden. This man did nothing; I had to do his work and try to hide his laziness. Most of the time he was in town amusing himself. Being white protected him from Marshall's bad temper, and I got the blame when his work was not done. Marshall did not knock us about with his baton or use severe physical violence, but I doubt if anything else can be said in his favour. He was not at the Mission for very long and we were all pleased to see him leave. A new manager was appointed and we were hopeful that our conditions would improve again.

Brain was the next manager; he had previously been at Angledool. The people from the reserve there were dispersed and most of them were moved to Brewarrina. Bert Groves* had been the handyman there, and it was good to have him living at the Mission for a while. Brain was a cruel man; he faked cheques and was merciless with his baton. For some reason he was quite pleasant to me, and offered me cigarettes or the occasional cup of tea. Despite this I hated him because he was so brutal to the others. A boy might be in some place which, according to Brain, was not the right place. There was never a warning word; suddenly he would bash the lad with his baton. In my opinion he was mad; this is probably the kindest way to describe his behaviour. When I say he did not ill-treat me, it would be more truthful to say that he did not hurt me as badly as the others. I remember that he asked me to go with him and look at some corn we were growing; when we reached the corn he hit me several times with the baton. There was no reason or warning. I had to visit the corn quite frequently, and it always sickened me. One day a lad was working with a hoe. Brain called: 'Come here, Johnny'. This was a boy aged fifteen who suffered from trachoma, and on this day he was wearing sandshoes. 'Didn't I tell you that you should not wear sandshoes? They are bad for your eyes.' The lad was bashed with the baton until he lay on the ground almost unconscious. For some reason Brain thought sandshoes affected the eyes. This was just one incident which showed his apparent madness. After Danvers' departure the Mission deteriorated rapidly.

Brain's dishonesty was flagrant. One old woman had a war pension which had been regularly received since her husband was killed in 1916. During the years that Brain was at the Mission she did not get her pension: he put her mark on the application and collected the money himself. One day

* Recorded Kamilaroi for A.I.A.S.

he sent me into the bank with some cheques and I noticed hers amongst them. He had been doing the same type of thing at Angledool. There is little doubt that he added a considerable amount to his salary by appropriating money from the residents and by his dishonesty in all money matters. He was one of the worst tyrants that we ever had, and we just had to suffer him. We could not complain to the police or anyone else. The police had no sympathy, and any complaint from us would get an angry response of: 'Get back to the Mission before I lock you up.' We all knew it was useless to fight the manager; with the exception of Danvers they were all dictators. The police came to the Mission periodically and the manager made certain that he was the one to complain about us; we were never allowed to mention our troubles. We had no privacy from a man like Brain: he could walk into our houses at any time of the day or night. He did this whether we were in bed or not.

One evening Brain strode into our house and yelled at me: 'Did you do that job for me?' I replied that I had not had the time but would do it the next day. He was furious and said that I must do it that night, but I refused firmly and said that I had finished work for the day. He swore horribly at me; it was not pleasant for my wife and children to hear. Another day he came along when I was in the workshop and knocked everything in front of me on to the floor. I asked him why he had done that; he replied that he wanted me to do the job in another place and not in the workshop. I was fortunate; these were my most unpleasant incidents. Many worse things happened to other people.

One night there was a fight and some of the men took Dick Macdonald to the manager. Certainly Dick had been beating his wife and was not blameless. I happened to be near by at the time and Brain told me to put handcuffs on him. I refused and said it was not right for me to do that sort of thing. The manager put on the handcuffs and told me to give Dick a belting. Once again I refused, but said that if he was not handcuffed I would not object to giving him some punishment. Neither Brain nor the others were pleased with me for refusing. Brain gave Dick a horrible bashing and injured him severely, so perhaps I should have done it myself.

Bill Johnson who worked in the country, came to visit his wife and children at the Mission. He found that his wife had not been issued with the various things to which she was entitled. He went to see Brain, who said: 'I'm sure she had some rations last week; she'll just have to wait until next week.' Despite Bill's protestations that the children had nothing to eat and that there was great hardship, he refused to help and told Bill to get some money for them. Bill explained that he had been out shearing and had sent her all his money, which she had not received. No more shearing was offering for a couple of weeks and there was nothing else that he could do. There was an argument for a little while, and Brain gradually moved closer and closer to Bill. Suddenly he hit Bill hard and repeatedly with the baton until he fell to the ground; he continued to hit him for several minutes where he lay. Eventually some of us had to carry him away. He had been seriously injured, and it was a long time before he was fit to work again. I suspected that Brain had collected the money that Bill had been sending to his family.

At times the Aborigines were so resentful that they made plans to retaliate and attack the manager. Each time this occurred I was able to talk them out of it with warnings that we had no say in what was right and nothing was in our favour. Any aggression from us could mean twelve months or twelve years in gaol; we must endure these unpleasant events. I prevented a rebellion many times, for I knew that the Aborigines would be the sufferers.

Brain left towards the end of 1936; we suspected that he had been sacked. A man named Dalley had been assistant manager for some time and he was now appointed manager. Dalley did not hurt anyone seriously, but he was not constructive in any way and made no improvements. It was during this time that a number of Aborigines were brought from Tibooburra and had to share our discomforts and lack of food. The Mission had sunk to a very low state, and the advent of another manager in 1940 did nothing to improve it. The new manager was not too bad with the adults but was shocking with the children. He used to beat them frequently with his hands; he would box their ears and hurt them horribly. This was probably better than being hit with a baton or a lump of wood, but he could hardly be called a good manager. Still, others were worse, and he was reasonably approachable when I had to speak to him.

I suffered less than the others from ill-treatment by the managers. My attitude was that they were in charge, and if they told me I was wrong or had incurred their disapproval I did not argue. Some Aborigines were quick-tempered when provoked by any injustice, and fought against it. Their punishment was severe when they did this. On the other hand, I have seen dark people who have neither said nor done anything wrong and yet have been horribly bashed with the baton. This use of the baton was cruel and wrong; it took away our pride and dignity and made it hard to accept authority. During the twenty-one years I worked at the Mission there was only one good and constructive manager: Mr Danvers. The years with him were a happy memory for us all. I think enough has now been said about the misery caused by bad managers.

My greatest worry was during Evelyn's last pregnancy, when she told me she did not feel well. It was unusual to see her sitting most of the time, and moving seemed to trouble her. I remember asking if she would do a little sewing on the machine for me: I was startled when she said that she did not feel well enough. This was when she had been pregnant for about six months. Many things seemed different and out of character, so I suggested that she should go to Dubbo for a thorough medical check. This was done and the doctor said she was normal, so she just returned to the Mission. In January I went to Pilliga to cut logs. There were fifteen inches of rain and it was impossible to return to Brewarrina for a month: in the black soil the lorries could not move. When I arrived home I found that Evelyn was in the Brewarrina hospital. It was not long before she was transferred to the hospital in Bourke, where a caesarean operation was performed. Our sixth child, Mary, was born but Evelyn was very ill. I had taken all the children to Bourke so that we could be near her, but there was little we could do for her. After Evelyn had been in hospital two weeks I could see that there was no hope for her. Although she was always brave, it was six long and agonizing weeks before she died on

16 April 1941. We brought her back to the Mission and she was buried there.*

I was left with our six children: four boys and two girls. We never know sorrow until we lose the one who is dearest to us. We had been married a little more than seventeen years. Evelyn had been wonderful during our life together, and our love for one another had become greater as the years passed. It is impossible to describe my feelings and the worry about caring for the children. Mary was minded by an aunt, while I worked and looked after the five older children. Added to everything else I had money trouble. When I received my wages I had always handed the money to Evelyn, and our savings were in the bank in her name. Neither the police nor the Commonwealth Bank were able to solve this difficulty, and it was a very long time before that money was made available to me. It was hard to support us all on my wages.

With all the good things that Evelyn had done for her family, she was unable to see them grow up. Seven children had been born. The boys' ages were about fourteen months apart: Jack, Billy, Gordon, Roy and Bert had arrived between 1925 and 1930. Gordon had lived for only one month. Margaret was born in 1937. My wife's sister, who minded Mary, helped a little, but things did not work out very satisfactorily. The older boys had to take any available jobs. Jack and Billy found work on the aerodrome at Bourke. Roy just walked out of school and started to work and in due course Bert did the same. He had less schooling than the others and was the most backward at reading and in general education. I regretted their loss of education, but this was the only way we could solve our financial problems.

When Jack's work was finished he moved to Tennant Creek, in the Northern Territory. He earned good money, but was never much good at keeping it. He enlisted in the A.I.F. but was discharged because of asthma; after that he worked on oil tankers and did a number of trips between Durban and Australia. He had various adventures at sea and later went to America, where he had a job on the railways. He went back to Durban where he became ill and eventually

---

* Jimmie was buried at the Mission in 1972.

had to return to Australia. He was overseas for a long time; I remember it cost me a lot of money occasionally. He has never worried much about money, and I was sorry he had not saved some of his earnings. He still talks about his travels, and those years were a great experience for him. He married an Australian and they have a large family; their home is in Brewarrina.

Billy was a fine lad; he died from cancer at the age of thirty-three. His main work was shearing. He married, and had five children when he died. Roy enlisted in the Army at fifteen and later spent some time in Japan with the Occupation Forces. He married the daughter of Blanche and Duncan Ferguson, very old friends of mine. Roy and June live at Lightning Ridge and have a number of children. Roy has worked hard during his life, but has not been very well recently. Bert is a real worker and has tackled many hard and heavy jobs. He has had to support a family of eighteen children and has lived in Brewarrina for a number of years.

It is strange to look back to the time when my brother Billy and I first came to Brewarrina and there were just the two of us. Billy died some years ago; five of his eight children are still living. They all have large families, and my own grandchildren are so numerous that I find them hard to count. When I think of our family it is interesting to consider skin colour. I am the darkest; Billy and my three other brothers were much fairer, and my sister Marcia was almost white. My own children vary in colour; this is always noticeable in a part-Aboriginal family. Mary is not as dark as Margaret, Roy is quite fair and Bert is very dark. Elizabeth, Margaret's daughter, appears to be a white girl. However, in about ten years she will be much darker than she is now. We darken as we become older, and my colour has changed through the years. It is possible to see an Aboriginal one day and then on seeing him again a few days later to notice that his colour is quite different. This has often puzzled me as I have noticed this colour variation in myself and in others. Some days I am much darker than on others, and there does not appear to be any rule or reason. The full-bloods also vary, and are not jet black. When one looks closely a slight copper colour may be visible; on other occasions an ashen sheen is seen on the dark skin.

After the boys had scattered and left the Mission I tidied the house and packed a number of belongings which were seldom used. I felt that I would like to leave the place if I could find a better job. The girls were always on my mind and Mary was still very young. From the beginning of 1942 the Mission was in the charge of a new manager. Twenty-one years had passed since I started the job of handyman. I had worked with ten managers and had been able to avoid arguments with all but four of them. Three of these men were not fit to be in charge of anyone.

I shall not forget the morning I walked off the job. There was a new assistant manager who was far from being worthy of the position. He was a nasty type and boasted about killing two people and hiding their bodies. Whether this was true or not I do not know, but he certainly appeared to be a man who would commit any crime. He hated me because I really had the better job. I suspected that I might have been his next victim if we had been living in a more remote area. It was about eight o'clock in the morning and I was at work repairing the flooring of the school veranda. The assistant manager suddenly appeared, with his sneaky, cat-like walk. He stood in front of me and said: 'Look, you, I'm in charge of all outside work and I'm taking over all your duties from today onwards. Gather up your tools and bring them to where I want you to work.' I replied that I was working on this job and it had to be finished. He waited for a minute and then said: 'So my name is just mud?' I told him that I had not said anything like that. Then he yelled: 'Pick up those tools and bring them to where I want them!' I said he could have the tools and put them where he liked, because I had finished working on the Mission now and for ever. His eyes blazed and I thought he was going to strike me as I walked away. I went to the office and told the manager that I was leaving immediately. He asked the reason and tried to persuade me to stay. My refusal was firm and I told him that I was finished with the place. After a while he said: 'Well, Jim, thanks for all your work here. I'm sorry I can't stop you leaving, because I have found you and your work really good. We shall miss you; if you need help at any time be sure to ask me.' I thanked him and we shook hands.

The boys were in town; I sent a message to them

Jimmie's house at the Mission, 1935

View of the Mission taken from the roof of his house, about 1930

immediately and asked them to send out a carrier. Most of my possessions had been packed in tea chests for months. Mentally I had been prepared and ready to leave at any time. We packed cases of clothing and sorted out the furniture. The house contained some Mission property which I left there.

I had almost finished getting everything out of the gate when the assistant manager appeared, accompanied by several young lads carrying picks and shovels. Straight away he made these lads dig up my roses. I had bought and cared for them myself and there were a number of beautiful standard roses. Simpson went into the house and tore down all the electrical wiring and fittings. His next effort was to carry away pot-plants which I had around the house. I owned them and had paid for most of the electrical fittings. It was no use bothering, but I had thought they could be used by the next occupant. I suppose this destruction satisfied his greed and spite. He walked around the house collecting anything else he could find while the others were destroying the garden. He questioned me about the contents of my cases and seemed disbelieving when I told him that everything belonging to the Board had been left in the house. Several times I thought he was going to hit me; his rage was almost beyond control. We had bought most of our furniture and the Board owned only a few beds. It was upsetting to watch his wanton destruction of my garden and those few belongings I had been unable to remove before he arrived. As we had never had much money our possessions were either cheap or home-made, but they had great sentimental value to me and my children.

By 4 p.m. I was well away from the Mission. That part of my life was over; somehow I had to try to concentrate on the future.

6   Brewarrina and Lightning Ridge

'More decisions had to be made'

I STAYED in Brewarrina for a few days before getting a job about thirty-six miles out of town. This was on a large station and involved mainly maintenance of cars and water pumps. By this time the four boys had jobs; Bert, the youngest, was not quite eleven years old. I worked on the station for four months, but was worrying about the children most of the time. A friend told me about a job as a groom at the hotel in Brewarrina. This was closer to the family, so I gave notice and started working at the hotel. I have no idea why I was called the groom; I was thankful to find there were no horses to bother me. It would have been more accurate to call me the handyman. I stoked the boiler-room fire, rolled kegs around and just did what I was told. People said that I was one of the driest men who had ever landed in a pub; I would neither shout a drink nor accept one. I am not a teetotaller and do enjoy an occasional drink. However, when working in a pub it seemed better to keep right away from it. I am very aware of the harm that alcohol has done to my people; while they abuse themselves in this way I see no future for them. While at the hotel I was offered several other jobs, mainly garage work. I was tired of repairing cars so continued working at the hotel until the war was over in 1945.

During this time there was little I could do for Margaret and Mary except worry. The place where they were staying was steadily going downhill and becoming nothing more than a house for parties. I did not like their environment and had to get them away. I tried several homes for girls in

Sydney, but they were overcrowded and I was told that it was unlikely that I would find a vacancy for some years.

In 1946 I had a break for two weeks and then started work at the Brewarrina Hospital. I liked my work there; I had my own room and was always on the job. Once again I was the handyman or general factotum. My work might be in the garden, the boiler-room, or sometimes helping with patients. A lot of the work was heavy, possibly too heavy. Once I cut ninety tons of wood for fires in ten weeks. There was a lot of work for one man, and I had to work on Saturdays and Sundays; I had a day off during the week. Everybody was very nice to me, and as the hospital became larger they put on an extra man to help me. This was not a success, as he did only the minimum and took time off when he pleased. On occasions I was unwell and saw the doctor; then they would put me to bed in the hospital for a couple of weeks. This happened fairly regularly and was caused possibly by heavy lifting. As well as the outside work I had to lift the heavier patients when required; these were very often large men.

At the hospital the matron and nursing staff were always good to me. I got on well with the domestic staff and gradually met a lot of interesting people. My association with the hospital went back for many years, as I had provided all the transport from the Mission; and during those years I had seen many changes. In the early days Aborigines had their beds on the veranda and were left there regardless of the weather. Either the rain or the scorching sun was pouring on to them. No other patient had to stand the bad treatment that was given to the dark people. For many years the veranda was called the Abo Ward, their sheets and towels were marked 'Abo' and they were the last patients to be given any attention. Around 1930 there was a slight improvement and the Aborigines were occasionally put in the general wards, but never in the intermediate or private wards. This was the situation until 1945 when a new matron was appointed. If a patient had the money she allowed him in any of the other wards, regardless of his colour. This matron was firm and refused to allow any discrimination; she was also sympathetic when an Aboriginal had any special request. The full-blood always likes to be on his own, perhaps somewhere around a corner. For the first time their

167

wishes received some consideration. Members of the nursing and domestic staff were told that their treatment of all patients must be the same and that there must never be discrimination because of colour.

I remember one incident when a white girl started work as a maid and her first job was to carry around the afternoon tea. I happened to be close to her and was able to observe that she gave all the whites their tea but gave none to the dark people. Matron appeared and asked one Aboriginal if he had been given his tea yet. He had not, which puzzled her, so she moved into the next ward and noticed that none of the dark people had tea. She spoke to the new white maid and told her to hurry with the teas as they should have been finished by now. Matron returned in about ten minutes and found that all the Aborigines were still without afternoon tea. Once again she spoke to the girl, who replied that she was not prepared to carry anything for blacks. I was in the kitchen and could hear everything they said. Then Matron asked the girl if she had put her luggage in her room; the girl said she had. Matron ordered her to accompany her to the bedroom, waited until she had packed and told her to leave the hospital. I shall always remember her words: 'If my shoes were boots I would kick you out. If you become ill don't come here for help. I have dark people working here and doing their jobs well; when they are patients we care for them. Leave here and never come back.' This matron had no feelings about colour; we were all the same to her.

Although my job was good, my worries about the girls continued. In 1948 I had a talk with the manager of the Mission. He was not a bad manager and seemed willing to help me. He said that a house was available, and I had already made arrangements with a woman who was willing to mind the girls. I put Margaret and Mary temporarily in her charge and installed them at the Mission. She looked after them fairly well. In October 1949 I heard of two vacancies at the Church of England Home for Girls in Burwood, Sydney. I wasted no time in sending them there. They were well looked after and did very well at school. Later they shared a flat together and worked at their respective jobs. During this time they met good people. Eventually they married, and both are living happily in

Sydney. It was very hard to part with them and to know there would be such a great distance between us. I was in hospital when they left Brewarrina. I asked them to work hard at school and learn everything possible, and to be ladylike at all times. I could only suggest that they should always remember these things and that they should never let me down. Today I am very happy that they have carried this out; I am proud of them both.

Soon after the girls left I built a crude sort of house just across the river from the hospital. I lived there for some time with the woman who had looked after the girls. She was kind and did everything for me, but I knew it was wrong. Man is weak, and I had taken the easy road and had fallen from grace. As time passed I became more worried about this situation and my way of living. Several times I considered moving elsewhere; other times I thought of just getting on a train and disappearing completely. I could never carry out this last idea. I had paid three hundred pounds for the maintenance of the girls; additional money was taken from my wages, and I could not default. In any case it was not fair to disappear. This woman had helped me greatly, and that could not be forgotten. There was no love between us; I had paid her to look after the girls and she had been good to them. My present life concerned me and I was worried about finding a solution.

Some time later I was at the hospital during my day off and decided to clean my room. As I was tidying I kept finding reminders of Evelyn: trinkets she had treasured, photographs, her hymn book and other oddments. Evelyn's photograph was always on my dressing table; I looked at it and suddenly knew the answer to my problem. My room was not much tidier, but my mind had been freed. The room could be cleaned later, I had another job to do. I went back and told the woman that I must leave, collected my belongings and established myself in my bedroom at the hospital. I have no idea what she thought of my behaviour. I was grateful for her help, but she seemed to manage all right without me. She died a few years ago.

The years at the hospital settled into a routine. Playing cards occasionally in the evenings was my only relaxation. Usually I read at night and tried to learn about science, astronomy and other subjects of interest to me. My life was quiet; I seemed to have enough money and had very few worries. In the later years I felt the work was almost too hard for me: frequently I was far from well. Additions were built on to the hospital; as it became larger the work increased. There is little of interest to remember from those years. Football games and pubs did not appeal to me; it was a peaceful and monotonous life.

It was a shock when the doctor told me that I was not well enough to continue with my job. He told me that I should stop work and apply for the pension. I refused, but the doctor was firm and insisted that I was not strong enough to continue doing the heavy work. For a couple of weeks he kept telling me that I must take his advice and eventually I agreed. It was an upheaval in my life and I felt horribly lost and bewildered. It was two years before I was due for the old-age pension, but the doctor assured me that there was no disgrace in taking the invalid pension when it was essential for me to stop work. This was in 1963; I had been working at the hospital for seventeen years. Bert was also working there, but his jobs were only temporary until after I left. He has continued working there for many years.

More decisions had to be made. I knew that I could go across the river and live near Bert. Jack lived farther along the Barwon River, and I could live there. I decided to move to Bert's place. I was more familiar with it, as I had always stayed there when he was away from home. It was only six weeks after I left the hospital that my first pension cheque arrived, and it has been coming regularly ever since. It is not very much, but it is much more money than I had in my early days. It is a great help to me. Some people say that I have worked hard enough during my life to have earned it. I do not really worry about money, and have never bothered about it too much. I suppose that is my Aboriginal way of thought. It is good to have enough, that is the main thing.

After years of work I found it hard to adjust myself to doing nothing. The time at the hospital had passed without incident, and I think I had expected to work there for ever. Bert owned five acres on the other side of the river and I moved into a shed near his house. There were always a number of odd jobs to be done and my time was reasonably occupied. I saw more of my family and spent a lot of time fishing in the river, but this was not sufficient and I needed some additional interest.

I have always loved opals and had often wanted to go to Lightning Ridge. In 1908 an old woman called Culgoa Mary had shown me my first opal; it fascinated me and I had thought of looking for them ever since. When my pension was arriving regularly I bought a tent and moved to Lightning Ridge. Roy came with me and stayed for eight weeks before returning to Queensland. I did not know anyone at the Ridge and after Roy left it was rather lonely. The local policeman was both helpful and good to me. It was unusual to be called 'Mr Barker' and to be treated with some respect. He did not seem to mind the colour of my skin. When I was registering my claim and getting a miner's right he took the trouble to give me some advice. 'Drive your pegs in well,' he said. 'Make sure those pegs are right down.' At that time I knew nothing about the way claim papers had to be displayed at the top of a stick. He told me that the papers could be thrown away after seven days. By then the claim could be presumed to be mine if no one had disputed ownership. He told me also to refer to him immediately if anyone tried to move on to my claim. He said that interlopers had been doing this to dark people and that he would remove anyone if I had trouble.

I felt reasonably well, and staked my claim at Cantwell's, a field close to the town. I lived in the tent and was able to do quite a lot of digging. I had been there for some time when Val Mingo, an Aboriginal friend, came to the Ridge. He did not have a claim but worked with others. One day when we were chatting he talked about getting a claim on Cantwell's. I pegged out a place next to mine for him and he registered it. Later we started working together, and we continued to do so for several years.

I had brought a motor from Brewarrina and made a puddler; it did not take long to collect the necessary equipment. I found a lot of opals but knew very little about their value or how to treat them; I am sure I broke a lot of good stones through my ignorance. I made models of the dumps with smashed opal and just gave them away. Later I learnt that I was breaking up good opals. This was after I had shown some of my collection to a man who assured me that they were fine-quality stones. He cut one opal for me; it was very thin, and when it was cut the lower part was black. It was really beautiful. After that I learnt how to do my own cutting. That first opal was very exciting and I sold it for twelve pounds. At that stage I knew very little about the value and it was obvious that I should learn about carats. Very few of the dark people at the Ridge knew of the existence of a carat, and the buyers were making large profits out of their ignorance. I studied the value of the opals and was able to ensure that the Aborigines had some chance of fair treatment. At that time there were not many professional cutters; only one man was reliable and honest. The Aborigines had their stones cut wherever they could and were defrauded most of the time.

As I had no scales I could not weigh the stones, so I made a little gadget which could measure them. Bill Gray, an Aboriginal, brought a stone to me one day. He had taken it to a cutter who said that it was four carats and he would cut it for two shillings. This low price had made Bill suspicious and he wanted my opinion. I measured it for him and told him that I should expect it to be eight carats and a valuable stone. We went to see a large buyer; I knew this man had been far from honest in the past, but we asked him to weigh the stone. He took his time doing it but eventually put the stone on the scales, which showed it was almost eight carats. I was able to help many of these people by warning them that they would be robbed if they did not study the value of their stones. It was not only the Aborigines who were being robbed; a lot of the whites were getting similar treatment. During this time I found quite a lot of good opals but it was impossible to get a reasonable price for them. In due course better buyers came to the Ridge and the miners knew more about the value of their stones.

I really loved this life of digging opals and could not think of anything else. In the hot weather the only bearable place was at the bottom of the hole. We stayed there all day, even if we were not working. We lit a fire at the top and cooked our dinner, then hurried back into the hole to eat it. While I lived in the tent I always cooked in the open. Living conditions were primitive for most of the miners. This was in

1964, and there were not very many people at Lightning Ridge. There were no others at Cantwell's and only a small number at Three Mile. This way of life brought back many memories of the times I had spent in the bush, and I enjoyed it immensely. We all lived for opals and seldom talked of anything else; there is a great fascination in the search. I did not make a lot of money as we did not find any memorable stones, but it was a small addition to my pension. The most I received for an opal was $200. Most of them fetched about sixty dollars; others would be priced at thirty dollars or as low as ten dollars. The buyers were tough and we had to battle for every dollar.

There was no colour discrimination, white men were working with black men and the common interest was opal. There were the usual arguments but most of these were between white men. As the population increased there were even more troubles. Two men may have been working a mine together and living some distance apart with their families. One partner might take home an opal and give it to his wife, then a few days later she would sell it, saying she had picked it up at Three Mile or some distant field. Once a man learns about opals he can tell exactly from which field a stone has come. In due course the husband's partner would hear of the transaction and there would be a fight which would end the partnership.

I visited Brewarrina occasionally; it was always good to see Bert and Jack. Roy visited the Ridge again and cut some timber for me. With this timber and some iron I built a little hut which I lived in until 1970. I could lock it when I visited the boys, and it was more comfortable than the tent. In 1968 Roy and his family moved to Lightning Ridge and built a house in Gem Street, where they still live. Soon after that I moved my hut to the back of Roy's house.

In June 1968 I was staying with Bert at Brewarrina when a policeman told me that a white woman was visiting the town collecting Aboriginal languages and music on a tape recorder. I told him that I was not interested and that I knew no Muruwari.* The following day Janet Mathews came to

---

*The policeman gave me this message. J.M.

see me. She persuaded me to record a tape with her, and then I confessed that I had a great interest in what remained of the Muruwari language. Just before her visit I had bought a little tape recorder with the idea of making an English-Muruwari dictionary. I had not realised how expensive the tapes were, and asked her for help with them. Through the Australian Institute of Aboriginal Studies I was provided with tapes and later was lent an excellent tape recorder. All my first recordings were made in the little hut at Lightning Ridge.

I enjoyed these years. I had friends, not too many but just as many as I wanted. I could have a chat with Jack McCrae* or Fred Reece** when I needed company. Both of these men were born on Bangate Station and remembered Mrs Langloh Parker with affection. Fred was a particularly good-looking man with striking features; his mother had been Juwalarai and his father was the book-keeper at Bangate for some time. There is little doubt that his father was a remittance man of aristocratic birth: this was acknowledged and known by everyone in the district.

Some of my friends were white, including a couple of Germans. There were a lot of foreigners looking for opals; I was not too keen on most of them, nor was anyone else. During the years that Val and I worked together we got on well. If we found an opal and I asked his opinion of it his reply was always: 'You are the man to deal with it.' This meant that he left everything to me and it was my job to find a buyer and get a fair price. We earned a moderate amount of money; it was hard to estimate the exact amount. It could be twenty or forty dollars for one week and nothing for the next. It was probably about ten dollars per week each, a welcome addition to our pensions. We enjoyed the search for opals and it was a great life. Neither of us was a drinker, and we seemed to have ample money to spend on the things we liked better.

In 1969 I began to find that the mining was a little strenuous for me. My arms and shoulders were troublesome and I could use a shovel for only a short time before having a

---

* Jack McCrae knew very little Juwalarai but was helpful.
** Fred Reece recorded many tapes of Juwalarai with me. J.M.

rest. My age was sixty-nine and Val was ten years older; he was unable to lift anything but could use a pick and shovel all day. He had no idea how to wind up the basket, nor did he know where to tip it. This was heavy work which I had to do on my own, and it was becoming too much for me. The work is easier down the hole; one only uses a small pick and it is just like chopping cheese. During this year I decided that I could not do the heavy work any more and that I was ready to move back to Brewarrina and live an easier life. Those were wonderful years at the Ridge. My love for opals remains and I can visit my old haunts occasionally. My claim is still worked by Roy when he has the time.

Before moving to Lightning Ridge I had packed away all my good books, little stories I had written, and photographs. I had a set of encyclopaedias and a large dictionary which had cost me a lot of money. When I opened the tea chests I found that all the contents were cemented together; this had been done by ants. Nothing could be salvaged, and it was a great loss.

I settled back into the little hut near Bert's house. It was a quiet life but my time seemed to be occupied doing odd jobs for myself or the family. I was recording more tapes: usually I had to do this at night. When I had bought my little recorder I had not intended to do more than record some vocabulary. When I realised how little was known of the Muruwari language I felt that I should try to construct sentences and record as much as I could remember. It took a lot of time and thought, but it was satisfying to know that I could still do something useful. I enjoy thinking about those days when I was young and also remembering the good and bad times in my life. When we are old it is probable that we mainly live in the past, and this is what I do when I speak into the microphone.

My mind wanders back to the way things have changed for Aborigines during my lifetime. When I was young I was familiar with the old Aboriginal customs which have gradually disappeared. There were rules which had to be obeyed, nothing was hidden from children, and we had to conform without argument. If we did not we were soundly chastised and 'put through the smoke'. This was a punishment that goes back to the tribal days; I have experienced it and so have many others of my age. A fire was made of green leaves and sticks which produced a lot of smoke. A blanket or kangaroo skin was placed so that it contained the smoke. The child was put under the skin until he was choking, breathless and completely subdued. There was something about this punishment that a child never forgot, and the result was absolute obedience. The Aboriginal laws and customs were rigid and were enforced by the elders for centuries, but they have broken down since we came in contact with white people.

Probably one of the first rules to disappear was that governing association with women at certain times. Women had to be avoided by everyone during their menstrual periods — the men were informed of a girl's condition by their own women in the camp. No one could go near a pregnant woman; she had to prepare her own food and it must never be touched by anyone else. If she became really ill another woman might give her some help. An old woman would probably assist during a birth, but the mother must dispose of the umbilical cord herself. This custom was related to fear of the witch doctor, who might use the cord for casting his spells. I have vague memories of these customs, which were not completely lost until 1912. During a birth the men disappeared until after the baby was born; there is still a tendency for them to do this.

Any woman with a deformed child was never helped, nor was the child. Their attitude was that the sooner the child came to an end the better it would be for everyone. If a child was weak and sickly the people would do everything possible to help, but deformity was not tolerated. Animals, fish or fruit with any deformity were quite unacceptable. The wild bananas or *mundinga* were often misshapen and we were always forbidden to eat them. I must admit that we did eat them when nobody was looking, but the custom of avoiding deformity was strong. Traces of this aversion still remain.

The urge for walkabout is still strong, but nowadays the mode of locomotion is more likely to be a motor car. Possibly this urge is one of the factors that prevents Aborigines from staying firmly in their jobs. In the old days when they really walked there was a certain procedure which involved good manners and behaviour. They were always quiet when they walked through the bush, for they were aware of the proximity of spirits. If they came to dense scrub they would stop and ask the spirits to let them pass through without trouble. Most of the small groups which made up the tribe were no more than thirty miles apart. If they were going walkabout from the Culgoa to the Warrego River the Aborigines would be very careful not to offend the spirits or people as they moved. It was usual for visitors to stop several hundred yards away from the camp they intended to visit; there they would wait until invited to join the residents. The travellers might be invited to go hunting with the crowd. If they wanted to hunt on their own they would always ask permission, which was usually granted. This was a strict method of procedure although they all belonged to the same tribe and spoke the same language. Probably this helped them to remain in their own little groups, since each group had to be treated with some respect by all others.

A Muruwari wrong-doer might escape and join the Galali tribe, who would keep him in their area. The result could be the death of a Galali man who strayed into our country, for he would be killed instead of the Muruwari deserter. This was how the small wars started: there were many skirmishes along the tribal boundaries. Until 1920 Aborigines tried to remain in their own territory, but since then it has been impossible to do this. The instinct for movement still remains, even if it is only a wish that cannot come true. Somehow just dreaming of movement can satisfy the urge. I have done it myself, perhaps when working or when just going to bed at night. I think of the bush and go walkabout in my imagination; it is the only way to stifle the longing for movement. This longing has been with Aborigines for many centuries, and when restrained in missions, reserves or compounds it just killed the old people. A Juwalarai man who was removed from his locality and made to remain in a reserve with Ngemba and Muruwari people would be miserable. He might have enjoyed a visit, but permanent restraint would be too much for him.

I remember how the old men took the youngest brides and the best food; they looked after themselves very well. If an older woman wanted a husband she would probably be given to a young man; this custom appeared to control the birth rate. There could have been some other method, but it was never discussed. A man could neither speak to nor look at his mother-in-law; if possible he avoided her completely and any other female relatives by marriage. This was still noticeable in 1940, but it is very rarely seen now.

The break-down of these rules has caused a lot of our trouble today. Until 1920 the old people worried about marriages which did not conform with our laws; it was hard for them to accept that all these rigid rules were being broken and destroyed. In the past a girl child was told which man was correct for her marriage, and she must never think of anyone else; this man might be quite old when promised to his bride aged about five years. These tribal laws were strict and the girl would be handed over to her husband at the age of fourteen or a little more. Once married the girl could only speak to another man on special occasions, and then she must keep her head lowered and the man must not look at her.

If the husband was going away for a long time he never kissed his wife when departing, nor would he kiss her when he returned. This custom can be observed in some Aboriginal families today, and possibly it has had some effect on their present-day home life. Where the wife might be doing jobs about the house, the husband just sitting and the children playing amongst themselves, there is a lack of companionship between the members of the family. Sometimes I have thought that there is not sufficient love between the individuals in a family, and this could be one reason why they do not have much pride in the family unit or the home. The husband is very jealous of his wife and her associations; this has been recognised in the tribe for centuries. This type of jealousy remains and comes into conflict with present-day life. There are a number of homes which I can visit comfortably, but there are others which I would avoid if the husband was not at home. This reminder of the past is still strong and can be noticed even in people who are only part-Aboriginal.

It has been hard for me to adjust to a life in town. My longing for the bush is still strong and I often dream of sitting around a fire with the sky overhead; those evenings are something that I shall always remember. Somehow speech is different when one is not restrained by walls. Fish, emu or porcupine cooked in the native way made a wonderful meal. I had a little of these experiences in the bush, but the Aboriginal who had many years of it must suffer a great loss now. Apart from my memories of the camp fire, I can still hear the songs; the singing of old Aboriginal songs around the fire is hard to forget. There is a lot of confusion and nostalgia amongst the older Aborigines; they try to revert to the old days in the bush and may go there to recapture what they are missing. When they have camped for a short time they want to return to the comforts of civilisation. For myself, I have found that when I go into the bush for some days, sleep on the ground under the stars, catch and cook my own food and live the natural life, my spirit is revived and it makes me feel well and happy. Several years have passed since I have been able to escape in this way. When recording I find that my memories take me back to some of the mysteries of the bush.

There is no explanation for what the Muruwari call *guwinjgu wiyi,* or 'spirit lights'. Sometimes they are called *wirlugu wiyi,* meaning curlew lights. I have seen them a number of times and cannot give any reason or explanation for their appearance. My first sight of one was in 1910. I was in a buggy with three men, returning home late at night. The men were seated and I was lying on the floor covered by blankets. We still had about fifteen miles to travel when the driver announced that there was a light ahead. Then they all started talking in Muruwari and decided that it was a *guwinjgu wiyi.* I was interested, and watched until it suddenly disappeared. The old man said he had seen many of them on the plains. I found my first experience rather eerie.

My next sight of one was when I was camping near Tottenham during my apprenticeship. One night I was amazed to see a light. There was no track or road in that direction, and I watched it for some time until it disappeared. During those months when I was alone I saw another one which was even more remarkable. The country is mountainous around Tottenham and Cobar, and occasionally I rode to the top of a mountain some miles from my camp; I liked it up there and it relieved the monotony.

One night I was returning from there and had to cross quite a large plain. When I came out of the scrub I saw a light which seemed as large as a football. It was not bright like the headlights of a car, but was yellow and dim. I realised that I was riding straight towards it, and suspected what it was. When I had approached it for several miles the distance between us still seemed the same as when I had first seen it. Eventually it disappeared and I returned to my tent.

My next sight was when walking to the Mission late one night. I had to cross a dry lagoon, and was startled to see a light in the middle of it. It was right in front of me and I thought it must be someone with a lamp. I kept walking towards it, but as I tried to draw closer it remained the same distance away from me. Suddenly it vanished. When I arrived at the Mission I asked if anyone had been in the vicinity of the lagoon. No one had been there, and I could only conclude that the light had been another *guwinjgu wiyi*.

Another incident occurred in 1930 when three of us, including my brother Billy, went about five miles down the river. Billy wanted some possum skins and had set a few snares near a bend. Although this was illegal we did it occasionally. We were collecting the skins at midnight when suddenly a light appeared quite close to us. Billy whispered that it might be the police. I said that I would not expect the police to have a light like that, nor would I expect them to be looking for people chasing possums in the middle of the night. We sat down and watched it; it seemed to move a little farther away. Billy had never seen one of these mysterious lights before, but the other man had seen a considerable number. He told us that one of the odd things about the *guwinjgu wiyi* is that a shadow cannot be cast from them. We found that this was true when we tried to cast shadows with our hands and bodies.

On a number of other occasions I have seen these lights, and they always appear somewhat similar in size and colour. Only once was the appearance quite different: this was when I saw some lights which were almost blue in colour. I walked across to them; they seemed to come up in a ball and then disappear when I got close to them. This was in the middle of a rabbit warren, and when I looked into the burrows a blue light seemed to rise and then return before it vanished.

Many of the older Aborigines are aware of these lights and some white people have seen them. They seem to appear after a few points of rain, although this may be a coincidence. The old people associated them with spirits and a witch doctor. They believed that the distant light was the fire of a witch doctor who was 'cooking' the hair or sputum of an intended victim, who would die if this magic was not counteracted by the skill of another witch doctor. The Aborigines never worried when a number of curlews were crying at night. However, if one bird whistled in the darkness they believed it to be a spirit in disguise. This single curlew was associated in some way with the mysterious lights, and that is why the name *wirlugu wiyi* was given to them by the Muruwari. This belief that the whistle of a single curlew was from a spirit was strong. It is an eerie sound, and I feel some fear when I hear it.

The loss of beliefs and customs has not been easy for people of my generation. I still feel that some part of me is closely linked with my heritage. I might have modern views in many ways, but there is another line of thought that draws me backwards. I feel that I am living between two worlds, and I am not even a full-blood. For those who were older the disruption has been much more severe. I remember Jack Murray, Tommy Carr* and a couple of other old men coming to the Mission from the bush; they talked about the early days and had deep regrets that their way of life had to change. They almost cried when old customs and beliefs were ignored, and were miserable when their laws were broken. Jack Murray had been through the *bora* and was a true Aboriginal in every sense. His age was ninety and he was normally a cheerful old man, but his distress was pitiful when our rules were not obeyed. The totem is inherited from the mother and it was permissible for the Muruwari to eat their own or another man's totem. This was allowed only if it was hunted, cooked and cut in the correct way. The animal must not be mutilated or the owner of the totem is insulted. Jack's totem was the emu, and I shall always remember his misery when some young fellows hacked up an emu and then cooked it on an open fire.

* Recorded Ngemba/Juwalarai for A.I.A.S.

Jack Murray, Tommy Carr, Clyde Marshall and others of their age knew all the laws and obeyed them rigidly. The importance of the totem was lost soon after 1920. In my case, I had a totem but my wife did not because of her Maori background. Consequently our children have no totems, and this is an example of how this system has died out so quickly. The marriage rules were completely lost at the same time. Soon after 1920 the custom of sharing food disappeared — it was no longer a rule and only occurred if the donor felt generous. It had been earlier, about 1915, that the custom of the donor tasting his food first had ended. This habit always appealed to me, it seemed to add some ceremony to the meal. In the early days it was done to show the absence of poison, but more recently it was a form of good manners. When a man had caught and cooked an emu he cut off a small piece and ate it in front of those who were going to share his meal.

Using smoke to confuse the spirit of a dead person has taken longer to disappear. Some fear of the spirit still remains, and the older dark people become unduly upset and concerned after a death. In some cases they burn dogwood in the fireplace and let the smoke creep into every corner of the house. It may also be used when someone is grieving after the loss of a close relative: they believe that the smoke prevents sad dreams and memories of the one they had loved. In other words, a number of Aborigines still believe that the spirit of a dead person can lurk in a house until removed by smoke. It was during the mid-thirties that the belief in good and bad spirits was lost. There is still the slight pull between two religions in some people of my age. Since all these customs and beliefs have been cast aside a lot of us have been left with a feeling of sadness and uncertainty.

During my life I have seen many of these Aboriginal ways disappear. None of the old fishing methods survive today, they finished soon after 1920. It was about this time that they stopped catching fish in the native way at the Brewarrina Fisheries. We all dived for mussels in the past, but that has not been done for many years. When guns became available our old methods of catching emus, kangaroos and other animals were never used. Even old Hippai used a gun. Several times he used the net for catching emu, but this was mainly to show me how it was done. Berries, roots and other food are seldom gathered from the bush today. Certainly the bush itself has changed considerably. In some remote places people might look for yams, but in general the taste for these growing things seemed to disappear twenty years ago. The old methods of tracking and catching goannas and porcupines are still used, as the natives still like eating them; in fact, porcupine is considered a great delicacy. But even these methods are disappearing rapidly, as dogs are effective trackers: their barking helps locate the quarry.

Now that I live such a quiet life I spend a lot of time reflecting on the past, present and future of Aborigines. Our customs have gone and their loss has caused a great need for readjustment. Life for dark people has been difficult in recent years, but the full-bloods are the worst problem. They need land and natural conditions to help them through this period of transition. It is unfortunate that most of the land which was used for missions or reserves is now lost to the Aborigines. In Brewarrina quite a lot of land was reserved for the Mission. As soon as it was known that the Mission was to be dispersed several Aborigines applied for some part of this land, but their applications were ignored. The manager told me that he would rather see the area returned to the administration of the Western Lands Commission than see it allotted to dark people. After a while more applications were invited for this land, and once again Aborigines applied. They were also unsuccessful, and eventually the land was divided into four parts and allotted to whites. This was a great disappointment, as the Aborigines felt that they could have made it self-supporting. They may have needed advice from white people, but some of these men had spent years working on stations and others were excellent wool-classers. It is always said that Aborigines are incapable of doing anything, but this should not be applied to all of them as there is a reasonable proportion who want to work and learn. The white people are not making a great success of working on these acres, and probably the Aborigines could have done as well or better.

After the Mission was closed new arrangements had to be made for the people. A housing settlement was built outside Brewarrina, not far from the Bourke road. This is a collection of fibro cottages clustered together and well apart from the town; it is known as Dodge City and there is evidence of all the unpleasant conditions of segregation. The fact that the Aborigines are isolated means that they are only mixing with one another and their advancement is being held back all the time. There is no one to set an example for them and they have no opportunity to see how the people in town care for their houses and possessions. In the old days in the bush they kept themselves clean, but now that they have houses and other responsibilities everything suffers from neglect. Dirt and unwashed belongings are seen everywhere, often due to laziness. At Dodge City everything is marked or stained and in a state of disrepair, rubbish lies around the houses and the standard of living is rapidly becoming lower. These people do not recognise that infection and illness are caused by filth; this is one of the most important lessons they need to learn and accept. Possessions are a problem to the native: he cannot look after them. This is caused by something basic in his mind; he had his happiest days when he owned nothing and shared everything. If the inhabitants of Dodge City had been scattered around Brewarrina and not isolated they might have attempted to behave better.

It is almost impossible for a full-blood to adjust to town life. He should be allowed to keep his beliefs and traditions until they gradually disappear. Robin Campbell* is a full-blood, and it is a little too soon for him to become adjusted to living in a town. He needs the bush, the river for fishing and some means of clinging to the past. He has these things at Weilmoringle, whereas life would be impossible for him at Dodge City. The part-white can assimilate more easily, and there are a number living next-door to white people in Brewarrina. They have been able to adapt themselves to the standards required and are respected by their neighbours. These people do not appear to have any problem with alcohol, they just drink a normal amount quietly at home.

One of the basic differences between white and dark people is the ability to worry. White people worry a lot about money and those things they want to possess or do possess. They may commit suicide because of their worries.

* Recorded Muruwari for A.I.A.S.

This does not happen to the dark man. I am sure he is happier when he has nothing. He does not envy the possessions of white people and finds it difficult to care for his belongings. He will not worry about money, all he wants is to be able to eat when he is hungry. It is not long since an Aboriginal handled money for the first time. In those early days he might just give it to his friends or family. This was probably less generous than it sounds, as his friends often demanded it. They might gamble with it, and if they won would possibly buy something for themselves, the rightful owner or others. The Aboriginal is not good at saving or keeping money; it disappears very rapidly.

It is bad when Aborigines are herded into a compound of houses like Dodge City because they drink together all the time. Boredom, inactivity and habit are the causes of their present drinking problem. The children of today should be more enlightened and when they have families of their own should be prepared to set a better example. These children must hate to see some of the things that happen in and around their homes when they are living in segregated groups.

Recently the white people have become more tolerant with us and seem willing to allow some assimilation; they are showing more sympathy and understanding. Some of the elderly people in Brewarrina would never say a good word for us, but their white grandchildren are friendly with the dark children; they walk down the street arm in arm and laughing together. This is the way it should be in the future. Some time ago I asked my daughters if they have ever had to suffer any rudeness or prejudice. They have not, although Roy has been subjected to a lot of difficult treatment. Bert has not had too much trouble, although he has had some unpleasant incidents. These have usually occurred when patients at the hospital have been rude to him during working hours. He does not put up with too much, and nearly punched a man who was ill in bed on one occasion. I warned him of trouble if he tried to hit a man in bed — he must carry him outside if he really wanted a fight! Bert is well liked in the town, and he receives very much better treatment than I did when I was his age. This indicates that there has been an improvement during my lifetime. The coming generation will have many more opportunities for education, and should be able to take a better place in the life of this country.

It is unfortunate that the Aboriginal does not look into the future and therefore does not consider an occupation until the necessity to earn money has arrived. Another reason for failure to settle into a permanent job is that if an Aboriginal is not within easy access of his own home and family he will not persevere to try to finish learning his chosen trade. I have seen this happen many times. One example was Dick Johnson, who had a good opportunity to work in a garage some miles out of Brewarrina; but he could not bear being away from his family, and just walked out of his job and returned home to the same old routine. I have noticed the same thing occurring with some children who were more intelligent than others. They should have progressed to the high school in Dubbo, as there is not one here in Brewarrina. When it came to signing the necessary papers the parents might refuse to let the child move or the child might insist on staying at home. Frequently I have seen one member of a family leave home for some good reason, then return suddenly without a reason. The urge which makes them want to remain together may go back to the tribal days: now that there is no tribe they need to remain with the family.

The fringe-dwellers have their own origin. A man might be removed from a reserve for reputed bad behaviour, and at the same time he would be denied the right to live in the town. He would build a shack on the river-bank or near the edge of the town; other Aborigines might already be living in the vicinity. He may want his children to go to school, but in earlier times not very many Aboriginal children were accepted. The result would be a mean little settlement; none of the children would go to school and the behaviour of the adults would be dissolute. An Aboriginal who feels he is an outcast loses his pride. The police may come and the children could be moved to foster-homes or missions. The parents may not have access to their children and the result would be further degradation and unhappiness. There has been an improvement since 1940: more children are accepted at school and missions have gradually been abolished.

The Aborigines are very fond of their children, but a lot of them are neglected. A small child might be dirty all day; both parents could be to blame for this and it is probably caused by laziness. There is a lack of discipline and the children are never restrained. The father might buy a new bicycle for his son and the next day it will be broken. On the Mission I have seen a child breaking windows just for the fun of it. His parents were close but would neither say nor do anything to stop the destruction. The children are allowed to be destructive and the lack of care for all possessions continues. It is hard for a child to change when he has grown up. He has never seen order in a house; he is used to seeing frying pans in the middle of the floor surrounded by food scraps and covered with swarming flies. There is very little concern about flies and the children probably eat them in their soup or with their meat. Their eyes are smothered with flies and the parents do nothing about it. The adults may spend their days playing cards while the children have to scavenge for scraps of food in the house. As a result they may eat something unsuitable, or nothing at all. I have also noticed that the feeding of babies is wrong in most cases. The babies may have a lot of teeth but are never given anything to chew. It is very hard to tell an Aboriginal anything; he shows disbelief unless there is visible proof. It is almost impossible to make them believe that germs breed in dirt: they want to be shown the germ. And yet in the past they believed in spirits and ghosts which could never be seen.

Although in recent times better houses have been built for Aborigines, they are not adjusted to living in them yet. They have a strong need for fresh air and freedom; there is something about the restriction of four walls and a roof that worries them.

There has also been an improvement in educational facilities for Aborigines, but it is still too early to know if they are going to be able to benefit from these opportunities. It is only recently that normal schooling has been compulsory for dark children, and it will take some time for them to adjust to the demands of a concentrated education. I have observed the children closely during the last six years and find it difficult to believe that there will be any rapid improvement. They do not do their required homework, largely because their living conditions are not suitable for it.

The parents are unable to help or encourage the children and the Aboriginal habit of never worrying is a handicap. I know that there are some parents and children who are trying their hardest to succeed, but even they are still not progressing as well as they should. The dark child does not seem to learn or understand easily, and he often has physical disabilities of hearing and sight, caused by constant infections since infancy.

The Aboriginal way of living only in the present is going to be difficult to alter. It concerns me that the young people aged fifteen years or more know so little. They may look at television all day, but will not be interested in discussions on current affairs, science or documentaries. I do not feel that I know much myself, but I have a lot more knowledge of these subjects than the younger people of today. During my life it has been obvious that learning was entirely a matter for the individual; and although education is more readily available today, probably a lot still depends on individual ambition. The fact that the young dark people have lost the knowledge of their forbears yet do not comprehend what is required for a normal Australian life is a serious problem. They are in between both ways of life, and appear to be stuck in a groove.

I predict that it will be close to a century before the Aboriginal is fully assimilated into the white community. By then it may be possible for him to still be Aboriginal but also take his place as a doctor, lawyer or scientist. The full-blooded Aboriginal will gradually disappear: this may be caused by mixed marriages or by environment. If he wishes to preserve his heritage he will need some help. Owing to infant mortality and epidemics it seems impossible for full-bloods to increase their numbers or to live for long. They cannot live in a town with comfort, and this is one of the most important reasons why they should be given land rights. But this could create another problem in that they may be sent to live in another State or some strange part of the country, and this too would make them miserable. I have had many talks with full-bloods and have told them that they are the only ones who have the right to speak for themselves and their land. Being of mixed blood, I have no right. Assimilation may be all right for the full-blood if he can keep to himself and be proud of his heritage. I do not feel that he should live as he did seventy years ago; there should be some educational facilities available for his children. In this way they would slowly become accustomed to the white man's way of life. The full-blood would still have his freedom and the opportunity to retain his customs, but a change would occur gradually. It is too late to worry about New South Wales, but the more remote full-bloods should be given a better chance to develop themselves under white supervision.

It must be recognised that the part-Aboriginal, also, still believes in many of the old ways. And it has to be realised that he has certain characteristics which do not help him to advance in the modern world. He is alert enough and has imagination, but we all have an inferiority complex. We have had years of being called 'no-good blacks' or worse. It has been drummed into us that we are the poorest type of humanity in the world and the lowest creatures in Australia. It was hurtful that sheep and other animals might be counted but the full-blood was never included in the population. That has been remedied, but there is still a lot to be done. So much damage has been done to us during the last century that it is hard to realise the possibility of getting fair treatment in the future. Public opinion indicates that we may be given some reasonable consideration, and that will help our confidence. Confidence is something that, once lost, is difficult to regain.

As the white men moved over the mountains many of the Aborigines were shot, even massacred. As these invaders took up land the dark people were pushed farther and farther away from the country they knew. The white men took their water holes, big companies had large holdings of land, and the stock destroyed the familiar bush. The native was robbed of his hunting grounds and ceremonial grounds and thereby of his normal way of life. They had to become scavengers, and it was an effort to exist. New diseases introduced by the white men killed many of the natives. Eventually some of the Aborigines learnt to ride and work with stock, but they had nowhere to go and very little remained that was related to their accustomed way of life. They had to live in little groups near large stations, and these camps were places of misery.

Jimmie at Janet Mathews' house, Bayview, 1970

White men might take their women at any time and their supply of food was meagre.

In due course the government marked out certain areas along the river-banks and these were called Aboriginal Reserves. The natives were herded into this small space; the land was undrained and most of it was flooded when the river rose. If the people were lucky they were supplied with a small ration of food; this had to be brought by wagon, and only arrived when the tracks were passable. The white preachers were continually shouting that all Aboriginal customs and beliefs were wrong. During those years the natives were miserable and confused. Approximately sixty years ago the old people were sure of their religious beliefs. They could not understand the forcefulness of the preachers; having to believe in a second religion was upsetting. The younger people were confused by the two religions, that of their parents and the garbled account of Christianity which came from some of the preachers. The result was a complete loss of stability which continues to affect the Aborigines of today.

During my life there has been a lot of kindness, especially from the white owners of Milroy. Amongst themselves, Aborigines are well disposed to one another and there is kindness in their disposition. I have noticed that an Aboriginal will do anything for a white man who is unknown to him or one who has been good to him, but a white man who has a bad reputation will be avoided completely.

When it comes to work, most Aboriginals are content with a roughly finished job. In the days when I had to be responsible for work done by other people, the result was frequently unsatisfactory. There is the occasional exception who enjoys doing a good job. I think that I should classify myself as one of those who try to achieve the best possible result. My impression is that at least half the Aboriginal people are very lazy. It is impossible to make any comparison between full-bloods and part-Aboriginals; I have seen a lot of the former who were very lazy in the camp, but many of the latter also lack energy and initiative. Frequently a man will walk into his house and sit down surrounded by a filthy and untidy mess. It also happens that a man will come home and clean up the house because his wife will not do it. On the job, men may be earning thirty or forty dollars weekly but all they want to do is sit down.

These traits are not helping the Aboriginal. He should fight for himself and realise that he must work before he can achieve any measure of success. I have worked for over fifty years and it pleases me that my family work hard and that I do not have to worry about their future.

I have tried to show how some of an Aboriginal's basic characteristics make his present life unsatisfactory. There is some element of his tribal past which remains and is contrary to what is required for modern living. All these things that I have mentioned have made us suffer and tend to keep us in our lowly position. There have been many improvements during the last twenty years, but conditions and opportunities need to become still better.

Ever since I was a child I have seen new ideas and inventions coming into our lives. These have always appealed to me: any invention fascinates me. This has meant that my thoughts have not stayed in the one place. Although I was able to get a job and remain in it when I needed work, I have always felt like an adventurer in an armchair: I have toured the world in my thoughts, and the smaller things in life have always satisfied me. My biggest worry has been life itself; life and living it has always given me my most serious thoughts. I have never worried about being poor and have not wanted to be a millionaire.

I regret that so many of the Aboriginal languages have been lost. And even though our customs are no longer in use, I feel that the people should know of our past beliefs. I have done my best to record as much of the Muruwari language as I can remember, and have enjoyed recording my memories of my own life and the Muruwari tribe. There have been many changes since I came to Brewarrina sixty years ago; those whom I have loved have gone and a lot of Aboriginal knowledge has disappeared with them. Looking at the Mission now it seems as if it could have been half a century since we lived there. The houses have gone and all that remains is part of the manager's house, the school and the medical treatment room. The small cemetery is still there and brings back many memories. There were troubles during those years at the Mission but there was also laughter and enjoyment.

My life is peaceful now, living near Bert's house at Brewarrina. I still like improvements, and started building myself a better house in 1971. This was quite an effort, but it is a good little house with two rooms and a veranda. I have made a small lawn and planted some flowers; I enjoy pottering in my little garden. I use the old shed as a workshop and still do odd jobs for the family and myself. As I get older there is not the same wish to do much; I enjoy living simply. Most of my life has been rough and I have not had the opportunity to learn to speak in the way I would like. Books have always given me great pleasure and I have been able to learn a reasonable amount from them. Sometimes I look back through the years and wonder what I might have achieved if my education had been better. I suppose most people look into the past with various emotions, perhaps satisfaction, nostalgia or regret. I have not many regrets.

Now I am absent-minded, I put something down and forget where I have put it. My life continues quietly, and I guess this is the normal pattern as one becomes older.

Postscript

IN APRIL 1975 I visited Brewarrina again, and during this visit Jack and Roy Barker gave me more details of their family life. Their memories add something to those of their father and help to fill in a few gaps in the Jimmie Barker story.

The first manager remembered by Jack, Jimmie's eldest son, was Mr Burns. He always carried a loaded revolver on his hip, and to break up a fight would fire shots over the heads of the participants. He also carried a stockwhip: it is doubtful if he ever hit anyone with it, but he used to crack it alongside children as well as adults. A baton hung on the wall of his office but he was not seen using it.

Mr Danvers was clearly remembered by both Jack and Roy. During his term the Mission was a different place: people were well fed and happy and conditions were good. Jack and Roy remembered how their father and Dudley Dennis had improved the water supply by designing an ingenious type of pump. They removed the tyres from an old T-model Ford and fitted a belt to its wheel-rims which was attached to a two-inch centrifugal pump. When the old car was started, the water was pumped up from the river into the small tanks.

After Mr Danvers left there was a rapid deterioration and conditions became shocking. Jack and Roy were both at school at this time and, along with the other children, suffered many bashings and beatings. For the purpose a length of hosepipe or a thick heavy stick from a river-gum was used. Most of the children had raised welts or scars as the result of these beatings. The baton was used frequently on the adults, and occasionally the stockwhip was employed. During the depression of the 1930s the police had a frightening amount of power over the Aborigines, many of whom were given jail sentences without legitimate cause. At that time the police were equipped with a motor-cycle and sidecar. The man riding in the sidecar would be holding an automatic rifle as they entered the Mission and as they drove up the street he would shoot every dog in sight, leaving perhaps twelve lying dead on the road. They would remain there until the sanitary man was due and cleared them away. By some miracle, although there were always lots of children playing in the street, none were killed when the dogs were shot in their midst. These episodes could have been caused by the white graziers who leased most of the Mission land at that time: if one of them had complained that a couple of sheep had been killed by dogs, the result was shooting in the Mission street. Packs of town dogs used to roam for miles; there was no investigation and the children's pets were killed indiscriminately. During these years most of the children lived in a state of fear and hunger and there was a lot of sickness and eye trouble.

When Mr Paull became manager there was some improvement for the children: he took an interest in them and taught a little carpentry and other extra-curricular subjects. During this term the Barker boys had some reasonable tuition. Apart from that they depended on their father, who taught them reading, writing and other subjects in the evenings. He bought a set of encyclopaedias, and most of his teaching was taken from them. Without this help Roy and Bert would have had very little education. Although there was always a manager-teacher at the Mission he was seldom in attendance at the school. There were two classes with approximately thirty in each; the older children were at the front of the schoolhouse and the younger ones at the back. The teacher might appear for an hour or two each day, never more. Before he left he would invariably hurl a question at some unfortunate child, who seldom answered to his satisfaction; then he would knock the child down and give him a beating. He would delegate the older children to keep the young ones quiet and teach them something if possible. Jack Barker did most of the teaching in his class of the older children.

Food was always a problem at the Mission. Malnutrition and the shock of their mother's death could have caused a lot of the subsequent ill-health suffered by the four Barker boys. Every Thursday when they were children their mother would have about six small rolled-oats bags and one flour bag washed and ready for them. In these they would collect sugar, tea, a very little rice, potatoes, onions and flour. That was all except for some meat occasionally. The meat was killed at the Mission but the animals were usually rejects from neighbouring properties: very old ewes, rams and bullocks. This meat was poor and in short supply. The boys managed to catch rabbits and fish, but as the Mission was surrounded by leased property there was no chance of gathering food from the bush. If any Aborigines were seen on a grazier's land he immediately telephoned the police and a jail sentence was the result.

Employment was often difficult to obtain for the men at the Mission. A squatter would telephone the manager and say he wanted six men for lamb marking or other jobs; the manager would nominate who would be sent. The man who wanted to get a job could not easily use his own initiative, and his earning capacity depended largely on the manager.

The issue of clothes varied little through the years. They were all made in New South Wales jails by the prisoners; most of these government-issued clothes had a distinctive red stripe which branded the wearer. Black jackets with tin buttons for the winter and khaki shirts and pants for the summer were not too bad to wear. The only other shirt was called a 'Harvard shirt' and was made of cotton so stiff that the garment could stand up by itself and washing never softened it. These had the usual red stripes, and both men and boys would cut the red threads and painstakingly pull them out. When visiting the town they felt that the shirts were not so obviously 'government' with the stripes removed. The children were given black flannel clothes for summer and winter; the old men had grey clothes. No pyjamas were ever issued, nor were underpants, socks or shoes. The old people were given military-type boots which were also made by prisoners. No underclothes for men were distributed, with the exception of an odd sort of black flannel undergarment which was worn under a shirt in the winter.

The women and girls were given material from which they made their own clothes: this was unbleached calico and dark grey flannelette. Summer and winter they had to wear the flannelette dresses, as the calico was needed for underclothes; it was a harsh and unpleasant material to wear next to the skin.

Occasionally blankets were issued; these carried the distinctive red stripe and the words 'Aborigines' Protection Board' in large letters. In those days the Aborigines used to be ashamed to take these blankets anywhere; they felt branded by possessing them. No sheets were distributed, and most people had to sleep in their clothes between blankets.

When Mr Danvers was manager he must have appreciated the difficulties of the Barker family. He arranged for their mother to be given child endowment in money; they were the first at the Mission to receive this. She was given seventy shillings a month and the family were taken off the list for the government issue. She managed to clothe them all on this allowance. She sent away for pyjamas, school shoes and other clothing that they had not been able to have previously. All her family say that she was wonderful at economising and doing the best possible with their small quantity of food and possessions. This addition to the thirty shillings a week earned by their father made it possible for them to live more comfortably.

Nineteen forty-one, when their mother died, is a year the Barker boys will never forget. They spent six weeks in Bourke with their father while their mother was ill; during this time they had no rations and there was some trouble over their father's pay. As he was paid only three pounds a fortnight and had to support his dying wife and five children, their circumstances were bad. When their mother died an old truck came over to Bourke to pick up her body. Their aunt was sitting in the front nursing Mary, the new baby. With their father and the driver also in front there was no place for the five children except on the back of the truck with their mother's body. The weather was cold, and they were forced to huddle under the tarpaulin with their mother during the seventy-mile drive.

During the first week after their return to the Mission the boys remained with their father while an aunt cared for the two little girls. Their father's distress was upsetting: he might walk into a room and try to speak to them while his eyes were full of tears. It was obvious that the family would not be able to stay together. They were a very close family and the impact of their mother's death and their father's grief was hard to bear. There was not enough money, so the only solution was for the boys to accept any job that was offered through the manager.

For a time Jack worked on a property between Bourke and Walgett; like his father many years earlier, he found that his living quarters were in the stable with the horses. His age was fifteen and he was handicapped by suffering badly from asthma. It was not very long after he left the Mission that he enlisted in the A.I.F., having put his birth date back two years. Because of his asthma he was discharged as medically unfit after four months. Then he was drafted to a construction camp in the Northern Territory where the Alice Springs-to-Darwin road was being laid. Asthma was still a problem and the dust made it worse, so he was discharged and sent back to Sydney. At that time men were being recruited for American small ships; he joined a ship and learnt about seafaring during visits to New Guinea and the islands. Later he joined the Merchant Navy and spent about three years out of Australia. He intended to stay overseas much longer, but was sent a photograph of his father which upset him. The picture showed an old man sitting down reading a paper: his hair was white and he was wearing glasses. This was not the father he remembered; he looked so much older that Jack felt he must return to Australia and see him again. Soon after that he married, and he has lived in Brewarrina ever since.

Bill's age was nearly fourteen when he left the Mission and went off droving. In a short time he was recognised as a very good drover and his wages had increased accordingly. Later he started crutching and shearing, although frequently he was not well enough to do such heavy work. From the age of twenty-six onwards he was treated for many different complaints without success. He had married, and when shearing became too heavy for him he and his wife took a married couple's situation as station hand and domestic help. Even that became too heavy and he moved back to

Brewarrina, where he was going to grow vegetables. He intended to build a small house near the river with the help of his father, who had helped all the boys with their building projects. Bill's illness was eventually diagnosed as cancer of the liver, and he was in and out of hospital until he died at the age of thirty-three — the same age at which his mother had died.

Roy's age was only twelve when he had to go out to work on a property belonging to a man called Beatty. Roy was fortunate: his boss taught him how to be self-reliant and self-supporting. The Beattys were a large family and had no colour prejudice. After leaving them Roy did various jobs in the Brewarrina district, mainly scrub-cutting, station work and shed work. When he was aged fifteen and quite a tall lad, he was pea-picking at Bathurst where they were calling for recruits. He put his age up to eighteen years, was physically fit, and was immediately enlisted in the army. This was early in 1944, and he remained in the army until late 1946. During that time he was sent to the islands and, after the war, to Japan with the Occupation Forces. When he returned to Australia he started shearing, but he had to stop later owing to trouble with his back. In his mid-forties he developed very high blood-pressure, and he cannot work any more. He and his family recently moved from Lightning Ridge to Brewarrina, where they are now living.

Bert, the youngest boy, remained with his father for a while after the others had gone. When his father left the Mission he stayed with an aunt at first, then did some fencing work near Dubbo. Later he returned to Bourke and did various jobs out on the stations. He married very young, settled in Brewarrina and later worked as handyman at the hospital, as his father had done. In addition to this he had the contract for the sanitary and garbage run and a licence for bringing wood into the town, as well as doing other odd jobs. In 1973 there was a tragic accident and he was shot in the spine; since then he has been unable to walk.

Margaret Brown and Mary Harris, Jimmie's daughters, are both married and live near Sydney. They are a credit to their father, who spent many years of his life worrying about their care and education.

Near the end of his story Jimmie Barker said: 'It is strange to look back to the time when my brother Billy and I first came to Brewarrina and there were just the two of us.' The Barker family is a large one now, and most of them still live in Brewarrina. Jack has nine children, Bill had five, and Roy has six. Bert has a family of eighteen, and Margaret has two. I have met a lot of them, and if Jimmie were alive now, I think he would be very proud of them.

JANET MATHEWS

APPENDIX

The Aboriginal station at Brewarrina

THE FOLLOWING information has been taken from the records of the N.S.W. Aborigines' Protection Board, later known as the Aborigines' Welfare Board. It covers the establishment of the Aboriginal station at Brewarrina and the official reports on its management and development up to and including 1936, followed by extracts from Proceedings of the Select Committee appointed in 1937 to inquire into the administration of the Aborigines' Protection Board. These extracts include comments referring to Jimmie Barker and his work.

At the end of this appendix is set out information about the Brewarrina station's final years, taken from a survey published in 1970.

1885. Police Report. Brewarrina.
Sergeant Steele reports: 'Since the removal of the blacks from the vicinity of the town there has been less drunkenness. A number of women who are able to find employment in the town go back to the camp in the evening. They are now in a reserve about two miles from the town, on the opposite side of the river. The half-caste children require special care.'

The establishment of an Aboriginal Home would be very desirable in this locality. The Board hope to be able to take action in this direction.

1887. The Aboriginal Mission, nine miles out of Brewarrina was first established.

1888. Manager's Report on Brewarrina Mission, year ending 31 December:
Just a year has elapsed since we took up our residence at the reserve set apart for this Mission. At the start of the year there was only one Aboriginal resident. After the first month twenty arrived. Mainly old people and a few children. Some additional natives came from Bourke and a contingent from Milroy.

The able-bodied men have fenced off two paddocks on two bends of the river, building a school house, forming a garden, etc.

The roll stands: Adults, 56. Children, 27.

1890. It is proposed to work the Station more as a sheep farm, rather than attempt to bring a large area under cultivation. A Provisional School has been started. Some 12 acres of the plain have been cleared of green timber and scrub. This has been fenced for cultivation. About 30 acres of land have been cleared of all but heavy timber and enclosed with a sheep-proof fence. Gates and sheds have been built. A dormitory for boys is being built. Improvements have been made to the schoolhouse.

Manager's Report:

About 50 Aborigines are living at the Aboriginal Station, which is under the control of the N.S.W. Aborigines' Protection Association. The Reserve is an area of 5,240 acres. There are about 2,000 sheep on the station. There is a five roomed weatherboard cottage used by the Superintendent as a residence, a schoolhouse, girls' dormitory, store, and a number of bark gunyahs occupied by the Aborigines.

1891. Manager's Report:

About 40 Aborigines are living at the Mission Station at Brewarrina. Half the area is open country, the remainder is thickly timbered with box-scrub. There are also several lignum swamps, comprising an area of 200 acres. In fair seasons the land is well grassed.

Extract from Annual Report of Aborigines' Protection Association:

Progress at the Brewarrina Mission has not been so marked as some others. It is, of course, of much more recent origin. Difficulty has been experienced in consequence of the great floods which covered the whole land, causing inconvenience and loss. 24 children are attending the school.

1893. The Mission Station at Brewarrina has been reduced 600 acres in area.

1894. Representations were made by numerous persons as to the mismanagement of various stations, including Brewarrina. These showed almost complete failure as regards any benefit which had been sought for the amelioration of the condition of the Aboriginal inmates of those places. The representations were to a large extent confirmed, and the Board at once determined upon the appointment of a Local Board of Advice and Management for each station.

1895. The Local Boards appointed last year have made good progress and are attributable to the present generally improved condition of Brewarrina Station.

1897. The Aborigines' Protection Board to the Principal Under Secretary:

'At the Brewarrina Station the ringbarked area of 3,000 acres has been suckered. Six boys and five girls from the settlement have been apprenticed to district residents. 474 sheep were shorn. The Local Board reports that the place is thoroughly clean, the Aborigines are well satisfied and the children are improving considerably owing to the care bestowed on them by the matron. When it is considered that upon the Board taking action at Brewarrina, the whole of the Aboriginal population were affected with loathsome disease, and were living near the town in a state of the utmost distress and degradation, the present satisfactory state of affairs is a subject of the deepest congratulation.'

1897. Extract from Report dated 7 March 1898 from the Local Board to the Aborigines' Protection Board:
'There were 43 people sleeping on the Station during the last night of the year. The weekly average for the whole year being 49. Health of the people was generally very good. Average attendance of school children, 18. 6 boys and 5 girls were apprenticed out.
Stock. 683 sheep, 33 cattle, 23 horses, 15 pigs. 401 sheep were killed for rations during the year. The Board feel that they cannot speak too highly of the manager and his wife, Mr and Mrs Hopkins, who still continue to give every attention to their duties.
'H. LORAINE CATHIE, CHAIRMAN, LOCAL BOARD.'

1898. Report from Local Board to A.P. Board, 5 April 1899: 'There were 50 people sleeping on the Station the last night of the year. School Roll, 19. Stock. 698 sheep, 7 cattle, 6 horses.
Dry season and some stock were trucked to Dubbo for grass.
'H. L. CATHIE, CHAIRMAN, LOCAL BOARD.'

1899. Repairs have been effected to some of the dwellings. 8 gates were constructed and hung at the entrances to paddocks. 53 Aborigines on the Station on 31st December.
Weekly average of people during the year was 40.5.
School Roll, 19 children.

1900. Manager, Mr Hopkins, died.
[See reference by Jimmie Barker to earliest headstone in burial ground at the Mission.]

1901. The appearance of the Station has been improved by the addition of verandahs to the houses and construction of fences. A new cottage was erected.
114 Aborigines on the Station on 31st December.
30 children on School Roll.

1902. New bunks were provided for the boys' dormitory. One new cottage erected and three others had verandahs added to them.
99 Aboriginal residents.
37 children on School Roll.
Schoolhouse accommodation very inadequate.

1903. 92 Aboriginal residents. School Roll, 38 children.
Stock. 830 sheep, 11 cattle, 7 horses.

1904. Local Board very pleased with management. Average number of residents during year was 92.6. 5 boys and 2 girls apprenticed out. Aborigines camped at Byrock are being pressed to move to the Mission. Stock. 1,008 sheep, 14 cattle, 8 horses.

1905. Average number of residents, 85.
School attendance averaged 30.3.
Stock. 1,063 sheep, 17 cattle, 7 horses.

1906. One new cottage built, three others being erected. Tender accepted for the erection of a new schoolhouse.
Residents, 81 adults, 53 children. Total population, 134. Apprenticed out, 7 girls and one boy.
Able-bodied men are not encouraged to remain at Mission. If it is absolutely necessary for them to do so, they have to perform certain work to earn rations.

1907. Five new huts built.
Health good, dominant illness tuberculosis.
Residents. 81 adults, 53 children.
School Roll, 28. Total population, 134.
Apprenticed out, 7 girls, 1 boy.
Stock. 850 sheep, 20 cattle, 5 horses.

1908. New school replaces the wretchedly overcrowded present one. Present building will be used as a carpenter's shop. Most of the girls, when old enough, are placed in domestic situations. Buildings needed to house the sick, sanitary improvements needed and also improvements to the water supply. No funds.
Residents. 73 adults, 94 children. Total 167.
School Roll, 41.

1909. Residents. 90 adults, 101 children. School Roll, 46. Total population, 191. Increase of residents as some Aborigines from detached camps have moved to the Mission. As there is no irrigation nothing can be done about cultivation.
Stock. 1,242 sheep, 40 cattle, 6 horses.

1910. The Local Boards at the various centres ceased to exist on 30th May. Local Committees and Guardians were appointed by the Board to replace them.
Mr R. S. H. Scott was appointed Manager and Teacher at the Brewarrina Mission.
Residents. 88 adults, 93 children. Daily average total being 175. School Roll, 44.
Stock. 1,388 sheep, 50 cattle, 1 bull, 6 horses.
Favourable season and the Station generally in a prosperous state.

1911. Education. To the subjects of reading, writing and arithmetic have been added picture and observation talks. Sewing taught by Mrs Scott, but not in school. Drill is regularly given. The children are firmly and sympathetically governed.

Improvements on the Station were: Flooring several cottages and erecting verandahs to each. Subdivision into 6 secure paddocks. Pulling down three dilapidated cottages and substituting three new ones.

Residents. Total, 130. School Roll, 39.

Stock. 1,362 sheep, 46 cattle, 6 horses.

Health and conduct good. An epidemic of whooping cough, three children died.

1912. Cootamundra Home for orphans and neglected children was opened.

Brewarrina Mission had an extensive examination by Dr Dickey when the manager developed typhoid. No trace of origin could be found and the doctor was impressed by the order and cleanliness of the place. Towards the end of the year there was a serious outbreak of measles. Station had to be quarantined and trained nurses were brought from Sydney. The staff had been added to by the appointment of an assistant teacher.

The whole of the Aborigines from the Culgoa River and Gongolgon Camps, though very loath to come at first, have been persuaded to take up their residence at the Station. They now appear contented and show no desire to leave. Discipline has been maintained, conduct showed a marked improvement.

Population. 135 adults. School Roll, 48 children.

1913. Extract from report furnished by Inspectors of the Department of Public Instruction:

'Brewarrina. The schoolroom is well-ventilated and kept scrupulously clean. The children are neatly dressed, clean and tidy in appearance. They are well mannered and attentive under instruction, and respond to the wishes of the teacher. Singing is a distinct feature of the school.'

Improvements. Repairs to huts.

This was a very strenuous year on the Station, being the worst on record from the health standpoint. At the beginning an epidemic of measles was raging, and nearly the whole of the population was affected. The outbreak was followed by a few cases of diphtheria.

Population. 85 people. There were ten deaths during the year.

Extract from report by Inspector of the Department of Public Instruction:

'Brewarrina. The children are well behaved and under good control. The attendance is good and the pupils are punctual. The teacher is to be commended for his work in swimming and life saving.'

Population on 31st Dec. Adults, 49. Children, 60. School Roll, 40.

Stock. 851 sheep, 18 cattle, 4 horses. Health good, except for a few cases of diphtheria. Good work has been done by the teacher, Mr Foster.

1915. Construction of buildings: 3 closets, repairs to verandah.
Report. The usual activities proceed under the management of Mr G. F. Evans.
Population on 31st Dec. 44. School Roll, 11. Health good.

During the years of 1916, 1917, and 1918 the references to Brewarrina Mission lacked detail.

1919. Epidemic of influenza broke out throughout the State. Reserves were quarantined.
[No specific reference to Brewarrina.]

1920-1. (1 July 1920 to 30 June 1921.)
Brewarrina Mission.
Population. 76 adults.
Stock was reduced to 200 sheep owing to drought. This was followed by severe floods. This necessitated the temporary abandonment of the Station, all the residents were moved to a ridge near the town.

1922-3. (1 July 1922 to 30 June 1923.)
'On several of the Stations, Sales Stores are stocked with such lines as groceries, etc. which find a ready sale amongst the Aborigines. The goods are purchased at wholesale rates and resold at a price which merely covers actual cost landed at the Station. The ability to obtain supplies on the spot tends to discourage the Aborigines from visiting neighbouring towns where they might obtain liquor.'

There were no details about the Brewarrina Station during the years 1924, 1925 and 1926.

1927. (Year ending 30 June.)
'The condition of the Aborigines in N.S.W. may be regarded as satisfactory. With a few exceptions which are receiving attention as funds become available, they are comfortably housed. The aged and infirm, children and those whose circumstances do not permit them to earn their own living, receive a regular supply of rations, meat, blankets and clothing. In addition they have medical treatment, hospital attention and medicine whenever necessary.'

There were no reports on Brewarrina during the years 1928, 1929 and 1930.

1931. (Year ending 30 June.)
'Satisfactory reports have been received from the various Aboriginal Stations which are under the immediate control of Teacher-Managers and Matrons. These Officers take personal interest in the well-being of those committed to their charge, see to their housing and rationing, exercise a general supervision over their health, and assist them to secure

employment. All Managers report an influx of Aborigines, and several of the Stations are suffering from the lack of sufficient accommodation, necessitating the provision of temporary shelter, such as tents, etc.'

No reports for 1933.

1934. (Year ending 30 June.)
Brewarrina Mission. Five new dwellings erected.
Health. The work of combating eye trouble was continued. A fully qualified nurse, who also acts as Assistant-matron, being employed to take charge of the treatment room previously erected by the Board.

1935. (Year ending 30 June.)
In all cases the Board follows the policy of, as far as possible, assisting Aborigines to assist themselves. This system, together with the supply of gardening implements, flower and vegetable seeds, and the planting of natural and ornamental trees, helps to create in them a pride in their homes and a sense of proprietorship. This is an important aid to the policy of graduating the Aboriginal from his former primitive state to the standards of the white man.

1936. (Year ending 30 June.)
Health. Unfortunately at certain western centres there have been epidemics of eye complaints. At Angledool a special medical inspection was made, as a result of which it was decided to close the Station, and remove the inhabitants to Brewarrina, where the Board already has a fine Reserve on the banks of the river, with a proper Treatment Room, and better housing and living conditions generally.

APPOINTMENT OF A PARLIAMENTARY SELECT COMMITTEE

This was appointed in September 1937 to inquire into the administration of the Aborigines' Protection Board, following upon the Board's action in dispensing with the services of one of its officers, and also upon certain criticisms levelled at the Board through the Press.

The Select Committee was called together on eighteen occasions, on five of which, however, the meetings lapsed owing to the lack of the necessary quorum. This was the case also on the final occasion of meeting, after which the Committee expired altogether with the termination of the Session prior to a general election, and before the Board had had an opportunity of presenting its case.

In addressing those who were present at the expiration of the Committee, the Chairman, Mr M. A. Davidson, M.L.A., in expressing regret at its termination, also expressed the view that one fact that had emerged out of the evidence taken was that the Board had had insufficient funds for the satisfactory carrying out of its functions.

The following information refers to the Brewarrina Aboriginal Station and is in the form of extracts taken from the *Proceedings of the Select Committee on Administration of the Aborigines' Protection Board:*

Committee consisted of Captain Chaffey, Dr Fleck, Mr C. E. Bennett, Major Reid, Mr Wilson, Mr Horsington, Mr Tully, Captain Dunn, Mr Davidson.

Mr A. C. Pettit to appear as representative of Aborigines' Protection Board.

Mr Roderick Roy Brain, ex-Manager of Aboriginal Settlement at Brewarrina.

Mrs Caroline E. Kelly. Represented Sydney University and also Association for the protection of Native Races.

Mr Ion Idriess addressed Committee on Aborigines.

Mr W. Ferguson representative of Aborigines of N.S.W.

Sister Ivy Pratt, trained nurse employed by A.P. Board.

2nd Meeting, 22nd Nov. 1937 [evidence].

Sister Pratt was the nurse at the Brewarrina Mission in charge of the eye clinic. Trachoma and impetigo were prevalent. Caused by unclean living. At this time there were about 100 Aborigines at the Mission. The average number of patients seen daily was 60-70. Conditions and people were dirty. There were 15-20 houses and a number of tents. She considered the food was not adequate. Seed for gardens could be given to residents, but they were not trained and did not know how to plant them. Whooping cough, sores and boils were common.

Mr Danvers helped in every possible way when Manager of the Station.

To Mr Marshall, who succeeded Mr Danvers, it was just a job. He cared nothing for the well-being of the natives.

Mr Brain seemed to do all he could and tried to teach them to make gardens.

Sister Pratt thought the residents were issued with one blanket a year. The doctor was nine miles away. There was no regular medical inspection by the Board. There was a reasonable amount of tuberculosis.

School building. She helped to clean it up. Was very dirty and untidy and the verandah was broken. Desks were broken, there was no garden.

There was a killing yard. No sheep were there. There were cows, and as fences were down the dogs chased them through the Station every night.

She made a second check of the Mission in January, 1936. At this time there was an increase in population. Number could be nearer 200 than 100 residents. There was an improvement, fences had been repaired and vegetables were available to the people.

Manager Marshall. She said that he spent two hours a day teaching in the school. On Thursdays his wife took sewing class while he was doing rations.

Sister Pratt said: 'Mr Danvers had turned a desert into an oasis. He taught the men how to grow vegetables and had a community garden. He saw to the stock, managed the Station, usually did his office work at night. Mrs Danvers assisted him in the school and visited people in their houses. I have seen her taking plants from her garden and teaching women how to grow them. I have also seen her working with the natives in the garden and helping them.'

Sister Pratt managed the Brewarrina Station for three weeks during Mr Brain's absence. She had the assistance of Jim Barker, the handyman, who was 'always there when I wanted him'. Her comments: 'One of the finest working men I have ever met. Reliable at every turn. Half Aboriginal. Once I told him to do anything there was no need for me to worry any more about it. He looked after the pump all the time when I was there alone, and saw to the milking, the stock and the issue of meat. I watched him do the rations. He was absolutely honest and reliable in every way. The men did the fencing, Jim was too busy with other work, watering gardens, etc.'

24th November, 1937.
Mr Brain being examined. The move from Angledool to Brewarrina was on 26th May, 1936. After amalgamation there were 212 Aborigines and less staff. He was given notice of his dismissal five months after the Angledool people arrived, before this there were 105 people at the Mission. Brain said that some complaint had been made to the Board and not to him about the inadequacy of the food by the inmates.
Housing Conditions. Unsatisfactory. Huts were built of iron in 1934 with board floors and were fairly comfortable. Two or three families might be living in the same house. This would be a four-roomed cottage.
Religious Teaching. Presbyterian minister from Bourke came once a month and held a service. Brain invited every minister or preacher he met to come and hold a service. The people were fairly amenable, but particularly liked singing hymns.
Employment. Neighbouring squatters applied for men to do stock work.
Sanitary Conditions. Pit system. Had to be a reasonable distance from the houses, but they would not walk that distance at night.
Brain said: 'Some of the people are good types. The handyman and his wife are as good as any people you would meet in the world. Probably quarter caste.'
[These remarks would have referred to Jimmie Barker and his wife.]
Baths. Conditions were impossible. People will not bathe in the river during the winter.
Rations. No trouble with the Board. Brain says that the responsibility rests with the manager. All people, other than the ill and the elderly, had to work for their rations.
Ill-treatment. Brain said that would apply to the individual manager. The manager had the authority to punish, and on one occasion he had had to use the baton.

Water. Brain said there were five taps, including one at the manager's house. The furthest distance of a tap from a house would be 50 yards. Women had to carry their water to do the washing.

Mrs Brain being questioned: 'Average children were very dull, only exception were the children of the handyman. He had a lot of Chinese and there was Maori on the mother's side. I think that accounted for it. The other children were very slow.'

Mr Brain giving evidence:
Community garden. Grew vegetables with the work done by the natives and supervised by the manager.
Doctor visited the Mission once a month. There were about 212-300 people at the Mission.
Stoves. Only a couple of houses had them. The people cooked on a camp oven or open fire.
Windows. The windows of the huts at Brewarrina were the type called 'shutters'. The sliding type that are lifted out. There was no glass. Very unpleasant when they had to be shut because of bad weather. Most huts had cement floors, some were partly wood and dirt. A number of people had beds and others did not.

25th November, 1937.
Mr Brain being questioned.
Baton. He only used it once when a man attacked him with a large stick and called him a filthy name.

When asked to submit reasons for the dismissal of Mr Brain the Chief Secretary said: 'The services of a married couple, who were in charge of the Aboriginal Station at Brewarrina as manager and matron, were terminated by the Board, following upon repeated neglect by the manager of correspondence, accounts, submissions of claims for family endowment, returns and other matters in connection with the administration of the Station. This action was taken only after the matter had received the fullest consideration by the Board, two of whose members visited the Station, and such action was endorsed by the Department of Education.'

The Board charged Mr Brain with neglect at Angledool and Brewarrina, and said that because of his neglect the people were deprived of their endowment and that conditions became dilapidated.

On 31st August, 1936, Mr and Mrs E. J. Dalley were sent to the Brewarrina Station as assistant manager and matron. Brain stated that Mr Dalley would do no office work, Mrs Dalley would not go near the dormitory. After their arrival Mr Brain admitted to doing no schoolwork. Mrs Brain and the handyman (Jimmie Barker) were ill and he had to do additional work because of this.

Question from Mr Pettit to Mr Brain: 'What was Jimmy Barker doing after the Dalley's arrival?'

Reply by Brain: 'He was fairly ill. Never at any time during 1936 was Jimmy a handyman to me, I always had to give him specialised work. Within a month of the Dalley's arrival he was in hospital for three weeks. I could not supervise anything that he had attended to formerly after he had recovered, like work in the garden. His time was fully taken up with other developmental work.'

Pettit: 'You had another man named Groves?'

Brain: 'Yes, he was pulling down houses at Angledool.'

It was stated that the Manager's house was surrounded by garden, others seemed to be deprived. Brain said that tons of pumpkins and other vegetables were sold elsewhere. Men received extra rations when they worked in his garden. Brain denied withholding rations, or forcing work so that they had to earn their rations.

Stated by the Chairman that Ernest C. Smithers, Inspector of Aborigines, of the staff of the Aborigines' Protection Board, had admitted that manager Danvers had turned the place into an oasis. A list of improvements were read out. Mr Pettit said these were carried out by Danvers and added to by Marshall, Brain's predecessor. They were:
Subdivision fencing and gates.
Planting of orchard and community vegetable garden.
Establishment of lucerne plot of more than half an acre.
Erection of cow bails and slaughter house.
Putting of gauze on meat house.
Engine room, two tank stands and tanks.
Handy man's quarters. [Jimmie Barker's house.]
14-15 huts, using old or new materials.
Lavatories, reticulation of water.
Renovation of manager's residence.
Alterations to dormitory.

Mr Smithers said that the tankstand to hold the 20,000 gallon tank was made by Jimmie Barker. Also admitted that Jimmie had designed and built it.

Question to Smithers: 'Barker must be a good tradesman?'

Reply by Smithers: 'He is a man of the best type. We have numbers of that type, but I think he is one of the best we have. Barker was the best man to build this and it was better left in his hands.'

Smithers was in charge of the move from Angledool. He made 10-11 trips over the 140 miles and received great help from the Aborigines. Brain was instructed to go to Angledool and collect a load. He was found asleep on a verandah by Smithers and the Aborigines were driving and loading his truck. They complained that Brain had been tough during the absence of Smithers. Brain said that he 'had to shake them up'.

211

Question: 'Assuming that the statement by Brain that he was working 12 hours by day and night to be correct, would there be anything unusual in him falling asleep?'

Smithers: 'No, but it was unforgivable that he should drive Aborigines out on a reserve to carry on work that he should have supervised and to take Jimmy Barker, who was nearly dead, and make him supervise while he had a rest. This is the part I took exception to.'

Chairman, to Smithers: 'You say that Jimmy Barker does all that fine work. What extra compensation did he receive for it?'

Smithers: 'Jimmy does not work for nothing. I think his salary is 37/6 per week. He gets concessions in the way of extra rations, and has a nice four-roomed cottage to live in, with electric light. We help him in different ways.'

Mr A. C. Pettit, Secretary of the Aborigines' Protection Board of N.S.W. Sworn and examined:

Endowment is classified as 'for the direct and indirect benefit of children, food nourishment and clothing. Also their sleeping accommodation, purchase of furniture, crockery, etc.'

Teaching. The manager is supposed to have sufficient education, and the standard required is said to be for third class. 3½ hours a day are supposed to be given to the teaching.

Expulsion of a man from a Station is allowed in an emergency. Then the manager is expected to notify the Board of his act and obtain confirmation.

Mr Pettit said that managers only possess limited powers.

Mr William Ferguson, Dubbo. Organising Secretary of the Aborigines' Progressive Association:

Mr Ferguson spoke firmly about the unpleasant power of managers, expulsion, etc. Complained about the dreadful treatment of Aborigines when they were apprenticed.

'Speaking generally, the managers I have come in contact with are not a proper type to be over Aborigines. They do not seem to have sympathy for the Aborigine. Their idea is to suppress rather than uplift. They are of a dominating character; they have to be that to keep the natives under. I find that in all cases.'

15th December, 1937. Parliament House Sydney.

Mr James G. Danvers, who was manager of the Brewarrina Station for three years. He describes his impression on arrival, and improvements achieved:

'When I went to Brewarrina I was astounded at the condition of things. There were two rows of houses, each of two or three rooms, I think. There was no vestige of a garden, except in one case. One person had tried to make a little garden and put a small fence around it. They were on the bank of one of our famous rivers, where there was ample water supply — it was deep enough for steamers to pass up and down. It was the best of water, yet there were no gardens for the people. There was only the manager's private garden, attached to his own residence. The children were suffering from malnutrition for the want of decent food, especially green foods. Their meat issue came from the local butcher who contracted at 7d. per pound and was delivering 150 lbs. of meat twice a week. The meat was the ends of ribs and shanks, pieces off the neck of beef, and the manager was given a roast. Very quickly I had that altered. I wrote to the Secretary and suggested that we should buy our own meat and kill our own sheep. During the first year I was able to supply meat at an average cost of 1½d. per lb. That was mutton. I was able to give two or three times the amount to each person, and it still cost the Board less. That went on during the three years I was there; perhaps in the following year the prices were a little more.

'In one purchase I bought 280 sheep for 5/- each and the skins were sold for 6/- and we also had all that meat.

'When I had been there a little while I established a community garden; I think that was the first of our stations — at any rate, as far as I know — where this was done. The result of that was extraordinary. There was a show in Brewarrina in which we took sixteen first prizes; in fact, we scooped the pool in vegetables and flowers. The people came in quite willingly and did their bit, and it was all done with mattock and shovel; we had no plough or horses. Within about four months we had vegetables on the Station for everybody.

'After that Mrs Danvers and myself got the people to make an effort on their own behalf. We requisitioned the Board for wire-netting and other things, and everybody then had a garden of his own. In the second year they worked in the community garden and also in their own gardens. We managed to give them a couple of fruit trees and some grape vines, and it made the people proud of their homes and they got on much better.'

Question: 'Can you give some idea of what you consider was the cause of that outbreak of eye disease?'

Danvers: 'I think it was generally accepted that the cause of the disease was malnutrition, and the filthy conditions in which the people were living, lack of vegetables and similar food. The people had no stamina or powers of resisting these things. They were certainly overcrowded in their homes, and they were up against it in every way. But things improved as time went on. The home conditions were more comfortable, verandahs were covered with vines, and the people were able to get out of the sun and away from the intense heat. But I think the state of the Station is much the same today as it was then, as far as eye disease is concerned.'

Question: 'The previous manager was retired because the Board was not quite satisfied with the way things were, and you were appointed to straighten matters up. Is that a fact?'

Danvers: 'Yes.'

Question: 'Your predecessor did have a garden there from which supplies were issued to the Aborigines. Is that so?'

Danvers: 'He never supplied anything from his garden to the Aborigines. I think you will remember that 7/6 per week was paid to Sam War, the Chinaman, for vegetables for the Aborigines.'

Question: 'I imagine that was to supplement issues, is that so?'

Danvers: 'He made no issues to the Aborigines from his garden. Whatever went out of the garden was sold, the same as the eggs were sold and the butter they made from the cows.'

Mr E. J. Dalley was sworn in.

'My wife is at the Mission as matron. We also have a trained nurse. 320 on the Station at the present time (1937). The assistant manager and the handyman help care for the people.'

Question: 'Who teaches at the Station?'

Dalley: 'I teach, but I get Jim Barker to assist me occasionally. He is a very handy man with tools, an all-round man, a coloured fellow. Any other coloured fellows that like to take it on are given the opportunity. They are not paid but I give them extra rations.'

Question: 'What wages does Jim Barker, the handyman, receive?'

Dalley: 'From 30s. per week and rations.'

In reply to a question about work Jimmie Barker was doing or had done Mr Dalley said: 'He has been very busily engaged in the erection of a power house, and he also assists in the laying of through lines and many other jobs. The power house is a very nice little job, especially for a coloured man.'

The following information is extracted from reports of the Aborigines' Protection Board:

RATIONS. These rations will be issued to managers and other officers on the Board's Sations:

flour	8 lb. per week
tea	¼lb. per week
white sugar	2 lb. per week
meat	7 lb. per week
potatoes	7 lb. per week
soap	1 lb. per week
butter	1 lb. per week
jam	1 lb. per week

Where butter can be made or potatoes grown on a station they must be taken from this supply.

Rations for aged, infirm or sick Aborigines:

flour	8 lb. per week
sugar	2 lb. per week
tea	¼ lb. per week

Children attending school may, at the discretion of the local committee or guardian, be allowed half rations. This issue will be withheld if the children do not attend regularly.

a. On the Board's stations where specially authorised, meat up to 7 lb. weekly, ½ lb. tobacco, salt and soap are to be issued as required.

b. Rations are not under any circumstances to be issued to the able-bodied without special reference to the Board. The men must go out and obtain employment and be made to understand that they must support themselves and families.

c. In cases of special urgency, rations not exceeding a week's supply may be issued in cases not authorised, but the particulars must at once be reported to the Board.

d. A quarterly return of all rations issued shall be furnished to the Board, giving particulars of the names, ages, sex and caste of the recipients, and the reason for the issue.

e. A supply of medicines and such medical comforts as rice, sago, arrowroot, oatmeal and maizena shall be kept in stock at the Board's stations, and may be issued to any Aborigines who may be sick or otherwise in need of the same, but the circumstances of such issue must appear on the quarterly return of rations issued.

SUPPLY OF CLOTHING. The following clothing will be supplied annually to Aborigines throughout the State in such cases where it may be considered necessary:

Men and Youths: One coat, two pairs trousers, two Harvard and two flannel shirts — the coat and trousers to be of diagonal tweed.

Boys: Two knicker suits (serge), two Harvard and one flannel shirt.

Women and girls: One winsey and two print dresses, one winsey and one flannel petticoat, two pairs of calico drawers and two calico chemises.

Infants (girls to 4 years and boys to 3 years): Two diagonal tweed frocks, five petticoats with bodices and three Harvard shirts.

SALE STORE. Where approved by the Board, articles in general use by the residents may be kept for sale at the Board's stations, for cash only. Duplicate books shall be kept in the 'Sale Store Account Book' of all goods received and disposed of.

GENERAL. Every able-bodied Aborigine resident on one of the Board's stations shall do a reasonable amount of work, as directed by the manager; and whilst so engaged shall be remunerated at a rate to be arranged by the Manager. Anyone persistently refusing to work when required to do so by the Manager shall have all supplies for himself and his family withdrawn until he resumes work, and shall be liable to be removed from the station.

APPRENTICES. The following are the conditions under which children may be apprenticed:

a. No child shall be apprenticed to a hotel or boarding-house keeper.

b. All apprentices shall be provided with sleeping accommodation, to be approved by the Board's officers or representatives, and such accommodation shall be liable to inspection by any person authorised by the Board at all reasonable times.

c. All apprentices shall be fed, clothed and lodged in a proper manner, and provided with medical attention when necessary.

d. All apprentices shall, in the absence of an agreement to the contrary, be paid wages at the following rates:

For the first year, Girls and Boys, 5s. per week, of which 1s. 6d. shall be paid to the apprentice as pocket money.

For the second year, Girls and Boys, 6s. 6d. per week, of which 1s.6d. shall be paid to the apprentice as pocket money.

For the third year, Girls, 6s. 6d. per week, of which 2s. shall be paid to the apprentice as pocket money.

For the third year, Boys, 7s. 6d. per week, of which 2s. shall be paid to the apprentice as pocket money.

For the fourth year, Girls, 7s. 6d. per week, of which 2s. 6d. shall be paid to the apprentice as pocket money.

For the fourth year, Boys, 10s. 6d. per week, of which 2s. 6d. shall be paid to the apprentice as pocket money.

The portion not paid as pocket money shall be remitted by the employer quarterly, to the Board, and shall be placed to the credit of a trust account in a savings bank, and paid to the apprentice at the end of his or her apprenticeship or at such other time that may be approved by the Board.

THE LAST YEARS OF THE BREWARRINA STATION

The following information has been extracted from *Aboriginal Settlements: a survey of institutional communities in eastern Australia*, by J. P. M. Long, published by A.N.U. Press, Canberra (1970):

This station [Brewarrina] was the oldest institutional-type community in the State that was still managed as such in 1965, but its population was by then greatly reduced and its final disappearance was imminent. The reserve was reduced from 4,638 acres to just 638 acres about 1953 but only a few acres of this were used in 1965 for the station buildings and a small cemetery. There remained in November 1965, eleven small cottages and a school, a garage, a small treatment room, a hall, and the manager's house and office.

The population fluctuated and fell to an average of fifty-eight in 1915. It increased again in the Depression years and particularly in 1936-7 after the station at Angledool was closed and many of the people from there and Tibooburra moved to Brewarrina. In 1939 the recorded population was 324 though the following year it had decreased to 242. After 1961 there was a fairly rapid decrease. In November 1965 only forty-two were recorded as actually living on the station. The station had in no sense become a refuge or home for the elderly as its population declined, since none of its residents was over 50 years old.

Living conditions. All the houses were old and apparently little or no new building-work had been done since the mid-1930s. No rents were charged. Materials from houses demolished as they became vacant had been used to repair and add to the remaining huts, but most had only two or three rooms. There were eleven huts on the station with an average of five people to each.

Water was pumped from the river and reticulated to the houses but only some of them had taps inside the dwellings. Most had outside coppers and tubs for washing and bathing and only two had bathrooms of any kind. The station handyman provided a garbage and sanitary service (pan system).

Community services. The matron provided a treatment room for minor complaints and patients were taken to Brewarrina hospital for treatment when necessary.

There was a school on the station from its early days as a mission and the Education Department still maintained a one-teacher school in 1965 with an enrolment of twenty-two children.

There was no shop or store on the station and daily trips were made to town in the station utility truck for shopping and to collect rations. No residents owned cars.

Employment and relief. None of the eight able-bodied men who were counted as residents was unemployed. One man (handyman) and one woman (treatment-room assistant) were employed on the station.

No resident males were receiving any pensions, the one invalid pensioner being in hospital. One woman received a widow's pension and five were supplied with rations by the Board.

Households and families. Only one house was shared by two families. The rest were occupied only by parents (or parent) and their children. Eleven families were recorded as 'resident' but two of these were actually living at Byrock at the time. Of the remaining nine families, five were 'fatherless families' and these accounted for nineteen of the twenty-eight children actually on the station.

The Board had had thirty houses built on a reserve on the northern outskirts of Brewarrina and all the families on the station were to move into these early in 1966, along with some of the many families living in humpies along the banks of the Barwon River near the town. No Board officer was to live on this reserve but it was proposed to station a welfare officer in the town. This is a conspicuously segregated Aboriginal residential area.*

* This settlement is approximately a mile from Brewarrina on the Bourke Road. It is known as 'Dodge City' and it is by this name that Jimmie Barker has referred to it.

When I visited the Mission with Jimmie in 1972 very few of the original buildings remained. It is probable that the small burial ground is the only tangible reminder of the life at the Brewarrina Mission between 1887 and 1966.

J.M.

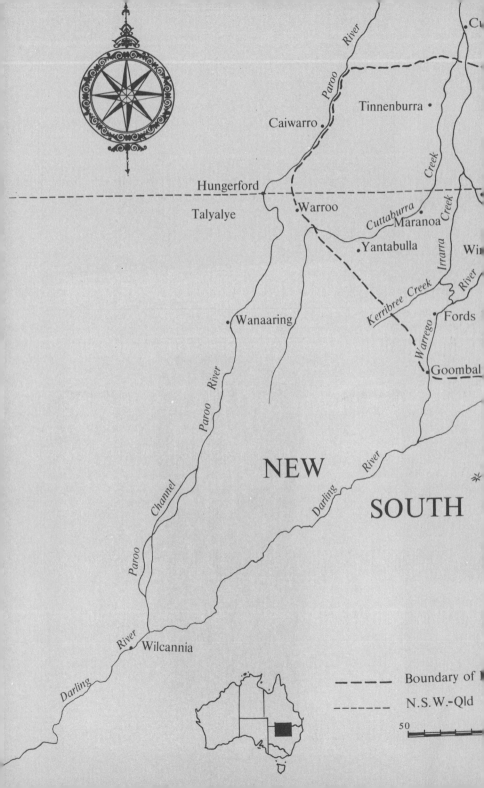

River

Paroo

Tinnenburra •

Caiwarro •

Creek

Hungerford

Talyalye

Warroo •

Cuttaburra

Maranoa

Yantabulla •

Irrara Creek

Wi

Kerribree Creek

Wanaaring •

Warrego

Fords •

Goombal •

Paroo River

NEW

Darling River

SOUTH

Channel

Paroo

Darling River

Wilcannia •

Darling

Boundary of

N.S.W.-Qld

50